OUTSOURCING TECHNICAL COMMUNICATION

Issues, Policies, and Practices

Edited by

Barry Thatcher
New Mexico State University

Carlos Evia
Virginia Tech

Baywood's Technical Communications Series
Series Editor: CHARLES H. SIDES

Routledge
Taylor & Francis Group

LONDON AND NEW YORK

First published 2007 by Baywood Publishing Company, Inc.

2 Park Square, Milton Park, Abingdon, Oxon OX14 4RN
711 Third Avenue, New York, NY 10017, USA

Routledge is an imprint of the Taylor & Francis Group, an informa business

First issued in paperback 2017

Library of Congress Catalog Number: 2007003763

ISBN 13: 978-0-89503-334-5 (hbk)

Library of Congress Cataloging-in-Publication Data

Outsourcing technical communication : issues, policies, and practices / edited by Barry
Thatcher and Carlos Evia.
    p. cm. -- (Baywood's technical communications series)
    Includes bibliographical references and index.
    ISBN 978-0-89503-334-5 (cloth : alk. paper) 1. Contracting out. 2. Information
technology--Management. 3. Business--Communication systems. I. Thatcher, Barry, 1964-
II. Evia, Carlos, 1971-

    HD2365.098 2007
    658.4'058-dc22   2007003763

ISBN 978-0-89503-334-5 (hbk)
ISBN 978-0-415-78465-8 (pbk)

Table of Contents

PART II
Management and Cross-Cultural Communication Issues

PART III
Legal, Ethical, and Political Issues

Acknowledgments

Many friends and colleagues helped with different aspects of this book and, particularly, my chapter on differences between training technical communicators in the United States and India. Russell Willerton helped me gather information in several stages of the process, and he was also helpful in recruiting collaborators. Phil Tietjen and Carolyn Gardner kept the outsourcing conversation going on for months and reminded me I had a project to finish. Victoria Sharpe helped with early drafts of my chapter. Carolyn Rude reviewed my chapter and was (is) my main source for information professionally. Barry Thatcher was a good co-editor and friend. In India, Gurudutt Kamath became a great contact and informant. His input is really appreciated. Dr. Kiran Thakur, from the University of Pune, was very helpful and friendly when sharing information about their program in technical communication.

Carlos Evia
Blacksburg, VA
carlos.evia@vt.edu

Introduction:
The Changing Face of Technical Communication in the Global Outsourcing Economy

Carlos Evia

This collection of essays examines the effects of outsourcing on technical communication and the work of its educators, students, and practitioners. If in order to connect with the audience, I had to introduce this book in terms of a common genre of technical communication, I would describe it as a user's manual. This book looks at an issue affecting the present of technical communication as a profession and academic discipline. Outsourcing is changing the face of the field as you read these lines, and the main purpose of this book, like a manual, is to give a state-of-the-art description of this situation in order to guide the user through a specific set of tasks. In academic environments, this book should assist administrators, faculty, and students (graduate or undergraduate) in their organizational or personal process of developing strategies for coping with the outsourcing phenomenon and dealing with opportunities that might arise because of this situation. Once that guiding purpose is accomplished, the authors and editors also intend to spark new ideas for research and discussion in the audience so they can generate their own action plan.

After reading this book, academic audience members should be better prepared to create or modify program specifications, course descriptions, and research or production assignments. These readers could embrace the international expansion of the field and develop skills with the goal of obtaining a competitive advantage. Workplace audiences could be represented by managers, staff writers, and

1

freelancers. These readers might already be involved in outsourcing projects and could be looking for ideas that would guide them in overcoming cross-cultural problems; or they could be gathering information about technical communication in other countries as a way of planning for the future. In academic or workplace environments, readers of this book can be in any country involved or planning to be involved in technical communication projects involving offshore outsourcing.

DEFINING OUTSOURCING

Authors in this collection write about outsourcing mainly as a synonym for offshore outsourcing or *offshoring*, a term that has been defined as "the procurement of goods or services by a business or organization from an outside foreign supplier, typically to gain the benefits of labor arbitrage" (Brown & Wilson, 2005, p. vii). It is important to point out that this book does not cover outsourcing as the general *vertical de-integration* process that takes place "when a company decides to purchase a product or service from a source outside of the company. It generally refers to products or services that were once done in-house, now purchased from a source external to the company" (Hira & Hira, 2005, p. 199). The chapters included in this book look exclusively at outsourcing cases involving international transactions and operations.

It is impossible to ignore outsourcing as a controversial topic. The outsourcing debate has generated discussion about exporting jobs and also concern for the complexity of managing the production of documents at a distance, for training offshore workers, and for the cultural differences that may result in different expectations for outcomes. The topic of outsourcing has been portrayed recently as a hot issue in news media, political campaigns, and even pop-culture representations. Some commentators say that "outsourcing and the motives behind it are simply destructive of our way of life" (Dobbs, 2004, p. 2), while others say that offshore outsourcing is a consequence of globalization and that "home-sourcing to Salt Lake City and outsourcing to Bangalore were just flip sides of the same coin sourcing" (Friedman, 2005, p. 38). Although some individual contributors might have strong ideas leaning toward any side of the debate, this book as a whole does not promote a general opinion or prescription about outsourcing. Instead, it presents a balanced gathering of perspectives that should enable the readers to come up with their own perspectives on this issue.

From a technical communicator's perspective, outsourcing projects are international by definition, vulnerable to cultural differences, and liable in legal and political dilemmas.

Outsourcing is international by definition because it involves offshore markets where writers are being hired to develop technical documentation for audiences that could be located anywhere in the world. The generic essence of the basic genres of technical communication makes the field susceptible to this kind of outsourcing. Unlike creative writing or even journalism, technical documents can be reduced to simple repositories of headings, subheadings, and list items. Any academic bookstore in the United States probably has a dozen technical communication textbooks that present the field based on principles of simplicity in design and composition. When fundamental deliverables in any profession can be apparently expressed in checklists and general rules, anyone with critical-thinking skills and average professional-English proficiency can become a technical writer—in any country. Non-native English speakers can write technical documents for American audiences, and technological advancements can integrate them to production teams regardless of their geographical location.

Outsourcing is vulnerable to cultural differences because those non-native English speakers might be able to write an effective set of instructions for household appliances, but they might not understand the context in which the tool will be used. Being in another country and trained in English exclusively for business or professional situations, these writers can be in *acontextual* or *bicontextual* situations, in which their native values and beliefs are not represented in the documents they produce for a living. These cultural differences are not related exclusively to nationality or language; they can also be present in organizational climate or managerial practices. The American offices of a corporation might have standards and procedures that the Indian office of the same company might not understand or follow, or vice versa.

Outsourcing is liable in legal and political dilemmas because we are writing the story on technical communication offshoring with every new project. There is not much written when it comes to rules and regulations for teams exchanging technical information overseas. Furthermore, every country has its own set of rules, and in most cases they are not 100% compatible with American regulations. In this area, technical communication projects involving offshore writers can take place in an environment of uncertainty and doubt. Likewise, the political climate of an organization can be very different in the American headquarters and its international branches, and these discrepancies have the potential to generate conflict among collaborators or between writers and managers.

This international nature of offshore outsourcing, characterized by differences in culture and management styles, and subject to misinterpretations and problems with legal and political repercussions, gives structure to the chapters in this book.

ORGANIZATION

Outsourcing Technical Communications is organized in three main sections: Outsourcing Practices by Region; Management and Cross-Cultural Communication Issues; and Legal, Ethical, and Political Implications. Each of these sections includes chapters addressing theoretical and practical implications of outsourcing in international environments.

Part I, Outsourcing Practices by Region, includes voices from different countries where technical writing is becoming a profession mainly because of outsourced projects. It also includes chapters analyzing problems caused by sending American documentation tasks to specific countries. The opening chapter, "Technical Communication and IT Outsourcing in India—Past, Present, and Future," justifies India's prominent role in today's international technical communication. Prashant Natarajan and Makarand Pandit, experienced technical writers and trainers in this field, explore the historical roots of technical writing in India, connecting it to religious texts written between 1500 BC and 1200 BC. The authors present a detailed account of the profession's development in India and also analyze the bilingual skills of technical writers in India, where millions of professionals speak English as their main language in business and technical environments. The core of this chapter is a survey that was applied to members of India's chapter of the Society for Technical Communication (STC) in order to determine their linguistic preferences and skills, and their experience in outsourcing projects.

Whereas Natarajan and Pandit portray the Indian perspective on the outsourcing debate, Carlos Evia brings in the American tradition looking for a contrasting effect. In "Defining Technical Communication in the United States and India: A Contrastive Analysis of Established Curricula and Desired Abilities," Evia compares what it means to be a technical communicator in the United States to what the Indian market expects from professionals in this field. Evia's chapter focuses on training and education options available for aspiring technical communicators in both countries. Upon analyzing course offerings and interviewing trainers and educators, Evia argues that the evolution of technical communication as a profession in India might lead to an interesting expansion of the field in the global economy. He also documents forces dividing the field in both countries, emphasizing the divide between academia and industry that affects technical communication in the United States.

In "Africa Goes for Outsourcing," Michael Bokor faces the difficult challenge of making a whole continent of over 800 million inhabitants look attractive for outsourcing projects involving technical communication. Bokor acknowledges the political, geographical, linguistic, and social problems that affect Africa's current potential for accepting outsourcing projects. However, he also presents success stories from call centers in Kenya, Ghana, and South Africa. His chapter includes a call for action that enables many African countries as potential outsource destinations in the same league as India and China for these types of projects. He also introduces the French component: many African countries have French-speaking professionals, who make the continent attractive for outsourcing projects aimed at French-speaking audiences.

If Bokor makes the audience look briefly at outsourcing from a non-English, non-American perspective, Petra Drewer and Charlotte Kaempf use that resource as the main element of their chapter. In "Outsourcing of Technical Communication Tasks from German-Speaking Contexts," these authors look at outsourcing from the sending end, but their senders are not American companies. As it turns out, German documentation projects are also susceptible to being sent to cheaper foreign markets from Austria, Germany, and Switzerland. Drewer and Kaempf compare definitions for terms related to outsourcing and technical communication in the United States and Germany, and then give data on the status of technical communication as a profession in German-speaking contexts, focusing on education programs and job opportunities.

The last region explored in this section is the United States-Mexico border. In "Approaching Outsourcing in Rhetoric and Professional Communication: Lessons from U.S.-Owned Maquilas in Mexico," Barry Thatcher and Victoriano Garza-Almanza study the history of rhetoric, outsourcing, and technology in projects involving collaboration between the United States and Mexico. Conducting case studies in American-owned *maquiladoras* or *maquilas* (subcontracting production plants) in northern Mexico, Thatcher and Garza-Almanza show how Mexican engineers "translated" technical information to lineworkers in a mainly oral approach. Then they present the well-documented profiles of some workers who, without being aware of it, were doing outsourced technical communication work in a country where, at least on paper, such a field does not exist.

Part II, Management and Cross-Cultural Communication Issues, ponders the repercussions of outsourcing on the production cycle and management of information products. Moving from organizational culture to international issues, this section also examines what kinds of cross-cultural competencies and technologies are needed to work effectively in the outsourcing environment. JoAnn and Bill Hackos, in "The Information Developer's Dilemma," denounce what they consider to be a disruptive innovation coming from low-cost economies obtaining outsourced documentation jobs originated in the United States and Western Europe. They blame this shift in the professional market on high–speed, inexpensive worldwide communications. These authors claim that because of new communications technology, technical writers do not need to be physically in touch with subject-matter experts or end-users; therefore, technical writing jobs can be sent to offshore markets. They propose a plan that urges technical communicators to take an aggressive position and understand market forces with business objectives. By learning how to save money in their projects, they add, information developers might be able to compete with cheap labor from foreign workers.

Continuing the skills-building recommendations for competitive advantage introduced by Hackos and Hackos, Jim Melton invites American technical communicators to get involved in international training programs. In "Language, Culture, and Collaboration in Offshore Outsourcing: A Case Study of International Training Team Roles and Communication Competencies," Melton wants to find out what competencies would assist technical communicators involved in international training projects. In order to answer his research questions, Melton conducted a case study inside a training program aimed at Japanese salespeople working for an American company in Hawaii. His findings and recommendations cover a wide range of skills related to translation, rhetoric, collaboration, linguistics, and social and cultural differences.

In "The Implications of Outsourcing for Technical Editing," Clint Lanier also urges American technical writers to gain specialized skills as a competitive advantage in the global economy. In this particular case, he introduces technical editors as mediators between outsourced writers and their client organizations in the United States. Lanier's research included a virtual focus group with technical editors, in which they expressed their opinions and experiences dealing with cultural and rhetorical differences in outsourcing projects.

Part III, Legal, Ethical, and Political Issues, stems from the question of what kinds of legal and ethical issues are associated with outsourcing and international collaboration in technical communication projects. In "The Privacy Problems Related to International Outsourcing: A Perspective for Technical Communicators," Kirk St. Amant uses a recent case of information blackmail to hypothesize on problems that could happen because of the exporting of personal medical or financial data to other nations. St. Amant talks about gray-market informatics: the process of an outsourced technical communicator stealing confidential information. He concludes the chapter by introducing a series of strategies that technical communicators can use to counter privacy threats in outsourcing.

St. Amant argues that gray-market informatics is possible because there is no actual regulation on privacy and confidentiality in outsourcing projects. In "Outsourcing Technical Communication: The Policy Behind the Practice," Keith Gibson investigates this apparent lack of legislation and looks at the way in which the future of outsourcing is presented in political speeches. Particularly, he looks at the 2004 presidential campaign in the United States and studies how each candidate addressed the outsource debate.

Continuing Gibson's analysis of outsourcing's legal implications, the last chapter of this collection, "Obligations and Opportunities: Legal Issues in Offshore Outsourcing Technical Communication," reviews policies and rules governing offshoring. Charlsye Smith Diaz writes in this chapter that most outsourcing projects rely on "soft law"—individual agreements between corporations, due to the lack of actual rules. She interviews legal specialists and suggests that technical communicators can work as facilitators who convene offshore outsourcing relationships.

The authors of this collection look at the controversial issue of offshore outsourcing from different perspectives based on nationality and personal bias, and grounded on professional specialization and interests. I hope their ideas can generate conversation and prompt readers to take action and get involved with technical communication in the global economy. The chapters should affect teaching and training programs in technical communication in countries interested in outsourcing for different reasons, and should also bring new knowledge to decision making in projects from academia and industry.

REFERENCES

Brown, D., & Wilson, S. (2005). *The black book of outsourcing: How to manage the changes, challenges, and opportunities.* Hoboken, NJ: Wiley.

Dobbs, L. (2004). *Exporting America: Why corporate greed is shipping American jobs overseas.* New York: Warner Books.

Friedman, T. L. (2005). *The world is flat: A brief history of the twenty-first century.* New York: Farrar, Straus and Giroux.

Hira, R., & Hira, A. (2005). *Outsourcing America: What's behind our national crisis and how we can reclaim American jobs.* New York: AMACOM.

PART I

Outsourcing Practices
by Region

CHAPTER 1

Technical Communication and IT Outsourcing in India— Past, Present, and Future

Prashant Natarajan and
Makarand Pandit

Writing in India has a long history and can be traced back to the Vedic and Harappan civilizations (2600 BC–1900 BC). The Brahmi script used in ancient Harappan texts of the period is "systematic" and appears to follow grammatical rules (Kak, 1994, p. 375). An early sample of Indian technical communication can be found in the *Rig Veda* (third millennium BC), a religious text that includes chapters on intricate astronomical code, grammar, and writing (Kak, 1994, p. 386).

The profession of technical communication in India, however, has humbler beginnings. It is only in the last fifteen years that technical communicators have been identified and recognized as practitioners of the field of technical and professional communication. Indian corporate recognition of technical communication as value addition appears to have been motivated by the needs of Information Technology (IT) outsourcing as opposed to the needs of the local economy. India is presently the favorite IT outsourcing destination for organizations located in North America, Europe, and the rest of Asia. According to India's National Association of Software and Service Companies (NASSCOM), "India's software and services exports business recorded revenue of $12.5 billion in the fiscal year that ended March 31, 2004, up by 30.5% over revenue of $9.6 billion in the previous year" (Ribero, 2004).

India, the "largest English-speaking country in the world" (Crystal, 2004) has a rich scientific tradition and is home to many renowned engineering and

11

science universities. Thanks to its linguistic, educational, and cultural strengths, India appears to be uniquely placed to address global technical communication/ information-development needs successfully. In *Offshore Information Development Benchmark Study,* Hackos (2002) states, "[. . .] to decrease operational costs and increase competitive advantage, offshore information development has, for some companies, become a viable alternative to hiring information developers in North America" (p. 2). In our opinion (Natarajan and Pandit), global trends and local business needs represent an increasing need for the services of Indian technical communicators, who are estimated to number fewer than 5000 today (exact statistics are not available).

Available scholarly research on writing and technical communication in the Indian subcontinent is almost nonexistent. Among the only published articles of significance are Kak's *Evolution of Early Writing in India* and Hackos' whitepaper for Dell Computers, *Offshore Information Development Benchmark Study.* However, Indian English (the Indian variant of British English) is well represented in linguistics research by authors such as Crystal, Mehrotra, Kachru, Schiffman, and Hohenthal, among others.

This chapter attempts to provide an up-to-date and detailed picture of the profession of technical communication in India. It briefly traces the evolution of writing and technical communication in the country's past, beginning with the *Rig Veda* and ending with the adoption of English as an official language. We also use responses from a national survey of members of the Society for Technical Communication's (STC) India branch to identify their current workplace roles and responsibilities. The chapter includes discussions on the roles of Standard American English (SAE) and Indian English (IE), global business trends, and academic support of future prospects for the profession in the subcontinent. We hope these findings and discussions are useful to researchers and professionals interested in learning more about language use, writing, and information development in India. This chapter is organized into the following sections:

- Writing and technical communication in ancient India
- English in pre- and post-independent India
- Outsourcing trends and technical communication
- Survey methodology and sample demographics
- Survey results
- Conclusions

WRITING AND TECHNICAL COMMUNICATION IN ANCIENT INDIA

India has a rich legacy of writing and technical communication. Early Indian technical communication appears to be a direct consequence of the country's scientific and mathematical tradition. In his seminal article on Indian writing, Kak traces the evolution of ancient Indian writing by using archeological artifacts and the discovery of astronomical code in the *Rig Veda* (or *Rgveda)*. He states, "The recent discovery of the astronomical code on the basis of the *Rgveda* also raises important questions regarding writing in ancient India. Even the most conservative estimates date the Rgveda to the second millennium B.C." Kak further states, "[. . .] the *Rgveda* was probably completed in the third millennium B.C." and "the existence of an intricate astronomical code suggests that the earliest Vedic phase was characterized by knowledge of writing" (Kak, 1994, p. 376).

The development of the Indian (also known as Hindu-Arabic or Arabic) numeral system (0–9) is well known and beyond the scope of this chapter. However, it is interesting to note that Indian numerals first appeared in European texts like *Codex Vigilanus* in 976 AD (Kak, 1994, p. 384). We think the evolution of science, mathematics, geometry, and algebra in ancient Indian civilizations is a direct consequence of the technical communication developed to support scientific thinking and processes. The Sanskrit texts *Shulba Sutras* (800 BC–200 BC) are examples of early technical documents that contain geometrical and algebraic formulae. Panini's (a prominent Indian rhetorician) treatise on Sanskrit grammar, *Astadhyayi* (460 BC), appears to be the first work on rhetoric and composition. O'Connor and Robertson (2000) stated, "[*Astadhyayi*] consists of eight chapters, each subdivided into quarter chapters. In this work Panini distinguishes between the language of sacred texts and the usual language of communication. Panini gives formal production rules and definitions to describe Sanskrit grammar."

The influence of Panini's *Astadhyayi* on both rhetoric and science has been seen as significant. According to O'Connor and Robertson (2000),

> Panini should be thought of as the forerunner of the modern formal language theory used to specify computer languages. The Backus Normal Form was discovered independently by John Backus in 1959, but Panini's notation is equivalent in its power to that of Backus and has many similar properties. It is remarkable to think that concepts which are fundamental to today's theoretical computer science should have their origin with an Indian genius around 2500 years ago.

Joseph stated that "[Sanskrit's] potential for scientific use was greatly enhanced as a result of the thorough systemisation (sic) of its grammar by Panini" (as cited in O'Connor & Robertson, 2000) According to O'Connor and Robertson, "[Joseph] suggests that algebraic reasoning, the Indian way of representing numbers by words, and ultimately the development of modern number systems in India, are linked through the structure of language."

Thanks to the economic and business opportunities created by outsourcing, Indian information developers may be able to use their ancient scientific and rhetorical traditions to create a positive impact on the knowledge creation and dissemination in the twenty-first century.

ENGLISH IN PRE- AND POSTINDEPENDENT INDIA

India's rhetorical and linguistic traditions would not be complete without an examination of the significant influence of English, first introduced in India following the bilingual language debate in 1835, which focused on "which language(s) should be used as the medium of education in India" (Hohenthal, 2000b). Despite the fact that Jones and other Orientalists found Sanskrit to "[have a] wonderful structure, more perfect than Greek, and more copious than Latin, and more exquisitely refined than either" (Schiffman, 1999, p. 437), Sanskrit lost its role as *apabrahmsha*—the more formal or the official language— and English soon became the language of administration in colonial India. English also became the preferred language for the elite Indian upper and middle classes, and the language for education (also known in India as English-medium education). After obtaining its independence in 1947, India decided to retain English as an important link language despite dozens of other languages and dialects, conferred it official status, and made it the language of law, adminis- tration, commerce, and education. The easy adoption of English by bilingual Indians in pre- and postcolonial periods is not merely a result of colonial dictates; unlike most former British colonies, the end of colonial rule did not mean the demise of English as a preferred language of the middle and upper classes or an official language of government. Independent India has continued to promote the use of English in bureaucracies, private businesses, and schools.

According to Kachru (1994), "The penetration of English in [Indian] societies is greater than it has ever been" (p. 542). It is important that we see the use of English in India as more than a second language (ESL). The use of English in India, in professional and personal spheres, should be viewed as symptomatic of multilingualism. *Webster's Encyclopedic Unabridged Dictionary of the English Language* (1996) defines multilingualism as the ability to "speak more than two languages with approximately equal facility" (p. 940). Additionally, Kachru described multilingualism as the "linguistic behavior of the members of a speech community which alternately uses two, three, or more languages depending on the situation and function" (as cited by Hohenthal, 2000a). Indian English, a national variant of British English, is now an official, integral colanguage (as opposed to being a second language). In her article, "Standard Englishes and World Englishes: Living with a Polymorph Business Language," Gilsdorf (2002) wrote,

Kachru (1992) diagrammed the spread of English as a series of inter-linked circles. The First—or Inner—Circle nations are those for which English has been strongly L1 (i.e., First Language) and from which English has spread to other countries. The Second—or Outer—Circle includes those where English has taken strong root as an intranational official language or co-language. The Third—or Expanding—Circle shows those nations now increasing their use of English as an inter- or intra-national language of business, technology, and/or government" (p. 368).

The development of Indian English is clearly in Kachru's "Second Circle" and appears to be poised for greater acceptance and growth in the future. The widespread acceptance of English in India as a colanguage appears to be one of the main reasons for the country's recent emergence as a hub for global technical communication and knowledge management.

OUTSOURCING TRENDS AND TECHNICAL COMMUNICATION

Outsourcing can be defined as "the act of obtaining services from an external firm." According to McIver (2004), Electronic Data Systems (EDS) pioneered the concept of Business Process Outsourcing (BPO) in the early 1960s. EDS was able to convince its potential clients that it could do a better job of creating, maintaining, and providing IT support services. According to McIver (2004), "The underlying theory is that the BPO firm can complete the process more efficiently, leaving the original firm free to concentrate on its core competency." Offshore outsourcing, or outsourcing to firms in developing countries such as China, India, Mexico, Sri Lanka, and Philippines, has become more common in the last ten years. Educated professionals in developing countries are able to work for lower wages than workers in developed countries. Though accurate figures are difficult to obtain, some studies estimate that organizations in developed countries can trim 25% to 60% of their costs by moving IT support services to developing countries. It is important to note that outsourcing is not driven by just cost concerns. In his book, *The World is Flat*, Friedman (2005) points out that ". . . India right now has a great advantage in having a pool of educated, low-wage English speakers with a strong service etiquette in their DNA and an enterprising spirit" (p. 189). Thanks to their emerging markets, pools of talented and educated professionals, and increased productivity, developing countries such as India are increasingly becoming obvious partners of businesses that are interested in achieving multiple gains through the use of outsourcing.

With its huge English-speaking population, India has particularly become an attractive destination for IT software and support services such as software documentation. NASSCOM estimates that more than 300,000 white-collar jobs have been created in India since 2000 to serve overseas clients, many of which are U.S.-based companies (Maher, 2004). However, the potential savings from outsourcing do not remain constant. Additional costs (political consider-ations, travel, long-distance communication, and increasing wages in developing countries) associated with outsourcing may influence the future of offshore information development. McIver (2004) warns, "Savings from the lower wage rate must exceed the increased costs of management and risk associated with offshore outsourcing for it to be economically viable."

SURVEY METHODOLOGY AND SAMPLE DEMOGRAPHICS

Survey Design

As mentioned earlier, we conducted a national survey of the 100 members of the India chapter of STC to elicit information on the current state of the technical communication. Our Web-based survey was developed and tested by the authors at their respective locations (Pune, India and Auburn, AL, USA) in mid-November 2004. After the test revisions, the survey was finalized in the following form, which contained 38 questions in nine sections. The nine sections were

1. Introduction to the survey
2. Demographics (name, age, education, and location)
3. Professional profile (title, experience, and organization)
4. Organizational profile (area of expertise, location of headquarters, number of employees, and outsourcing relationships)
5. Job roles (document genres, preferred language for workplace writing, and translation)
6. Linguistic profile (native language(s), language proficiency, English education, and English as a first and a second language)
7. Outsourcing (optional part on specifics of outsourcing relationships between the participant's organization in India and clients located outside India)
8. Professional development (career development and skills enhancement)
9. Additional comments (open-ended questions on the current profile of the profession, future of outsourcing, and recommendations)

To assist participants in describing their professional roles and personal qualifications, the survey provided possible answer choices and open text fields. For example, the question on title/designation provided a list of multiple workplace job titles (taken from the STC Web site) and an open text field for recording an unavailable option. To improve the usability of the survey and to ensure better survey management, we organized the 38 questions into eight sections and ensured that each section did not contain more than five open-text or multiple-choice questions. Additionally, we designed the survey to allow multiple interruptions and continuations from the same Internet Protocol (IP) address. As a result, participants had the option to continue with and complete the survey over multiple login sessions. To answer the various mandatory and nonmandatory questions, participants could choose from binary, multiple-choice, and open-text answer options. The complete list of questions is available at www.calanus.us.

Survey Dissemination and Sample Selection

After the final version was uploaded on a paid online survey management Web site, two survey rounds followed. In the first round, we e-mailed an introductory message and the link to the online survey to the 100 members of India chapter on December 2, 2004 through their Yahoo Groups listserv. This listserv is an online mailing list for members of the STC India chapter and serves as the primary contact mechanism for chapter members. Listserv subscribers are invited to join by the listserv owner after they join STC under the India chapter affiliation. From the Yahoo Groups e-mail archives for 2004, we obtained the list of 22 members who had joined STC in the latter half of 2004 but were not yet members of the listserv. We added these e-mail addresses to the directory of listserv subscribers for a total of 100 survey invitees.

On the first closing date of December 15, 2004, 31 participants had responded to the survey for a relatively low response rate of 31%. In the second round, we sent out e-mail reminders to all subscribers of the listserv requesting their participation. Between December 15 and December 22, 2004, we received 19 additional replies for a total of 50 participants. Our response rate of 50% "is consistent (under 50%) with most writing research" (MacNealy & Heaton, 1999, p. 44). Responses from both rounds are combined and reported in our discussions.

Our sample size of 100 may appear to be relatively small compared with rough estimates of 5,000 technical writers in India. We decided to restrict the survey-participation requests to the STC India chapter because these members are more likely to have at least two years of continuous professional experience and may be expected to have a better understanding of national and international trends in information development. Additionally, other recognized international professional organizations (such as IEEE PCS and ACM SIGDOC) have minimal representation in India. As a result, the analysis and responses of the 50 participants can be assumed to provide a representative picture of people, workplace roles, organizations, customers, language, and outsourcing of technical communications as a profession in the Indian IT outsourcing industry.

SURVEY RESULTS

The survey results are presented in the following sections: Demographic Profiles, Professional and Organizational Profiles, Job Roles, Linguistic Profiles, Outsourcing Relationships, and Professional Development. Responses to the professional development and open-ended questions (in the last two sections of the survey) substantiate our discussions and conclusions. The complete survey results are available at www.calanus.us.

Demographic Profiles

Survey participants had the option of providing their name, e-mail address, and age. Of the 50 participants, 41 participants (84%) provided their age. The age distribution of the respondents is given in Table 1.

The age distribution of the participants (76% between the ages of 26 and 40) reflects our assumption regarding the recent emergence of technical communication as a profession in India. Outsourcing of information development to India, a relatively new trend that goes back to the last 10 to 15 years, appears to be a significant contributor to the current and future growth prospects of technical communication in the country. Based on this trend, it is valid to assume that the overall age distribution for non-STC members who work as technical communicators may be similar to the ranges for STC members. Though data for comparison is unavailable, the only significant difference between age ranges for participants and non-participants may lie in the 21–25 range. This difference may be a result of the work-experience filter of two years that we used to define our sample.

The educational qualifications of the participants mostly include undergraduate and graduate degrees in commerce, English, engineering, science, mathematics, journalism, mass communication, or information systems. Most English degrees have been obtained at the master's level in literature. None of the participants has an undergraduate or graduate degree in technical writing, information design, rhetoric, or professional communication; our interviews with academic and industry professionals in India indicate that Indian universities do not offer

Table 1. Age Distribution of Participants

Age range (in years)	Response percentage	Response total
18–20	0%	0
21–25	12%	5
26–30	29%	12
31–35	27%	11
36–40	20%	8
41–45	<5%	2
46–50	<5%	1
51–55	<5%	2
56–60	0%	0
	Total = 100%	Total = 41

academic-degree programs in rhetoric and professional/technical communication. At present, the need for basic and continuing adult education appears to be met by employers and short-term courses by smaller private institutes (as opposed to being met by public and private universities). However, recent announcements on the Yahoo Groups mailing list regarding courses offered by a few universities in India indicate an ongoing interest in the development of university-level courses and programs in technical communication and rhetoric.

Most respondents are located in Bangalore, Chennai (Madras), Delhi, Gurgoan, and Pune. These results are in line with the distribution of India's IT industry. Bangalore, home to the largest concentration of local and multinational IT companies, is the residence for the largest number of participants (20 out of 50, comprising 40%). Pune, with nine participants (22.5%), ranks second among the five cities. The other three cities share the third position for the largest concentrations of technical communicators.

Professional and Organizational Profiles

Technical communicators in India are called by a variety of professional designations. Table 2 displays the different designations and the distribution in the industry/workplace.

"Technical Writer" is the most frequent designation for professionals who are not in management. Participants who chose "Other" provided designations like senior technical writer, lead information developer, and principal technical writer. Designations such as lead technical writer and documentation manager occur at a higher rate in this sample compared to the IT industry as a whole. The difference in these rates arises from our sample selection, which was designed to encourage participation by professionals with at least two years' experience.

Table 2. Distribution of Job Titles

Designation	Response percentage	Response total
Technical Writer	20%	10
Information Developer	6%	3
Technical Communicator	0%	0
Lead Technical Writer	12%	6
Technical Editor	<5%	1
Content Developer	<5%	2
Documentation Manager	24%	12
Other (please specify)	32%	16
	Total = 100%	Total = 50

A majority of participants (approximately 60%) started in the profession after hearing about it from family, friends, or co-workers. Twelve (24%) saw job advertisements for technical communicators and decided to join the profession. The remaining participants learned about the profession from newspaper articles, Web sites, and career counselors in university or training institutes.

Our assumptions on outsourcing and its impact on the development of technical communication as a distinct profession are supported by the responses on participants' professional experience as technical communicators. Figure 1 provides the responses to the question "How many years have you been working as a technical communicator?"

Thirty-one participants (62%) had 4–10 years' experience. The percentage of technical communicators with more than 10 years' experience was quite low and reflected the relative inexperience of the technical communication community in India (in contrast to other well-established professional communities in North America and Europe). These results also support Hackos' (2002) contention that "In India and most other countries outside out North America and western Europe, technical communication is still in its infancy" (p. 12).

Figure 2 provides the responses to the question "How many years have you been working as a technical communicator in your current organization?"

Seventeen participants (34%) worked in the same organization for more than four years. The vast majority of participants (66%) worked in the same company for less than four years. This distribution appears to support the assumption that the profession is still in a relatively early stage of evolution in India. The distribution of responses may also indicate that job prospects are bright for experienced and qualified professionals because the field is relatively uncrowded.

Organizational Profiles

Participants could choose more than one answer for the question "What domain/area of expertise does your organization/business unit specialize in?"

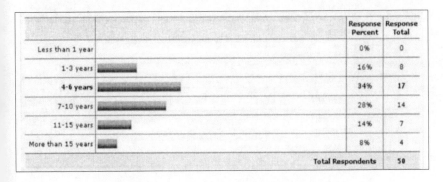

		Response Percent	Response Total
Less than 1 year		0%	0
1-3 years		16%	8
4-6 years		34%	17
7-10 years		28%	14
11-15 years		14%	7
More than 15 years		8%	4
	Total Respondents		50

Figure 1. Years as technical communicators.

Participants' employers specialize in various industrial specializations or areas of expertise. They include computer software and hardware development, manufacturing, embedded software (such as chip-based real-time operating systems), and training and development. As we expected, the software-development industry is the primary employer of Indian technical communicators. The total distributions for this question are given in Figure 3.

The employers of seven participants (14%) function as corporate-training institutes. The six (12%) participants who chose "Other" mostly worked for organizations that offer only technical communication products and services. The

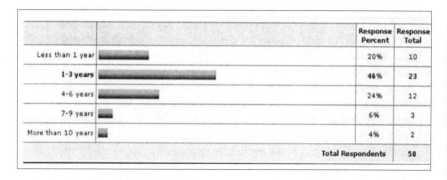

Figure 2. Years as technical communicator in current organization.

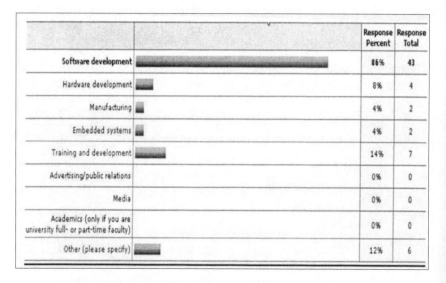

Figure 3. Industry distribution of technical communicators.

corporate headquarters of participants' organizations were located in India (26%) and the United States (64%). Corporate headquarters were also located in Canada (6%) and Finland (4%). These percentages demonstrate that many technical communicators in India currently work for either United States or India-based organizations.

In response to the follow-up question "Does your organization in India provide outsourcing or offshoring services for a parent company or a client that is located outside India?" 32 participants (64%) selected "Yes" and 14 (28%) selected "No." Four participants did not know the answer to the question. The 64% who selected "Yes" indicated that their outsourcing partner's customers/ end-users are mostly located in the United States, the United Kingdom, and Australia. Other answers included Japan, China, Germany, Scandinavia, Canada, and India. The prevalence of end-users in English-speaking countries like the United States, the United Kingdom, and Australia suggests that India is increasingly being recognized as a production center for information development and knowledge management in English.

Job Roles

Multiple roles and responsibilities appeared to be a part of the average participant's job. When asked to select the multiple roles in their jobs, participants selected the following primary responsibilities: technical writing, such as user guides, installation guides, configuration guides, Application Program Interface (API)/software code documentation, and other hardcopy documents (39 entries); editing (33 entries); online help development (30 entries); project and team management (40 entries); and corporate training and development (23 entries). Secondary responsibilities included proposal/grant writing (98 entries), quality assurance or testing (9 entries), and education (3 entries).

At their workplaces, technical communicators primarily write their documentation in SAE. Of the 50 participants, 44 (88%) chose SAE as the primary language for workplace writing. One participant responded that she wrote her documentation in SAE, British English, and IE based on end-user language requirements. Apart from demonstrating the location of most end-users/readers in the United States, this result may indicate that SAE (as opposed to other "flavors" of English) is the primary language for global business communication. Figure 4 shows the complete distribution of responses.

These results also appear to prove that technical communicators must develop competency and excellence in SAE in order to be more successful professionally. Participants chose to answer the follow-up question "Is your documentation primarily written for foreign countries (outside India)?" by selecting "Yes" as the clear favorite. Regardless of the company they worked for or its location, an overwhelming 46 participants (92%) wrote their documents for clients located outside India. This statistic also supports our assumption that the profession owes

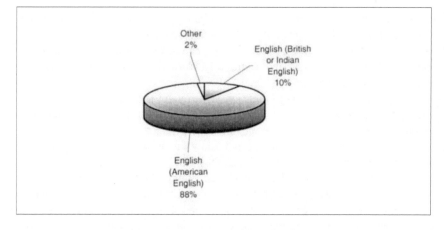

Figure 4. Documentation language.

its current recognition to IT outsourcing and global business trends instead of local professional needs.

The documents of 32 surveyed writers (64%) are translated from English into other languages. Fourteen (28%) writers' documents were not translated from English (as discussed earlier, SAE is the overwhelming choice for most Indian information developers). Four (8%) did not know the answer to the question. Hackos (2002) stated, "Participants in [her] study noted that technical communicators for whom English is a second language produce non-standard writing that is difficult, time consuming, and very costly to translate" (p. 13). Data on ease of translation of documents written in SAE by Indian technical writers is not available presently. It is possible that the difficulties involved during translation arise from cultural differences, lack of face-to-face contact, and other constraints of virtual communication. However, we recognize that differences exist between the rhetoric and language used by native English speakers (English as a First Language or L1) and non-native speakers (ESL or multilingual or L2 speakers).

Linguistic Profiles

In his article, "India: Bursting at the Linguistic Seams," Choudhry (2000) states,

> India with a population of around one billion people is often regarded as a model of harmonious linguistic coexistence within a single state. It has two official languages (Hindi and English), 18 major languages Scheduled in the Indian Constitution, and 418 "listed" languages, each spoken by 10,000 people or more. All-India Radio broadcasts in 24 languages and in 146 dialects; newspapers are published in at least 34 languages; 67 languages are used in primary education, and 80 in literacy work.

Our survey reflects the rich linguistic diversity in India; Table 3 displays the distinct native languages for the 49 participants who answered the question. One participant chose not to answer this question.

Of the four who chose English as their native language (L1 or mother tongue), one is a native-English-speaking American national who is a member of the STC India chapter. The other three participants are Indians whose L1 is British English or IE. Kachru argues that "in the multilinguistic and culturally pluralistic context of India, the English language has developed its regional, social and occupational varieties: typically Indian registers of legal system, business, newspapers, creative writing" (as cited in Hohenthal, 2000b, "The Question of Standard English"). Research on English use in India by Crystal, Hohenthal, Kachru, and others indicates that the linguistic development of IE displays a definite influence of Indian history, attitudes, and culture.

In addition to being home to several native languages, India has "a special place in the English language record books—as the country with the largest English-speaking population in the world. Ten years ago that record was held by the US. Not any more" (Crystal, 2004). According to Crystal (2004), in the 1980s, "only about 4%–5% of the population were thought to use the language." He also stated, "given the steady increase in English learning since 1997 in schools and among the upwardly mobile, we must today be talking about at least 350 million [English speakers]." Though "many [Indians] still think of Indian English as inferior, and see British English as the only 'proper' English," it may take only a few years for popular and scholarly opinions in India to recognize and accept the local Indian English variant (Crystal, 2004).

Table 3. Native Languages of Participants

Native language	Response percentage	Response total
Assamese	2%	1
Bengali	4%	2
English	8%	4
Hindi	12%	6
Kannada	16%	8
Konkani	2%	1
Malayalam	12%	6
Marathi	10%	5
Punjabi	4%	2
Tamil	18%	9
Telugu	10%	5

Of the 48 participants who answered the follow-up question on when they first learned English, 36 (75%) answered that they learned English at school because it was the language of instruction. Nine (19%) learned English at school as a second language. The remaining participants learned the language at home as a native language (L1). Thirty-seven participants (77%) claim to be "very comfortable" with using English (or as our survey shows, SAE) to produce documents for a native-English-speaking (L1) audience, and 23% claim to be "comfortable" in using SAE to create documents for L1 speakers. Not a single participant chose the "Neither comfortable nor uncomfortable," "Uncomfortable," or "Very uncomfortable" options. For the reasons mentioned earlier (experience in international communication and linguistic expertise), the high levels of comfort in using SAE to communicate to native audiences are to be expected for our survey sample. However, these results cannot be extended to the larger professional community in India because published research appears to suggest otherwise. For example, Hackos (2002) states, "[t]he majority of [U.S.-based] managers interviewed argue that using non-native-English speakers significantly increased the amount of editing required to produce a sound product for North American audiences and translation from English into additional languages" (p. 31). In the open-ended-question section (last section of the questionnaire), some participants recognized the need for excellent English communication skills. One participant pointed out, "Technical writers in India must make that extra effort to learn the English language well, if they want to shine in the international market."

Outsourcing Relationships

Beginning with this section, the remaining questions in the survey were optional. This was done in order to facilitate survey completion for the limited number of participants who worked in organizations that do not collaborate with customers/partners outside India. In response to the first question "Do you/does your documentation team have a native-English speaking editor and/or a documentation manager located outside India?" 22 participants (52%) answered "Yes" and 20 (48%) answered "No." According to Hackos (2002), controlling editing costs can be effectively accomplished by "assigning North American mentors, providing training on basic English, educating in the technical subject matter, and establishing rapport to facilitate better feedback channels" (p. 35). We agree with most of Hackos' recommendations because we think their adoption can facilitate the establishment of successful outsourcing relationships, especially in the earliest stages of partnership. However, we think the advanced nature of IT research and product development in India and the colocation of development and documentation may result in decreasing reliance on technical-knowledge transfer to Indian professionals in the near future. We are also of the opinion that corporate/organizational-level-English training should focus on teaching the L1 speaker's formal and idiomatic use of SAE, gender-neutral/non-sexist language, and plain/international English as opposed to teaching basic English skills.

Indian professionals interact regularly with documentation/information-development team members and counterparts in other countries. In order of decreasing frequency, the countries chosen by participants include the United States, the United Kingdom, Canada, Finland, Korea, Ireland, Italy, Singapore, Sri Lanka, and Sweden. These interactions occur daily (53%), twice or thrice a week (27%), or once a week (10%). The other 10% interact with their international colleagues on a less-frequent basis. In this sample, the diverse list of countries indicated by the participants suggests that Indian professionals are mostly a part of and regularly interact with larger international technical communication teams. Hackos' (2002) study appears to support our results; the American organizations in her sample outsourced their information development to countries such as Argentina, Belgium, Germany, France, India, Italy, Japan, and Russia, among others (pp. 37, 38). The establishment of multisite international teams also indicates that information development may increasingly become part of the global economy.

In response to the last question "What are the challenges involved in producing documentation for clients located outside India?" participants chose time zone differences, lack of face-to-face interaction with clients, and unclear requirements as the top three challenges. Cultural and linguistic differences were the fifth and sixth choices. The "Other" option included challenges such as project planning, network bandwidth (one participant), and client-specific tool and domain knowledge. Two participants answered that they faced absolutely no challenges in their relationships. Figure 5 provides the complete distribution of challenges involved in document distribution.

The results here appear to correspond generally with the findings in Hackos' study (p. 58). However, there are a few minor differences arising from the

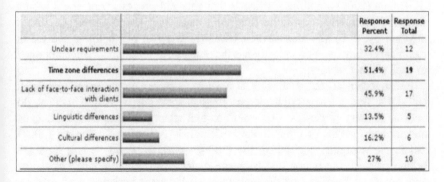

		Response Percent	Response Total
Unclear requirements		32.4%	12
Time zone differences		51.4%	19
Lack of face-to-face interaction with clients		45.9%	17
Linguistic differences		13.5%	5
Cultural differences		16.2%	6
Other (please specify)		27%	10

Figure 5. Challenges in document distribution.

different sample profiles used in the surveys; Hackos' study also collected responses from U.S.-based managers of technical communication teams.

Researchers (Adams, Bosley, Campbell, Cook, Fukoka, Gonzalez, Hackos, St. Amant, and Ulijn among others) have demonstrated that cultural differences have significant effects on rhetoric and technical communication in international settings. We agree with their conclusions and accept Campbell and Ulijn's (2001) observation that "culture affects language, even when people of different cultures use the same language" (p. 78). We think the linguistic and cultural differences are underestimated. Possible explanations include

- The sample's expertise and experience in international communication reduces the impact of cultural and linguistic differences
- Linguistic and cultural differences between India and North America/U.K. are not fully understood by the sample because of the lack of published research
- Unclear requirements, time zone differences, and face-to-face interaction with clients create more challenges compared with cultural and linguistic differences in outsourcing relationships (It may be useful and interesting to reexamine this assumption as a part of further research on challenges facing global multisite information-development teams.)

CONCLUSIONS

This section uses responses from the "Professional Development" and "Additional Comments" sections of our questionnaire to analyze the future of both the profession and the professionals in India. The creation of a global marketplace of ideas and resources appears to represent the future of trade and commerce in the twenty-first century. In his *Intercom* article "Trends for 2000: Thriving in the Boom Years," Carliner predicts that technology has the potential to create continuously functioning offices and production facilities (2000, p. 13). St. Amant (2001) amplifies Carliner's thoughts and suggests "one could use the Internet in combination with the time shifts caused by the rotation of the earth to create a cyber factory that never closes" (p. 291). In our opinion, the Indian technical communication industry has the potential to be an important component of such a cyber factory.

Indian technical communicators, as a whole, possess a unique set of knowledge and skills. They are a part of the largest English-speaking population in the world, and the country possesses a rich multilingual talent pool that can be educated and trained in ASE or other flavors of English. According to Crystal (2004), "India has a unique position in the English-speaking world. It is a linguistic bridge between the major first-language dialects of the world, such as British and American English, and the major foreign-language varieties, such as those emerging in China and Japan." Future research on the rhetorical and linguistic differences between technical documents written by Indians and L1/first-language users has the potential to provide interesting results.

Asian product development organizations are likely to exhibit more mature information development processes. Technical communication teams in countries such as India "are similarly more likely to follow a set process and value efficiency in their operations over individual creativity" (Hackos, 2002, p. 10). Indian technical communicators may be able to use their process maturity and expertise in software technology to contribute to practices such as single sourcing and process measurement/management. A comparison of process maturity levels in Indian and North American information development teams is an area for further research.

Corporations and members of the global information development community appear to be recognizing the potential of Indian technical communicators. In 2004 and 2005 the STC India chapter won STC's distinguished and meritorious Chapter Achievement Awards. The newsletter of the India chapter, *Indus*, also won STC newsletter awards for two consecutive years. In the absence of formal university courses, the India chapter's city-specific learning sessions and annual conference play an important role in providing continuing education to members and nonmembers. Despite its relative youth, inexperience, and paucity of resources, the India chapter appears to be developing a framework to address the needs of existing and prospective technical communicators.

To address future business opportunities effectively, schools and universities should support the profession academically. As discussed earlier, as of early 2005 India does not have a single university-level-degree program in rhetoric, professional communication, technical writing, and usability. In their answers to open-ended questions, survey participants bemoaned the absence of academic programs and its negative influence on hiring. One participant wants "more university courses"; a second one asks for "formal academic programs." Others "would definitely like to see universities offering degrees in Technical Writing" and are interested in "[academic] research." Mandatory courses in writing and technical communication in universities appear to be an immediate necessity. In our opinion, academic programs will not only increase awareness of the profession in universities and create a richer talent pool but also provide much-needed research opportunities for existing professionals.

As seen in this survey, many Indian technical communicators in the IT outsourcing industry create documents for users in North America and Europe. Organizations and universities must focus on teaching SAE, plain/international English, intercultural communication and rhetoric, and translation to their employees and students. Effective and successful participation in a global economy is not possible unless we make an attempt to understand different cultures and rhetoric. Indian professionals must also make the attempt to keep abreast of the latest management strategies, business concepts, technologies, and technical communication trends.

Given its rich and ancient scientific, linguistic, and communication traditions, it is not surprising that India is increasingly becoming a significant player in global information development. Thanks to outsourcing and India's own economic growth, future prospects appear to be bright for the profession. Indian technical communicators may be able to address the opportunities and challenges of simultaneously addressing global and local users by developing a clearly defined professional-brand image similar to the one developed by their counterparts in the IT/software design and development industry.

REFERENCES

Bosley, D. S. (Ed.). (2001). *Global contexts: Case studies in international technical communication*. Needham Heights, MA: Allyn and Bacon.

Carliner, S. (2000, January). Trends for 2000: Thriving in the boom years. *Intercom,* pp. 11-14.

Choudhry, A. (2000, April). *India: Bursting at the linguistic seams*. Retrieved December 28, 2004 from the UNESCO Courier Web site:
http://www.unesco.org/courier/2000_04/uk/doss24.htm.

Crystal, D. (2004, November 19). *Subcontinent raises its voice*. Retrieved December 22, 2004 from the Guardian Weekly Web site:
http://education.guardian.co.uk/tefl/story/0,,1355064,00.html.

Dennett, J T. (2000). Going beyond the native speaker in technical communication. *IEEE Transactions on Professional Communication, 43*(3), 327-336.

Fukuoka, W., & Spyridakis, J. M. (2000). Japanese readers' comprehension of and preferences for inductively versus deductively organized text. *IEEE Transactions on Professional Communication, 43*(4), 355-366.

Friedman, T. L. (2005). *The world is flat: A brief history of the twenty-first century*. New York: Farrar, Straus, and Giroux.

Gilsdorf, J. (2002). Standard Englishes and world Englishes: Living with a polymorph business language. *The Journal of Business Communication, 39*(3), 364-378.

Hackos, J. T. (2002, August 1). *Offshore Information Development Benchmark Study*. Retrieved September 15, 2004 from the Comtech Services Inc. Web site:
http://www.comtech-serv.com/white_papers.shtml.

Hohenthal, A. (2000a, December 17). *Definition of the concept of multilingualism*. Retrieved November 21, 2004 from The Literature and Culture of the Indian Subcontinent (South Asia) Web site:
http://www.postcolonialweb.org/india/hohenthal/contents.html.

Hohenthal, A. (2000b, December 17). *The question of standard English*. Retrieved November 21, 2004 from The Literature and Culture of the Indian Subcontinent (South Asia) Web site:
http://www.postcolonialweb.org/india/hohenthal/contents.html.

Kachru, B. B. (1994). English in South Asia. In R. Burchfield (Ed.), *The Cambridge history of the English language* (Vol. V, pp. 497-626). Cambridge: Cambridge University Press.

Kak, S. C. (1994). Evolution of early writing in India. *Indian Journal of History of Science, 29*(3), 375-388. Retrieved December 20, 2004 from the Indian National Science Academy Web site: http://www.insa.ac.in/html/search.asp?search=yes.

MacNealy, M. S., & Heaton, L. B. (1999). Can this marriage be saved? *Journal of Technical Writing and Communication, 29*(1), 41-63.

Maher, K. (2004, March 2). Next on the outsourcing list. *Wall Street Journal*, p. B1.

McIver, R. (2004, June 1). *Outsourcing 101*. Retrieved February 9, 2004 from the Outsourcing Times Web site: http://www.blogsource.org/blog/2004/06/outsourcing_101.html.

Mehrotra, R. R. (2001). English in bereavement advertising in India. *English Today, 17*(3), 31-35. CSA Internet Database Service, Auburn U. Library, Auburn, AL. Retrieved April 7, 2004 from the Web site: http://md2.csa.com.

Mehrotra, R. R. (2003). A British response to some Indian English usages. *English Today, 19*(3), 19-25. CSA Internet Database Service, Auburn U. Library, Auburn, AL. Retrieved April 7, 2004 from the Web site: http://md2.csa.com.

Nayar, P. (2004, May). A remarkable summer: Looking back. *Indus*. Retrieved October 18, 2004 from the Web site: http://www.stc-india.org/indus/052004/indus_distinguished.htm.

O'Connor J. J., & Robertson, E. F. (2000, November). *Panini*. Retrieved November 15, 2004 from the Web site: http://www-gap.dcs.st-and.ac.uk/~history/Mathematicians/Panini.html.

Ribero, J. (2004, June) *Study: India's outsourcing industry continues to boom*. Retrieved November 15, 2004 from QuickLink# 47309 on the Web site: www.computerworld.com.

Schiffman, H. F. (1999). South and Southeast Asia. In J. A. Fishman (Ed.), *Handbook of language and ethnic identity* (pp. 431-443). Oxford: Oxford University Press.

St. Amant, K. (2001). Cultures, computers, and communication: Evaluating models of international online production. *IEEE Transactions on Professional Communication, 44*(4), 291-295.

St. Amant, K. (2000). Expanding translation use to improve the quality of technical communication. *IEEE Transactions on Professional Communication, 43*(3), 323-326.

Ulijn, J. M., & St. Amant, K. (2000). Mutual intercultural perception: How does it affect technical communication? *Technical Communication, 47*(2), 220-237.

Ulijn, J. M., & Campbell, C. P. (2001). Technical innovation and global business communication: An introduction. *IEEE Transactions on Professional Communication, 44*(2), 77-82.

CHAPTER 2

Defining Technical Communication in the United States and India: A Contrastive Analysis of Established Curricula and Desired Abilities

Carlos Evia

A recent survey of technical communication practitioners in the United States reported that "certainly, the top global concern for technical communicators in the United States is the notion of sending technical communication work offshore" (Giammona, 2004). That concern is the main reason for this book's existence, and chapters in this collection address from different perspectives the "threat" that offshore outsourcing might represent to the profession of technical communication in the United States. Offshore outsourcing of industry processes is not a new trend, but some authors have identified a second wave of outsourcing (Bardhan & Kroll, 2003) that moves beyond manufacturing jobs and has started using foreign workers for telecommutable white-collar jobs. As part of that wave, high-tech companies have started outsourcing writing projects, with downsizing and job-market shrinkage as the consequences for professionals in the United States. Some authors talk about thousands of jobs in technical documentation lost to outsourced workers (Rainey, Turner, & Dayton, 2005).

Because of factors like a stable democratic political system, incentives for new investors, telecommunications infrastructure, and "a huge pool of talent and lower costs" (Kobayashi-Hillary, 2004), India has become the main destination for most of the jobs included in that second wave of outsourcing, which includes positions in technical writing. In the chapter they cowrote for this book, Natarajan and Pandit refer to India as "the favorite IT (information technology) outsourcing destination for organizations located in North America, Europe, and the rest of Asia." Most technical writing jobs in India, according to the Technical Writers of India's (TWIN) jobs database, are related to IT and their clients are or represent American companies (Technical Writers of India, 2005). As a result, it is valid to conclude that some IT technical writing jobs from the United States are being outsourced to offshore markets, and India is currently the main destination for these types of jobs.

The number of technical communication jobs from American companies sent to India notwithstanding, there are concerns about the quality of work produced in third-world countries. For example, Rainey et al. forecast that the "mostly mediocre English translations that technical documents receive in third-world countries will eventually moderate the trend to outsourcing" (2005, p. 334). One way to explore the actual strengths of offshore technical communicators is to compare their education and training options to those available in the United States. In the specific case of India, most Indian practitioners do not have formal education in technical writing or communication, and the main reason behind this is that their country does not offer academic programs in this field as of late summer in 2005. Positioned in that gap in training and education, this chapter analyzes similarities and differences in the professional definition of technical communication in the United States and India. It does so with the main purpose of assessing how real the "threat" from Indian writers is on their American counterparts. The chapter attempts to show what competencies Indian technical communicators offer to outsourced projects and how they compare to their American counterparts, based on the education and training they are receiving. The chapter focuses on India because as of mid-2005 it was the main market for technical writing outsourcing projects.

In order to conduct this analysis, the chapter first looks briefly at the complex American definition of technical communication and establishes what it means to be a professional in this field from the U.S. perspective. Second, it presents a snapshot of some key aspects of the technical writing industry in India (for information on the Indian tradition in this discipline, see the chapter by Natarajan and Pandit in this book), contrasting it to the situation in the United States. In both cases, the chapter focuses on available options, academic and corporate, for training aspiring technical writers in these countries. Lastly, it analyzes relevant differences and intersections in the professional description of the field in both countries, offering recommendations for coping with the growing outsourcing phenomenon.

Because the emphasis of this chapter (and this book) is on outsourcing, the section about defining technical communication in the United States will be purposely brief and is included mainly as a reference to contextualize and compare the Indian definition. Recently, several authors (Giammona, 2004; Dayton & Bernhardt, 2004; Pringle & Williams, 2005; Rainey et al., 2005; among others) have conducted detailed studies on what the field of technical communication means and represents in America.

THE AMERICAN DEFINITION OF TECHNICAL COMMUNICATION

Trying to define technical communication in the United States is a difficult task, because it can be described both as a skill and as a profession or discipline. As a skill, technical communication has been recently defined in textbooks as the "process of managing technical information in ways that allow people to take action" (Johnson-Sheehan, 2005, p. 6). The Society for Technical Communication (STC) defines technical communicators as professionals who "take technical information and make it understandable to those that need it" ("Press-Related FAQs," 2005c). As a discipline or profession, technical communication in the United States can mean many different things. This section uses the dual term of discipline/profession because one of the main characteristics of this field is the "ideological split between technical communication practitioners and academics" (Moore & Kreth, 2005, p. 305). From the practitioner perspective, technical communication is a profession that might or might not require an academic degree. For aspiring technical communicators, STC "recommends a college degree, though a major in technical communication is not necessary" ("Interested in Technical Communication?" 2005b). It can be a grant-writing job for a nonprofit organization or a software-documentation project for a major IT company. From the academic standpoint, technical communication is a discipline that includes everything from the introductory service course that students from any field can take in order to acquire technical writing skills, to fully developed undergraduate, master's and PhD programs majoring in technical communication.

In an outstanding attempt to specify what the profession means in the United States, Rainey et al. (2005) proposed a list of core competencies for technical communicators. Based on results from a survey and interviews with technical communication managers, these authors determined that "the most important competencies for technical communicators are:

- Skills in collaborating with both subject-matter experts and coworkers
- Ability to write clearly for specific audiences directed by clearly defined purposes
- Ability to assess and to learn to use technologies
- Ability to take initiative (be a self-starter) and to evaluate one's own work and the work of others" (Rainey et al., 2005, p. 323).

These authors also list secondary (technological skills, ability to write, edit, and test documents) and tertiary ("usability testing, single-sourcing and content management, instructional design, budgeting, oral presentations, research, multimedia, and awareness of cultural differences") competencies for professionals in the field of technical communication.

Nevertheless, these competencies are not officially taught in every academic program in technical and professional communication in the United States. As a result, the academic definition of technical communication might seem different from the definition used in industry. At the fifty-first annual conference of the Society for Technical Communication in 2004, Dayton identified the differences between academics and practitioners as one of the "major fault lines creating tension in technical communication." He claimed, among other things, that academics critique corporate culture and technological determinism, and practitioners question academia's lack of practical tools expertise and real-world experience. Moore and Kreth (2005) also analyze this division and point out that "part of the problem is that many academics within the field of technical communication are too committed to forms of critical rhetorical theory and exclude all other relevant non-rhetorical theories and strategies" (2005, p. 305). Allen and Benninghoff confirm that "rhetorical analysis currently receives extensive coverage in (technical and professional communication programs)" (2004, p. 180).

If anything, the topic of offshore outsourcing has deeply widened that fault line between industry and academia, as evidenced by the concern on this issue expressed in journals and professional conferences. Whereas practitioner-oriented publications and presentations worry that outsourcing is a sign of the end of technical communication as a profession, academic journals and conferences show little concern about this situation.

Although professionals see offshore outsourcing as the main concern for technical communicators (Giammona, 2004), academics are more concerned with the "current downturn in the job market, noting that students were having trouble finding jobs, were having to relocate, or were choosing to continue their education" (Dayton & Bernhardt, 2004, p. 35). Offshore outsourcing can probably be included as a cause of the downturn in the job market, but the academics did not use that specific term. Similarly, in 2005 STC's annual conference featured three panels dedicated to the topic of offshore outsourcing, including two moderated discussions. ATTW's conference that same year offered only one presentation about (anti) outsourcing, inside a "Global Issues" panel.

The core of this difference in perspectives about technical communication between academic and industry professionals might be in the different approaches available for training and educating technical communicators. If technical communicators in the United States are to be competitive in the global marketplace, they need to offer value that their colleagues in other countries do not yet offer. Yet the education emphasizes competencies that can easily be outsourced. The following section addresses the contradictory nature of some of the options available for aspiring technical writers in the United States.

Education and Training

In the main navigation bar of its Web site, the Society for Technical Communication has a link labeled "Education," offering information on academic programs and seminars for aspiring technical communicators. This section of STC's site emphasizes academic degrees in technical communication, and even states that one of the Society's incorporating principles is to "guide and inform students and to aid colleges and universities in the establishment of curricula for training in the arts and sciences of technical communication" ("Academic Programs," 2005a). In late August 2005 STC's academic database listed 122 bachelor's, 89 master's, and 27 PhD programs in technical communication and related areas being offered the United States. However, as mentioned before, STC also has on its Web site a paragraph stating that a major in technical communication is not necessary to work professionally in this field. This case exemplifies the contradictory shape of education and training in the discipline. An aspiring technical writer in the United States could run into STC's academic database and decide to obtain a degree in technical or professional communication; however, she can also follow the advice of "get a degree in computer science or engineering and take a class in technical writing," that one of Giammona's practitioner interviewees expressed (2004, p. 356). Furthermore, Harner and Rich (2005) mention that definitive information describing a typical technical communication program in the United States simply does not exist.

Adding a level of confusion to this situation, in the summer of 2005 STC announced its own training program, "consisting of five two-day courses taught by some of the most respected names in technical communication" ("STC Training Program," 2005d). The Society says this program "provides a unique, in-depth educational opportunity that will help you advance your career. You'll gain new skills, techniques, and hands-on experience that you can use to do your job better. You will have the opportunity to network with other highly motivated professionals. Certificates will be awarded upon completion of the course" ("STC Training Program," 2005d).

STC does not mention if there are any academic or professional prerequisites for participating in this training program. The Society does not say either if this program is for starting or advanced technical communicators, or if it should be taken after, before, or instead of one of the academic degrees included in its database. STC's training program includes the following courses:

- The Architecture of Content
- Creating and Using Personas to Improve Usability

- Focusing on Content: Making Web Sites Work for Users
- Leadership in Information Management: Developing the Business Framework and Implementation Roadmap for Single Sourcing, Content Management, and Knowledge Management
- XML: From Hand-Coding to WYSIWYG Authoring

This list of topics directly addresses issues included in the group that Rainey et al. (2005) identified as tertiary competencies for technical communicators. However, the courses also touch on some of the core competencies identified by these authors, such as writing for specific audiences and purposes, and learning to use technologies.

STC's training program supports the position adopted by many authors who think technical communication's future involves more than writing. Giammona, for example, says that technical communicators "are becoming more than writers. We are also becoming product usability experts" (2004, p. 351). In academic programs, this "more than writing" movement is also gaining strength. In his 2004 STC presentation, Dayton talked about a group of "techno-specialists" in academia who wants to connect technical communication to content/knowledge management and develop curricula stressing information architecture and usability. This is already being reflected in some academic programs. For example, Texas Tech University describes technical communicators as "information designers and developers" on the Web site promoting its Bachelor of Arts in English with a specialization in technical communication (Texas Tech University, n.d.).

However, this is still a new trend in academia. Allen and Benninghoff identify the following topics as the most frequently featured in academic programs in technical and professional communication in the United States: audience, genre, visual rhetoric, document design, rhetorical analysis, collaboration, ethics, user-centered design, and project management (2004, p. 165).

Regardless of these new approaches and their repercussions in course content, the field's main application in the workplace still is writing and documentation. According to Rainey et al., "it is not surprising that managers seek in their new hires many of the skills that have long been associated with the work that most technical communicators do" (2005, p. 332). The second wave of outsourcing seems to be affecting this job scenario, because offshore technical writers might also be showing those skills that managers still see as fundamental in the profession. In order to assess the actual threat that foreign workers constitute to U.S. technical communicators, it is necessary to understand the way in which offshore professionals see the field and how they define and study technical communication. This chapter looks at the specific case of technical communicators in India.

THE INDIAN DEFINITION OF TECHNICAL COMMUNICATION

It would be pointless to make any general assumptions about professionals from any field in a country as big and diverse as India. Regardless of the evasive nature of an absolute definition of technical communication in the United States, defining this profession in India is much more difficult. After all, India is a country with more than one billion inhabitants and very few formal programs in technical writing or communication. Therefore, probably nobody knows for sure how many Indian workers are technical writers and how they would define that profession. India has several organizations grouping technical writers (physically and virtually). These include major groups like the India chapter of the Society for Technical Communication (STC, 2005) and Technical Writers of India (TWIN, 2005), but also contain smaller Web-based communities like the Technical Writers in India branch of Meetup.com, which had more than 650 members from Bangalore, Delhi, Hyderabad, Mumbai, and Pune as of August 2005. This abundance of options only makes it harder to define technical writing under Indian parameters. Because the evidence presented here is preliminary and does not necessarily give a complete picture of technical communication as a profession in India, the chapter concentrates on a few cases of professionals and education programs obtained from the STC India chapter and TWIN.

Kiran Thakur, head of the Department of Communication and Journalism at the University of Pune, describes technical writers as professionals who "are prepared to take pains to understand the production processes and write the manuals for commoners, the end-users, in simple English," and he adds "They should only be prepared to spend time in interacting with technical staff to turn the jargon-filled production literature into easy-to-understand manuals for the commoners" (Thakur, 2004). An article published in The Times of India covering the local STC conference in 2003 described technical writers as people who "write user manuals for products, online help files, multimedia presentations, installation guides for software, among other things," and added that in India "the highest demand for technical writers is generated by the IT (information technology) industry" (Times News Network, 2003).

Following that description and information obtained from many individuals and organizations, the main keyword in most definitions of technical communication in India would be its connection to the IT industry. Makarand Pandit, president of the STC chapter in India for 2005 (and a contributing author to this book), said, "today, the biggest contribution of technical writers is to software companies. This is because they are involved in a lot of product and project development programmes" ("Demand for Writers," 2003). Frederick Menezes, also a former STC president in India, acknowledges this connection to the IT industry, but implies that technical communication cannot be limited to it. Menezes denounces that some practitioners in the field think "technical writing is an easy backdoor entry into software companies" (2001), probably implying that new technical writers would expect to move on to better-paying jobs as programmers or interface designers. The majority of technical writers in India interviewed or contacted for this chapter attribute those overlapping and conflicting ideas about technical writing to lack of formal education in the field.

Education and Training

In the chapter they cowrote for this collection, Natarajan and Pandit conclude, addressing the topic of education for technical writers in India, that "mandatory courses in writing and technical communication in universities appear to be an immediate necessity." Many of their peers support that opinion. Gurudutt Kamath, founding president of STC India, has been a longtime advocate for formal technical writing education in India. In an online column from 2002, Kamath asked "when will this country wake up to the need for technical writing education?" and "why can't schools of journalism and communication include technical writing as part of their curriculum?" (Kamath, 2002). In 2005 Kamath was still asking the same questions:

> Why are we having so many mediocre technical writers? Because we do not have schools and colleges teaching technical writing. A few institutions are doing their best in such a bleak scenario. A majority of technical writers just accidentally get into the jobs and bumble along. Many learn technical writing through web sites and emailing lists (personal communication, March 31, 2005).

In light of the scarcity of structured training programs, technical writing in India frequently follows a mentoring model. Some experienced Indian professionals become mentors to aspiring technical communicators. These mentors, in the cases observed for this chapter, are experienced Indian writers and journalists and can call themselves trainers (like Kamath) or promoters (like Pandit). In a debate conducted by the STC India publication INDUS in 2004, the importance of having a mentor was listed as a key element when hiring technical writers. Usha Mohan, Director of Triumph Research & Holdings, a software development and documentation firm in Bangalore, asked in the debate (when supposedly revising the credentials of a new technical writer): "Who was his Mentor? Was he under the close supervision of an experienced writer or a good project manager?" ("Formal Education," 2004). As an educational resource, having a mentor (even an excellent one) cannot compete with an actual degree in technical communication. However, for Indian technical communicators the role of a mentor apparently does not have to be that of a teacher or instructor. Kamath described his mentoring job simply as e-mailing encouraging words to a colleague. Regarding his responsibilities as a mentor, he added,

One of my biggest achievements has been as a mentor and as a guide. Many regard me as their role model. I have served as an inspiration. In India, people have a lust for foreign jobs and have too high a regard for anything foreign. If I am held in so high an esteem, it is mainly because of all the foreign jobs that I have done (personal communication, March 31, 2005).

Academic Initiatives

Natarajan and Pandit indicate in their chapter that India, as of early 2005, did not have formal academic programs in technical or professional communication. The STC chapter in India highlights two academic initiatives on its Web site: "an optional paper in the Master of Communication and Journalism (MCJ) course offered by the Dept. of Mass Communication, Calicut University and a short-term program offered by Stella Maris College, Chennai" (STC India, 2004). The Technical Writers of India (TWIN) Web site highlighted a "workshop-cum-training programme on 'Technical Writing Fundamentals'" offered by the University of Pune (Technical Writers of India, 2005).

Out of these three initiatives, only one is being offered in an English department. Stella Maris College offers a technical writing course among its "inter-disciplinary electives common to all postgraduate students" in English (Stella Maris College, 2005). The universities of Calicut and Pune have their related courses and programs inside their Communication departments.

The most developed of these programs is the one offered by the University of Pune. Thakur explains the structure of this program as consisting of "45 sessions of 90 minutes each, spread over two months," and adds that the prerequisites are a university degree in any discipline, and a test in English language skills. Also, "knowledge of *MS Word* is a must" (personal communication, August 27, 2005). The syllabus for this program covers

- Basics of Communication and Introduction to Technical Communication, containing communication models; history of technical communication; technical writing in India; and needs, roles, and deliverables.
- Information Organization and Development, addressing the documentation development life cycle, writing and editing issues, graphics and illustrations, and document design.
- Tools and Technologies, teaching *Microsoft Word, Adobe FrameMaker,* and *RoboHelp.*
- Assignments, including templates, a user manual, and an online help system.

The University of Pune also plans to offer a certificate in technical com-munication, consisting of "about 240 sessions of 60 minutes each, spread over six months," according to Thakur, but "it will take some time before we launch the course" (personal communication, August 27, 2005).

Corporate Training

TWIN's Web site offers a list of training programs from institutions in different Indian cities. These programs range from one-day courses to six-month seminars, and most of them focus on teaching editing functions of Microsoft Word. There is very little content about communication or writing theory.

For example, TechnoPoint, a training company in Bangalore, offers a course divided in five modules, four of which are dedicated to software tools (XML and *FrameMaker*, HTML and *RoboHelp*, Advanced *MS Word*, and *Adobe Photoshop*). The first module is titled "fundamentals of technical writing and grammar" (sic), as posted on the company's Web site (TechnoPoint, 2005).

The emphasis on tools and the connection between technical communication and IT is dominant in most of these programs, and many of them define technical communication as "technological communication." S. A. International Limited, with technical writing training programs in Chennai, Bangalore, and Kochi, is the only company listed on TWIN's Web site that tries to separate *technical* communication from *technological* communication. However, their joint program with Simon Fraser confers a diploma in "Professional Writing for Hi-Tech Industries" (SAI, 2003).

The emphasis on software tools seems to contradict what two past presidents of the STC India chapter think about the field. The main point of conflict among Indian professionals in this field is in the content about software tools that should be included in courses. This might be a direct consequence of the dependence on IT that some in India see as a characteristic of technical communication. Menezes said about seeing proficiency in software tools as essential to being a technical writer:

> A lot of people seem to believe that knowing how to use tools like *Word* and *RoboHelp* can make one a technical writer. No doubt, knowledge of such tools is essential, but laying more emphasis on tools over language, writing, and technology grasping skills is wrong. Learning to use tools is much easier than learning to write well. In fact, writing is a skill that has to be nurtured from a young age. The affinity for technology and technical details also does not come about easily (2001).

Kamath, for example, says that a good professional should have technical writing skills, designing abilities, experience with tools, and project-management skills; and the most important part is putting all those elements together.

> Therefore, I never include tools training in my seminars. I feel anyone— more so technical writers—can quickly pick up and use any tool. It may just take a few days to a few weeks to master a tool. Many companies would call me and ask for tools training in *RoboHelp* and *FrameMaker*. I would tell them that it is not necessary and they can learn it on their own (personal communication, March 31, 2005).

Another point of contention might be in the fact that some technical writers in India seem to regard the profession as an exclusive club threatened by "fake writers" and impostors. Menezes, for example, pointed out that "a growing field like this could be infiltrated by the wrong kind of people. Indications are available that this is already happening" (2001). Kamath added that he still receives "laudatory e-mails" for a column he wrote in 2003 about the phenomenon of the "fake technical writer," which he defined as "an upstart with no talent or skills (who) is out there competing against you" (2003). He also said, "Joining mailing lists on technical writing does not make you a technical writer. Similarly, being a member of an international association does not make you a good technical writer" (2003).

However, this seems to contradict Kamath's own advice to aspiring technical writers. After all, he wrote in a column published online in 2002,

> If I could become a technical writer, 15 years ago, without even knowing about the field, you too can become a technical writer. Today, it is so much easier. Books are available. The Internet is a goldmine of information on technical writing. The mailing lists are a great support group for novices. So why don't you too consider becoming a technical writer? (2002).

It would be fair to emphasize that Kamath wrote those opinions in different years, but they do reflect the contradictory advice that aspiring technical writers in India might be receiving when starting their careers. Therefore, the lack of formal education programs might keep those aspiring professionals as "fake technical writers" for a long time.

ANALYSIS OF INTERSECTIONS AND DISCREPANCIES

If we compare the history of technical communication as a field to an evolutionary chain, it might appear that India is at a very early stage of a path that the United States of America started a long time ago. According to the training they receive mostly from corporate instructors, it seems that technical writers in India are being prepared to address the core competencies for technical communicators identified by Rainey et al. (2005). Indian technical communicators are learning to collaborate with subject-matter experts, write for specific audiences, use technologies for writing, and probably evaluate their own work and the work of others. Additionally, some technical communication programs in India are addressing the secondary competencies identified by these authors, which include "using technologies to accomplish documentation work in various media and the ability to write, edit, and test various technical communication documents" (2005, p. 323).

To the academic observer in the United States, it might seem as if the training and education programs listed in the Web sites for the STC chapter in India and

TWIN have the collective purpose of preparing professionals for jobs as "grammar cops, wordsmiths, and software application experts" that Moore and Kreth (2005) see as once the main type of occupation for technical communicators in the United States. The course offerings in India analyzed for this chapter probably aim to create technical communicators as technicians "in the engineering sense of the word," which Pringle and Williams see as part of the past of the profession in the United States, when professionals "documented and edited the work of others rather than creating and designing information" (2005, p. 363). Moore and Kreth add that these jobs are still available for American professionals, but "are diminishing in value as the global information economy becomes more cost-conscious, profit-driven, and focused on designing and delivering better experiences to individuals, groups, organizations, and entire cultures" (2005, p. 303). However, Rainey et al. (2005) mention that technical communication managers still look for those skills in new hires; therefore it is valid to conclude that technical communication can be outsourced. In this specific case, technical communication jobs can be outsourced to India.

At this moment, training and education programs in that country are teaching mostly about core and secondary competencies for technical communicators because that is what the market demands of them. Technical writers in India are also aware of the tertiary competencies and the "more than writing" approach (as evidenced by Kamath's description of relevant skills in the field and the University of Pune's program), but they are not aspiring for those jobs because the field there is still undeveloped and the market is not demanding them. In no way does the research conducted for this chapter indicate that technical communicators in India are not interested in usability, content, and information management or are not smart enough for those jobs. As Sivakumar (2004) and other authors have pointed out, one of the main anti-outsourcing arguments is that Indian workers cannot "think outside the box" and are limited to routine and systematic jobs. If anything, the interviews and analysis of Web pages and "blogs" only indicates that Indian technical writers are very creative and interested in the future of technical communication. Furthermore, it is impossible to tell if in the future, with the right technological applications, jobs involving those tertiary competencies could be outsourced and thus adopted by foreign professionals.

The evolution of technical communication as a profession in India might have similarities with past moments of the field's history in the United States; however, most likely the path will not be parallel or verbatim. Based on the research conducted for this chapter, two main forces might take Indian technical writing in a new and unique direction: cultural and language differences, and the role of Communication departments as home to technical communication programs.

Regarding the quality of technical documents produced in India, and after analyzing samples of work from Indian practitioners, there is no way to measure how cultural and language differences will modify and adapt genres and conventions of technical communication to Indian patterns in the future. Documents will probably be reduced to plain sentences and may rely heavily on visuals in order to avoid conflicts related to context and language. India may produce 2.1 million college graduates a year who can speak English (Kobayashi-Hillary, 2004, p. 139), but many of those graduates speak English as a second language and live in two different cultures. For some of these professionals, as it happens to most outsourced workers in any field, the "job" culture is influenced by American traditions and policies, but the "home" culture is autochthonous. As Natarajan and Pandit mention in their chapter for this book, Indian English has different types and classifications, which affects the work of professional writers. I found many spelling, grammar, and style errors in the course description of the corporate training programs from India analyzed for this chapter. This could be an interesting area for further research on the topic of outsourcing technical communication to India.

The second force is that academic programs in technical writing seem to be coming out of Communication departments in India. In the United States, most academic programs are housed in English departments, and technical- and professional-writing students are frequently seen as "English majors." Indian academic professionals might not be aware of this, as evidenced by Thakur's comment regarding how "in USA and Europe, there are regular full-time courses at undergraduate, graduate, Master's levels in several Communication schools" (2004). It would be a good experiment to analyze how, in the near future, technical communication graduates from India compare with their American colleagues.

Technical communication is hard to define as a field and profession in the United States. It is also hard to define in India, and harder to define globally. Giammona described technical communicators with the following statement: "We are, as a breed, an eclectic and unusual group of people" (2004, p. 351). That definition also applied to technical writers in India, where lack of formal education, purists denouncing "fake writers," and the old tools vs. theory forces are creating a workforce as diverse and versatile as the collective of technical communicators in America. For the time being, U.S. technical communicators should be trained to address the three levels of competencies identified by Rainey et al.; and an option to obtain a competitive advantage in today's global marketplace is to look at the profession as "more than writing." However, that might change in the future if skills related to tertiary competencies are outsourced thanks to new technologies.

The professional community of technical communication has expanded internationally and now includes offshore colleagues from India and other countries who are competitors, just like the guy from the cubicle next door or the high school student who can design a Web page for $10. This expansion, however, is not perfect and is affected by differences in training and education, language and culture (which can have negative repercussions in the quality of work), and salaries. In a field defined by the eclectic nature of its members and gaps between academic and industry perspectives, the challenges represented by the offshore outsourcing expansion are nothing new. Worrying about lost jobs is a narrow concern in light of a discipline's concern for global effective practice. A short-term disparaging of a relatively fledgling practice in India would have long-term negative consequences for the field, not just because of jobs and who does them but because of the quality of work that a technical communicator does, whether in the United States or abroad.

REFERENCES

Allen, N., & Benninghoff, S. T. (2004). TPC Program snapshots: Developing curricula and addressing challenges. *Technical Communication Quarterly, 13*(2), 157-185.

Bardhan, A. D., & Kroll, C. (2003). The new wave of outsourcing. *Fisher Center for Real Estate & Urban Economics. Report #1103.* Retrieved May 10, 2005, from http://repositories.cdlib.org/iber/fcreue/reports/1103.

Dayton, D. (2004, May 10). *The future of technical communication according to those who teach it.* Paper presented at the 51st Annual Conference of the Society for Technical Communication, Baltimore.

Dayton, D., & Bernhardt, S. A. (2004). Results of a survey of ATTW members, 2003. *Technical Communication Quarterly, 13*(1), 13-43.

Formal education in technical writing—Is it really a manna from heaven? (2004). *INDUS, 6*(2). Retrieved April 14, 2005, from http://www.stc-india.org/indus/052004/debate_main_page.htm.

Giammona, B. (2004). The future of technical communication: How innovation, technology, information management, and other forces are shaping the future of the profession. *Technical Communication, 51*(3), 349-366.

Harner, S., & Rich, A. (2005). Trends in undergraduate curriculum in scientific and technical communication programs. *Technical Communication, 52*(2), 209-220.

Johnson-Sheehan, R. (2005). *Technical communication today.* New York: Pearson.

Kamath, G. (2003). Wanted: Fake writers! *IT People.* Retrieved April 14, 2005, from http://www.expressitpeople.com/20030317/careers1.shtml.

Kamath, G. (2002). Education and certification. *IT People.* Retrieved April 14, 2005, from http://www.itpeopleindia.com/20020826/careers1.shtml.

Kobayashi-Hillary, M. (2004). *Outsourcing to India. The offshore advantage.* Berlin, Germany: Springer.

Menezes, F. (2001). Can anyone become a technical writer? *INDUS, 3*(1). Retrieved April 14, 2005, from www.stc-india.org/indus/archives/May2001.pdf.

Moore, P., & Kreth, M. (2005). From wordsmith to communication strategist: Heresthetic and political maneuvering in technical communication. *Technical Communication, 52*(3), 302-322.

Pringle, K., & Williams, S. (2005). The future is the past: Has technical communication arrived as a profession? *Technical Communication, 52*(3), 361-370.

Rainey, K. T., Turner, R. K., & Dayton, D. (2005). Do curricula correspond to managerial expectations? Core competencies for technical communicators. *Technical Communication, 52*(3), 323-352.

SAI. (2003). *Technical writing course.* Retrieved April 15, 2005, from http://203.199.194.122/sai_techw3.html.

Sivakumar, N. (2004). *Dude, did I steal your job? Debugging Indian computer programmers.* Bridgewater, NJ: DivineTree.

Society for Technical Communication. (2005a). *Academic programs.* Retrieved May 10, 2005, from http://www.stc.org/academic.asp.

Society for Technical Communication. (2005b). *Interested in technical communication?* Retrieved May 10, 2005, from http://stc.org/interestedTC.asp.

Society for Technical Communication. (2005c). *Press related FAQs.* Retrieved May 10, 2005, from http://www.stc.org/pressFAQs.asp.

Society for Technical Communication. (2005d). *STC training program.* Retrieved May 10, 2005, from http://www.stc.org/training/.

Stella Maris College. (2005). *English.* Retrieved May 10, 2000, from http://www.stellamariscollege.org/departments/english.asp.

STC India. (2004). *Activities.* Retrieved April 15, 2005, from http://www.stc-india.org/activities.htm#acad.

Technical Writers of India. (n.d.). *Courses.* Retrieved April 15, 2005, from http://www.twin-india.org/.

Technical Writers of India. (2005). *Jobs.* Retrieved May 10, 2005, from http://www.twin-india.org/Jobs.html.

TechnoPoint. (2005). *Course details.* Retrieved April 15, 2005, from http://technopointindia.net/course.htm.

Texas Tech University. (n.d.). *Bachelor of arts in English. Technical communication specialization.* Retrieved May 10, 2005, from http://www.english.ttu.edu/tc/BA/BAhome.htm.

Thakur, K. (2004). Technical writing: Emerging opportunities. The University of Pune's Department of Communication and Journalism has now taken an initiative to organise a workshop-cum-training on technical writing fundamentals. *Education Times, 25.* Retrieved April 15, 2005, from http://epaperdaily.timesofindia.com/Repository/ml.asp?Ref=VE9JUFUvMjAwNC8wOC8xNyNBcjAyNTAx.

Times News Network. (2003). Demand for writers is high, "technically." *The Times of India.* Retrieved April 15, 2005, from http://timesofindia.indiatimes.com/articleshow/356111.cms.

CHAPTER 3

Africa Goes for Outsourcing

Michael Jarvis Kwadzo Bokor

I argue in this chapter that Africa can expand its participation in the outsourcing of jobs related to Information and Communication Technology (ICT) if prompt and appropriate measures are taken to improve the continent's business environment. Though some of the 54 African countries have begun attracting some outsourced jobs, there are indications that more could be achieved if existing constraints are removed. Some of these constraints include low levels of scientific and technological development, inadequate material resources to support ICTs, the low status of technical education (in fields such as technical documentation and business communication), and lack of a reliable labor pool. The Outsourcing Institute projected in 2004 that the overall outsourcing market (including U.S.-based jobs outsourced to other countries) would grow to $234 billion by 2005. African countries must not miss the chance to profit from this growth because they already have the potential to maximize productivity in outsourcing.

My position is that African countries should enunciate clear and workable policies to solve the technical and human resource problems if they want to succeed in luring foreign companies seeking to outsource their jobs. Such measures should have a wide scope to eradicate the geopolitical risks caused by civil wars and political instability; to facilitate investment and the unimpeded use of telecommunications and ICTs; and to produce a reliable labor pool through technical training. In effect, there is need for good governance to eradicate corruption and other unproductive tendencies that hinder the provision of appropriate infrastructure (such as reliable electricity supplies, good roads, and

47

efficient telecommunication facilities) to meet the requirements of foreign corporations that may want to do business in Africa.

In arguing for the creation of a congenial business environment to attract foreign companies involved in outsourcing, my main strategy will be to draw attention to what some African countries have already begun doing in outsourcing vis-à-vis current developments in ICTs on the continent. Solving ICT-related problems means doing the groundwork to widen the scope for outsourcing in the future. Second, I will discuss the impact of the technical, political, sociocultural, and economic constraints on any attempt by Africa to emulate the examples of countries in which outsourcing is already well established. Finally, I will suggest that though the existing constraints may not allow Africa to immediately outdo those countries, the situation could be different in the future if the problems are addressed sufficiently and early enough to push the continent forward in its bid for a much bigger chunk of outsourced jobs.

Several factors justify why Africa should become a viable outsourcing destination. The continent's geographical location and time zones are favorable. There is a high proficiency in the use of English and French on the continent, which will facilitate contacts with companies in Europe, North America, and Asia that want to do business on the continent. The rate of ICT penetration into the continent has improved tremendously, and the various countries are doing more to open up for efficient communication. For instance, in South Africa the stable communication network and the support of the Western Cape provincial government and the national Ministry of Trade and Industry have boosted call-center operations. Concerted efforts are being made for skill acquisition through technical education in the schools and industry, which will allow workers to cope with the demands of the job market. Additionally, work ethics are encouraging, and workers do their assignments with zeal and interest. Wages are generally low on the continent, especially in the public sector, and workers currently doing outsourced jobs consider their earnings and conditions of service as a "blessing." In Ghana, for example, where Affiliated Computer Services operates, an employee earns $4 to $5 a day, which is three times higher than the legal minimum wage of 13,500 Cedis (1 U.S. dollar = 9,125.73 Ghanaian Cedi as of February 8, 2006). These factors, among others, indicate that Africa is gradually drawing attention to itself. I now turn to what is currently being done in outsourcing by some African countries to confirm that a prompt solution of the technical, political, economic, and infrastructural problems could ensure a more productive and meaningful participation. This modest trend suggests that the continent is not completely left out of outsourcing.

CURRENT STATE OF OUTSOURCING IN AFRICA

Remarkably, much of the outsourcing in Africa is focused on telemarketing. According to the *Outsourcing Times Online* (2005), the increasing wages in principal call-center outsourcing areas such as India, Ireland, and China is one main factor boosting this trend in Africa, where a number of countries are expanding their efforts to attract outsourcing work. Though less profitable than other ventures such as processing medical forms or acting as the customer service department of an overseas corporation, telemarketing is a viable job on a continent that has begun seeing an improvement in ICT infrastructure in less than 10 years. Call-center operations dominate the outsourcing tasks and employ workers who do not have good quality training in ICT but can do their assignments assiduously because of job satisfaction. Datamonitor (2004) estimates that there are 54,000 call-center jobs in the most advanced countries in Africa, out of a total of 6 million such jobs worldwide. The 54,000 figure includes only South Africa and the countries of North Africa. Emerging call centers in places like Ghana and Kenya are not included.

Ghana provides a unique example. The country has the first and only English-language call center (called Rising Data) in West Africa. Established in the national capital city (Accra) in 2003, the company sells mobile phones to people in the United States. Additionally, Affiliated Computer Services (ACS), a company based in Dallas, Texas, runs an outsourcing operation in Accra. Its 2,000 Ghanaian employees type in health records for U.S. clients served by Aetna Insurance Company (Hale, 2003a). Their duties do not demand any high degree of qualification as they copy handwritten notes taken in dental practices. The workers process American health insurance claims, working around the clock in three shifts. As Hale observes, "They speak English, type at least 50 words a minute on a computer, take data from paper claim forms supplied by U.S. health insurers via satellite in electronic form, put it into new digital forms, and ship it back to the United States. So connected are these workers that their forms can be reviewed—as they fill them in— by an American supervisor 8,000 miles away." With this workforce, the ACS is currently Ghana's largest employer in the private sector. The employees also receive health insurance (a rarity in Ghana), meals, and subsidized transport. Comparably, this job offers relief because only a small number of Ghanaians employed elsewhere (especially in the public sector) can earn much more.

Some of the call-center operations elsewhere include "KenCall" of Kenya, which has enough clients to keep its 200 telephone operators busy (*Foreign Dispatches Online*, 2005; Lacey, 2005). South Africa is far ahead, having an estimated 500 call centers and employing about 31,000 people. Proficiency in English and a time zone the same as some parts of Europe make it easy for companies to do this type of business with South Africa.

The vast population of French speakers in Africa has created good opportunities for the French-speaking African countries to claim that part of the outsourcing market. French-language call centers are operating in Morocco, Senegal, Tunisia, and Madagascar, reaching out to customers in Paris. Datamonitor (2004) reports that offshoring from France to Africa has begun yielding good results. In Tunisia, for instance, a technical support and customer service outsourcing provider (called Stream) opened a site that operates as a satellite to Stream's current facilities in Velizy and Angers, France. It provides French-language support to its clients and, since September 2004 when it began its activities, the company has employed professionals to provide technical support, customer assistance, and distance-selling activities. The choice of this destination was largely influenced by the country's stable political and economic environment; high proficiency in French as well as Tunisia's proximity and cultural ties with France are other factors. The benefit of this partnership is that Velizy and Angers provide onshore and nearshore solutions to high-value-added questions, while Tunis provides lower-value-added solutions for a high volume of transactions at reduced costs.

According to Datamonitor (2004), countries in North Africa are likely to become the destinations of nearshore call-center jobs because of their proximity to Western Europe, available workforce that is located relatively close to major EU centers, and modern telephony infrastructure favorable for nearshore call-center outsourcing. As predicted by Datamonitor, the number of outsourced nearshore agent positions in Central and Eastern Europe and North Africa was to rise from 4,400 in 2003 to 13,700 by 2008. Morocco and Tunisia will remain focused on French customer care, though Morocco is likely to diversify into Spanish- and English-speaking services. These business transactions are a good cause for optimism.

Other outsourced jobs in Africa involve assignments that include transcription of the minutes of conference calls from companies in the United States and Britain. This trend shows that the continent has the potential to attract more outsourced jobs if the various countries speed up their scientific, technological, political, and economic development efforts. The modest gains made so far by the various countries in creating a congenial environment to attract foreign businesses should be heartwarming, considering the long-lasting negative impact of events such as the Trans-Atlantic slave trade and colonization on Africa. These events not only hindered growth but also engendered perennial problems of poverty, political instability, and insufficient infrastructure. As Zachary (2004) observes, "To be sure, Africa is a far better place to do business (today) than (it was) five years ago." He identifies the spread of mobile telephony, which has revolutionized ordinary life on a continent with the world's lowest penetration of fixed-line telephones, as an important reason for the positive business environment. Furthermore, satellite links have vastly improved Internet access, and a new undersea cable that runs along the coast of Africa (SAT-3) promises to improve and reduce the cost of all types of communication. I share this optimism, because by all indications, the continent has room to maximize its participation in large-scale outsourcing.

HOPE FOR THE FUTURE

Since the late 1990s African governments have been adopting better strategies for the continent's involvement in the ICT revolution. The initiative to train people appears to be coming from the private sector, especially in South Africa and Ghana. This has led to the introduction of computers into the classrooms and the inculcation of technical writing skills at workshops, mostly through lectures on a modular basis. The upshot is that although Africa may not currently have the labor pool with the expertise to do high-quality outsourced jobs in the software or hardware industry, the incorporation of ICTs into the curricula of schools should begin boosting technical training to change the situation for the better. A few examples of what is being done in two countries (South Africa and Ghana) and the continent in general will throw more light on my claim.

What South Africa is Doing

According to a report by *Offshore Outsourcing World Staff* (2005), South Africa is the top offshore contact center destination, relegating India to the second place. The ranking is based on the findings of the U.K.-based marketing services specialist, Ion Group. In the Ion Group's own study that rated locations according to call-handling quality, technological infrastructure, and linguistic capabilities, South Africa garnered 51.1% while India received less than 50% in each category. Though this difference may not be considered profoundly significant, it is an encouraging development, which suggests that South Africa is positioning itself as a serious participant in the outsourcing industry. Furthermore, the *India Daily Online* (2005b) reported that South Africa's success is due to its better infrastructure, call-center operation capabilities, and mastery of the English language. This success is not adventitious. Most Africans regard South Africa as the continent's economic giant. It is the twentieth largest market for ICT products and services, accounting for 0.6% of worldwide ICT revenues. According to the 2001 report of the Cape Information Technology Initiative, with 10% growth per annum over the past five years, the sector is worth 43 billion ZAR or South African Rand ($7,035,915,896 USD, where $1USD= 6.1115 ZAR at current exchange rate) (see http://www.citi.org.za/).

South Africa's Western Cape ICT industry is vibrant. The *Technews Online* (2003) reports that as of 2003, there were about 1,200 companies employing 27,000 people in the region, confirming that the ICT sector is the Western Cape's second largest industry after tourism. Furthermore, the Western Cape's excellent skills base opens opportunities for software development, Web services, outsourcing, and training. Marc Spendlove, Marketing Director of The Dialogue Group (one of the largest call center companies in Cape Town, South Africa), said that "firms were showing a keen interest in the fast developing call-center industry in South Africa" (*India Daily Online*, 2005). This trend evokes optimism that the call-center industry in Cape Town will grow exponentially.

The Internet is booming in South Africa, a country considered an early adopter of this technology, having two million Internet users today. Specialist service, connectivity, and content providers are available for both corporate and private users. Corporate access provision to the Internet is among the most profitable Internet activities, with Internet Service Provider revenues yielding some 700 million South African Rand ($114,538,165 USD) in 2000 alone (Cape Information Technology Initiative, 2001).

Furthermore, the Computer Sciences Corporation (CSC) has over the past few years secured offshore outsourcing multiyear work from its northern hemisphere counterparts that is worth more than one billion South African Rand ($163,625,951 USD) (for details, see http://za.country.csc.com/en/ne/pr/676.shtml). The offshore outsourcing projects being done on behalf of CSC's international clients include Business Process Outsourcing (BPO), Application Managed Services or applications outsourcing, and international network security management. Thus, the CSC offers the South African market a wide range of services, including systems integration, application and infrastructure outsourcing, and BPO. It also provides services for customer relationship management (CRM), and health care and financial services. The CSC also provides offshore BPO services to manage the policy processing and administration for its U.S. and U.K. financial services customers who include life and pensions providers, short-term insurers, and bankers. Information available in the online directory on outsourcing in South Africa indicates that other companies such as Sun International, Unisys Africa, and TPI Corporation are deeply involved in the practice (see http://www.citi.org.za/Companies/1000/1009/1041.html).

According to the *Cape Business News Online* (2003), a group of tech-savvy Cape marketers formed a marketing consultancy company— iKineo—in Cape Town by converging marketing and technology to propel themselves into the consumer-brands-driven Asian market. They spent the last quarter of 2002 rolling out an innovative Customer Relationship Management (CRM) communications strategy and solution for British American Tobacco in Japan with their Tokyo advertising agency. Since the successful completion of this project, iKineo has been approached by the company, Bates 141 Japan, to develop strategy and solutions for other multinational brands in the Asia-Pacific region. The company hopes to penetrate China and the United Kingdom; its strategy elements would include ways to facilitate one-to-one interaction with customers, personalizing databases, and offering partner services to increase sales and profitability, to elevate brand awareness, and to add value to customers. There are other success stories.

South Africa's success in these ventures is the result of concerted efforts, as explained by Mandisi Mpahlwa, Minister of Trade and Industry (South Africa Department of Trade and Industry, 2004). Since the inception of multi-ethnic democratic governance in South Africa, the government has effectively adhered to disciplined, predictable economic measures to support the country's efforts for economic growth. Some of these measures included tariff reform, trade and investment promotion, an industrial strategy that focuses on supply-side, and a reform of the regulatory environment. Through government efforts to liberalize trade and to modify the country's industrial-development policies, South Africa has been established as a dynamic and internationally competitive location for investment.

An additional factor is the postapartheid environment of political stability, which is a major positive signal to investors. Consequently, through the arduous process of opening up the economy, South Africans developed a strong entrepreneurial culture and were prepared to jointly develop their country in concert with international partners in economic practices, including outsourcing. The measures are cumulatively instrumental in creating a promising medium- long-term economic agenda to ensure that local and international firms can operate profitably in South Africa (South Africa Department of Trade and Industry, 2004). Nor is that the end of the prospects. With this posture, South Africa has the ability to support and facilitate other members of the Southern African Development and Coordinating Council (SADCC) in creating conditions for outsourcing through a wide array of skills and technical facilities.

South Africa has also established links with organizations involved in technical communication. It currently has three registered international and national associations for technical writers—the ACM/SIGCHI (Association for Computing Machinery/Special Interest Group on Computer-Human Interaction), IABC (the International Association of Business Communicators), and ITCSA (Institute of Technical Communication South Africa). It is debatable whether the mere presence of these associations in the country means that progress is being made in the training of people to do technical documentation. We can, however, infer from such linkages that the country is opening up to external influences, which in itself indicates that local technical education is being pushed into an international spectrum.

Realizing the importance of skill acquisition, South Africa is vigorously pursuing the training of people for ICT-related jobs. This intensification echoed the results of the "Software Skills 2004 Survey" compiled by ITWeb and Software Futures, which revealed that shortages existed in terms of business analysis skills (23%), project management (14%), process management (10%) and team leadership (10%), according to the South African Broadcasting Corporation (2004). As part of the skills-development program, 117 students from the ICT Academy at the CIDA City Campus were trained in IT Technical Support Learnership, involving courses such as applications fundamentals, computer-hardware basics, operating systems, and computer environments by July 14, 2003. Financial support for training institutions was also forthcoming. For example, the Carnegie Corporation of New York in June 2002 awarded a $1 million grant to a research team headed by the University of the Western Cape for research into information and communication technology (ICT) in higher education. The grant would fund a three-year project to look into the applications and benefits of ICT in higher education. A team of developers would also investigate innovating technologies to meet the demands of teachers and students (South African Broadcasting Corporation, 2002). With these developments, South Africa is certainly geared up to propel Africa into the broad outsourcing market.

The Situation in Ghana

In Ghana, efforts at training people for ICT-related and technical documentation jobs take various forms. There is what I will call an "Apprenticeship Model" that involves workshops and seminars during which facilitators—mostly foreign-trained private individuals—teach selected participants from industry and governmental or quasi-governmental institutions certain technical communication practices and genres such as grant-proposal writing, bidding for jobs, technical or formal report writing, and feasibility-study report writing. Like the South African training model, the Ghanaian approach is modular, lecture-based, and involves few hands-on exercises. The participants are expected to return to their various workplaces to practice what they are taught and to impart their skills to others through some kind of "innovation diffusion" process. Generally, however, the tendency is for on-the-job training by which subordinates either emulate the writing styles of their supervisors or use boilerplates to write technical documents. One company—Busy Internet—has begun activities in graphic design for industries in addition to the Internet services it provides to its clients. Workers do 40 hours a week and enjoy an eight-hour benefit of training in graphic design when they are allowed to use the computers for free. This concession creates room for self-advancement in technical communication training, though at a minimal pace.

Some enterprising Ghanaians have also begun making breakthroughs in the ICT sector. In 2002 Hermann Chinery-Hesse, a Ghanaian computer scientist based in the United Kingdom introduced software that is not only "tropically tolerant and able to cope with frequent power cuts" but that competes with Bill Gates' Microsoft in Africa (Hale, 2003c). Chinery-Hesse's software company, known as Soft, plans to expand its operations in Africa and has already set up business partnerships in Nigeria, The Gambia, Senegal, and Kenya. The emergence of this company may be a harbinger of better things to come. As a beginning, India's largest software firm, Infosys, intends to enter the Ghanaian market and is set on using Soft as the local agent for marketing and support services. This local initiative is likely to set the pace for a continent-wide interest in ICT use.

At the official level too, something concrete is being done to boost accessibility to ICT. The Ghanaian government has made some strides with its direct involvement in the ICT sector. For example, in 2003 it established the Ghana-India Kofi

Annan Centre of Excellence in ICT (AITI-KACE), Ghana's first Advanced Information Technology Institute, to stimulate the growth of the ICT Sector in the Economic Community of West African States (ECOWAS). This state-of-the-art facility is a partnership between the governments of Ghana and India, and it houses West Africa's first supercomputer. Nearly 1,000 information and tech nology professionals, researchers, visitors, and trainees can be hosted at any given time. This facility has a subregional scope and should help the beneficiaries to maximize their business transactions. Furthermore, the training of Ghanaian youths in ICT has improved because of the government's direct involvement. The educational institutions are being equipped with computers for that purpose. So far, 12,500 people have been trained in employable skills under the government's Skills Training and Employment Placement (STEP) program. The government also provided an initial five billion Cedis for disbursement through the micro finance institute (*Ghana News Agency*, 2005).

Africa-Wide ICT Developments

Technological developments on the entire continent are also encouraging. According to the African Studies Center of the University of Pennsylvania, the United Nations Development Program (Africa) launched the "Internet Initiative for Africa" (IIA) in July 1997 as a further development of its initial program in March 1996. The goal of the IIA program is to promote the development of Internet Services to sub-Saharan Africa. This program focuses on assisting Sub-Saharan African countries to develop or enhance Internet connectivity, to build capacity, and to develop policies that are conducive to an information-rich society. The good news is that all 54 countries and territories in Africa now have public local dial-up Internet-access services in their capital cities, according to the July 2002 status report of the African Internet Connectivity on the use of the Internet in Africa (Jensen, 2002; Tillin, 2003). According to that report, the use of the Internet has grown relatively rapidly in most urban areas in Africa in much the same pattern as the adoption of the mobile phone, which followed shortly thereafter. This development is refreshing, because five years ago only a handful of countries had local Internet access. The situation has improved drastically such that the Internet is now available in every capital city. Ghana's capital city of Accra alone has about 500 Internet cafes, which is roughly six times as many as in London (Hale, 2003b).

The spread of mobile telephony has revolutionized ordinary life on a continent that has had the world's lowest penetration of fixed-line telephones. Satellite links have vastly improved Internet access, and a new undersea cable that runs along the coast of Africa (SAT-3) promises to improve and reduce the cost of all types of communications. Though these are encouraging trends, the differences between the development levels of Africa and the rest of the world are still wide (Zachary, 2004). More importantly, governments appear to be more flexible than they were in the past. The upshot is an encouraging private involvement in decision making concerning how to solve the problems hindering economic growth. With the proliferation of computer technology in teaching and learning, additional measures are being taken to broaden the curriculum for technical education and to create the requisite labor pool for participation in outsourcing.

The work of institutions that provide technical assistance to users on the continent makes it possible for an encouraging pattern to develop. For example, AfricaLink provides support to the United States Agency for International Development (USAID) partner networks in Africa that seek Internet access to facilitate the exchange of information among their members. Environmental, agricultural, and natural resource-management networks are specifically targeted for assistance. Furthermore, the Capacity Building for Electronic Communication in Africa (CABECA), which is a three-year project to promote computer-assisted networking throughout Africa and implemented by the Pan African Development Information System (PADIS) of the United Nations Economic Commission for Africa (UNECA), also assists African countries in their ICT needs (see African Information Society Initiative (AISI) and The African Internet Status Report, 1992). These developments in the technology industry give clear indications that Africa is waking up to the reality.

Notwithstanding the gains being made by some countries on the continent, some crucial problems still continue to hold back progress. As Zachary (2004) rightly observes, Africa's "economic appeal" may be increasing as the outsourcing environments in India or elsewhere become gradually saturated; but these countries are ready to widen the gap between themselves and prospective competitors by continually taking prompt steps to improve their environment more quickly. And unless African countries also do so, their cities that are increasingly attracting the attention of outsourcing experts as corporate locations for investment may lose out to their Asian counterparts. For example, when the Dallas-based Affiliated Computer Services decided to expand its outsourcing operations in 2003, it opened a new center in India rather than in Ghana or another African country (Hale, 2003a). The motivation for this decision is not difficult to fathom. The company's smaller facility in Bangalore (India) has better facilities for handling more analytical and high-tech work while the facility in Accra (Ghana) could be used mostly for more routine data entry requirements.

THE CONSTRAINTS

Most of Africa's political, economic, scientific, and technological problems are systemic. Until quite recently, Africa did not actively engage in scientific and technological developments mainly because of scarce resources, though some people continue to blame colonialism for the continent's woes. One common view is that "colonialism inhibited the development of indigenous technology in Africa to a large extent . . . colonial domination brought with it a shift into a cash crop economy and de-stabilized some of the existing processes of technical growth" (Emeagwali, 1998). Others (Michael & Michael, 1998) hold the view that the superimposition of western technology, sociopolitical institutions, and ideologies on the continent was "violently disruptive of the old familistic order" of African societies, creating "new values and symbols, new techniques for the acquisition of wealth, status, and prestige, and new groups for which the old system had no place" (Coleman, 1954). Both Fortner (1993, p. 198) and Ali Mazrui (1980, p. 208) agree that colonization is partially responsible for some of Africa's systemic problems. But the problems go beyond colonialism.

Other constraints such as inadequate workforce resulting from the low status of technical education (in ICT and related fields, including technical documentation and business communication), lack of institutional capacity and expertise, inadequate material resources, linguistic and cultural differences, and political instability made it difficult for African countries to readily create the kind of attractive environment that foreign businesses need.

Geopolitical Risks

The geopolitical risks are largely caused by political instability and civil wars in many African countries, though some countries began addressing some aspects by the 1990s. At the local level, erratic attitudes by the various countries toward enunciating and implementing policies on science and technology often delayed the adoption of pragmatic measures for national development. The cumulative effect of these external and internal factors hindering sustainable development in Africa is the often-severe difficulty in building stable political institutions, implementing economic development projects, and promulgating policies to get rid of tribal animosities and other issues that create instability (Fortner, 1993, p. 198). These geopolitical problems appear to have resulted in Africa's having a bad image that doesn't attract as much foreign investment as is possible. The situation is, however, gradually improving because of the democratization process penetrating the continent.

Bad Government Strategies on Science and Technology

Bureaucracy and red tape, government monopoly over the telecommunications sector, and the existing situation in which telecommunication and Internet traffic is routed outside the continent at an extremely unbearable cost to the African end-user compound problems. For example, when Rising Data (the first ever English-speaking call center in West Africa) was to be established in Ghana in 2003 to sell mobile phones to people in the United States, it took more than a year for the owners to explain to the Ghanaian Communications Ministry what Voice-Over-Internet technology was all about (Hale, 2003a). It was not until the owners threatened to move their operations to India if the government forced the company to work through Ghana Telecom that Rising Data was granted its license to use Voice-Over-Internet technology via satellite. There is something peculiar about this problem into which one can read some political connotations. Hale notes that although it is legal for U.S. citizens to call Ghana over the Internet, it is illegal for people or Internet cafes in Ghana to offer that same service. Yet, it is a certainty that the reliability and cost-effectiveness of a country's communications infrastructure is an important requirement for any successful cross-border business transaction.

Another problem is that the governments do not provide much-needed resources for investment in the ICT sector. The necessary institutional arrangements and financial investment to create subregional and regional backbones are also not available to facilitate direct connection between African regions and the exchange of network information between African Internet Service Providers. Apart from these problems, the high-handed policies on ICT are a disincentive. Most tax regimes in African countries still treat computers and cell phones as luxury items, which makes these almost exclusively imported commodities all the more expensive and even less accessible to majority of the people (Jensen, 2002). Although there have been notable efforts in some countries to reduce duties on computers, the rates charged on communications equipment and accessories are still too high for users. Thus, the current environment does not match with vibrant ones in India and China, which continue to catch the eyes of business concerns in North America and Europe.

Obsolete Infrastructure

Africa has the world's lowest level of telecommunication development, resulting in a scarcity of lines, even in urban areas. Compared to the United States and others in the developed world, African countries often lack basic infrastructure such as reliable electricity, driveable roads, efficient public transportation, and modern communication networks. Many countries have extremely limited power distribution networks, which do not penetrate significantly into rural areas, and power rationing is a common occurrence, even in some capital cities such as Lagos (Nigeria), Accra (Ghana), Abidjan (Ivory Coast), and Durban or Johannesburg in South Africa (Jensen, 2002). As noted in the July 2002 report on the status of the Internet in Africa, the main communication networks (road, rail, and air transport) are quite narrow—though costly—and often in poor condition. The movement of people and goods needed to support a pervasive ICT infrastructure is hardly smooth.

Inadequate Labor Pool

Mainstream technical education in Africa has not created an adequate labor pool with the requisite technical communication skills to handle large-scale outsourced jobs. Lack of experience and the high cost of training constrain the creation of a reliable labor pool. Evidence from some of the companies handling outsourced jobs (in Ghana and Kenya, for example) indicates that workers currently doing ICT-related jobs are mostly products of institutions providing general education in the Humanities and Sciences. They have limited skills in typing, computer technology, and technical communication but endeavor to learn on the job so that they can hone their skills. Until technical education in ICT-related jobs is intensified, it is not likely that the reliable and well-trained workforce needed for outsourced jobs would be available soon. This problem appears to be the result of the low status that technical (or business) communication has in the curricula of African educational institutions.

Sociocultural and Linguistic Problems

Cultural and linguistic differences among the diverse African communities affect cross-border commerce. As Gupta (2003) points out, the fundamental need to deal with cross-cultural communication problems, the fact that employees who hold most of the knowledge about a certain system may also be adversely affected by translation problems, the unavoidable reality that offshore vendors lack company-specific understanding, and the problem of high turnover among offshore IT professionals are problems that those wishing to outsource jobs should know about and solve promptly. Africa's business and social cultures are often very different from what happens in the home countries of the corporations seeking to outsource their jobs there. For example, there are different standards of work ethics, risk taking, and organizational structure, among others. More importantly, the attitude toward time—which metaphorizes as "African Time"— cannot be glossed over. To most Africans, time is "circular" and not "linear," which impacts their understanding of how to handle schedules. In Ghana, for example, where the concept of "African Time" is entrenched, the attitude toward time and business schedules is erratic, which often disrupts business transactions. In most cases, culprits get away with a mere reprimand or no sanction at all, though their disrespect for time and schedule could cause financial loss. Doing business in a society with such a generally "flexible" attitude to business appointments could create unforeseeable problems.

There are other cross-cultural problems. Earley (2003) explains that knowledge transfer problems emanating from such cross-cultural differences, especially in the case of outsourcing of ICT and technical documentation jobs, delay business. The offshore workers' lack of programming experience and knowledge about the project and its origins, together with their faulty understanding of users' needs and misperceptions about what constitutes a successful project, could also have adverse effects on schedule and budgetary allocations for the technical documentation tasks. Thus, for example, the process of transferring knowledge from a U.S. client to an offshore vendor in Africa—everything from hard skills such as programming knowledge to more tacit knowledge such as an understanding of what the company and its users expect from a system—can make or break a project that is outsourced to the multicultural and complex environment in Africa if the proper homework is not done in advance. Earley (2003) notes again that on quality assurance and project management, there could still be problems. It is important to determine clearly what standards for the technical documentation process are to be adopted. Should the prerogative to determine standards lie with the local supervisors or the original owners of the tasks being outsourced? How these standards should be determined and implemented efficiently is another likely source of friction. These problems need to be solved.

SOLUTIONS

There are compelling reasons why African countries must solve the problems that hinder the continent's participation in outsourcing on a large scale. First, the outsourcing environment in India is gradually becoming unattractive for a number of reasons, according to forecasts by outsourcing monitors. For example, the international research agency the Gartner Group has predicted that India's overall share in the Business Process Offshoring (BPO) market would slip from the present 80% to 55% by 2007 (Saha, 2004). According to Gartner, the global offshore BPO market was likely to be around $27 billion by 2007, with India's share rising from $2.3 billion to $14 billion during the same period, though its overall share will fall. As explained by Sujoy Chohan, Vice-President and Research Director of Gartner's "Offshore BPO," even though India would continue to be a dominant player, other countries would come up fast. The rising wage problem is another setback for India. A recent survey by Hewitt Associates, the Global Human Resources Firm, indicates that the rapid increase in wages, especially within the IT industry, is quickly shrinking margins and eroding the attractiveness of the region (Siddharth, 2005). The survey revealed that India showed the highest average salary increase in Asia, followed by China, the Philippines, and Korea. It said while India reported an 11.6% overall pay hike in 2004, salaries grew by 6.4% to 8.4% in China, about 7.4% to 7.7% in the Philippines, and 6.4% to 6.8% in Korea for the same year.

Second, a number of countries such as China, South Africa, the Philippines, Australia, New Zealand, Mauritius, and Malaysia have woken up to the job-creating potential of BPO ventures and are trying to put together integrated strategies to develop them (Datamonitor, 2004). In a research report, Datamonitor predicted that the number of agent positions (APs) in South Africa would increase from 38,400 in 2003 at a compound annual growth rate (CAGR) of 13% to reach 69,600 APs in 2008; and that the number of call centers was set to almost double, increasing at a CAGR of 14% from 494 in 2003 to 939 in 2008. Furthermore, the most optimistic Datamonitor forecast predicted that the number of offshore outsourced APs would quadruple from 1,400 in 2003 to reach 6,200 in 2008, which represents a CAGR of 34%. In Datamonitor's estimation, therefore, "South Africa offers outsource providers a higher quality more culturally-aligned front-office and back-office location where labor costs run at two-thirds of their US or UK equivalent." Additionally, the number of jobs to be created is expected to increase from just 60 about two years ago to more than 1,000 within the first three months' emergence of the call-center business, according to forecasts made by the Cape Information Technology Initiative (2002).

Other factors likely to turn the attention of businesses to destinations other than India may emerge with time as outsourcing intensifies and workplace politics become more rigorous and unpredictable. In spite of predictions pointing to a drop in India's share, it is important that we understand what India did to become the leading participant in outsourcing. With its English-speaking, educated, and technically proficient workforce, India has made strides and will continue to benefit from the projected 30% annual growth in outsourcing. Undeniably, the growth of the software industry in India is the result of investment in education and training of software engineers to form the labor pool, which is a positive model for development. Zachary (2004) tells us that the Asian countries succeed in attracting many jobs by creating "industrial parks," with more reliable services, including ultrareliable communications networks, and a reliable labor pool, which are offered at competitive prices. By restructuring their secondary schools and universities to equip graduates with the skills demanded by multinational corporations, these Asian countries also create more competitive labor pools by supporting the education of their citizens either at home or abroad. China and India are known for sending students annually to the United States for training in Information Technology. These graduates are encouraged to return home to use their training for their countries' well-being. Over time, the opportunities are created to supply the labor pool with the workforce from local initiatives. According to the Gartner Group, between 150,000 and 200,000 contact-center workers are employed in India, the Philippines, Ireland, and other emerging destinations such as Russia and Mexico (Earley, 2003).

The claim is often made that India has continued to be the choice of many companies seeking to outsource technical functions because of the seriousness with which the country tackles the factors that influence outsourcing. According to the Gartner Group's 2003 survey, about 70% of businesses with plans for large-scale outsourcing were planning to outsource to India in 2004. Furthermore, the Giga Information Group, citing Indian outsourcers for both cost and quality benefits, expected outsourcing to India to grow by 25% in 2004 alone (Earley, 2003). China's example is also noteworthy. According to the Outsourcing Institute (2004), China will overtake India in outsourcing in about 10 years because of the measures it is taking to improve the business environment. Apart from a high literacy rate of 82% (one billion literate people), China has improved its infrastructure and human resource base. The country has the prospect of graduating 200,000 IT professionals from colleges, starting in 2006; it hopes to add about 50 million to its workforce annually; it currently has 400,000 IT professionals, which is just 100,000 fewer than the United States; and it has 175 million phone lines, while India has 34.5 million. Thus, with a wage rate 40% to 50% less than that of India, the software outsourcing revenue for China was projected to more than double to $5 billion by 2005 (Outsourcing Institute, 2004).

The successful operations of North American companies in these Asian countries indicate that corporations will do business wherever the environment is conducive. With the persistence of globalization and expansion of ICTs, corporations in the advanced world will continue to look for destinations at which to use outsourcing as a means to maximize profits at the minimum cost. It is imperative that Africa also create such a business-like environment to promote large-scale outsourcing on the continent.

Solutions to these problems could come from four main areas: (1) favorable government policies and actions; (2) effective language instruction and technical education (at any level possible) for the creation of a reliable labor pool; (3) infrastructural development; and (4) adoption of business-oriented attitudes (including acceptable work ethics) and effective use of techniques for cross-cultural communication. The objective is to ensure greater competitiveness to boost transactions.

Governments must deregulate and privatize the ICT sector and other facilities. For increased economic and social activity, which could be stimulated through greater use of ICTs (Jensen, 2002), it is important that steps be taken to improve the communication network. Telecommunication costs, especially for international calls, should be reduced and tariff barriers to data communication removed. Governments should also support outsourcing ventures as in India and China, for example, where the governments provide financial incentives to companies looking to set up call centers there (Gupta, 2003). These incentives are often in the form of tax credits, government-funded infrastructure, or eased regulatory requirements. African governments must go beyond lip service in order to stamp out corruption and to reform the economy. Such issues as intellectual-property protection, labor laws, data protection, and an overall ability to enforce contracts need to be tackled to assure investors of the security of their businesses.

As suggested by the African Technical Advisory Committee (ATAC), the transformation of regulatory and legal frameworks in Africa is vital to the introduction of new regulatory framework and capacity building for regulators in order to promote policy and regulatory harmonization that would facilitate cross-border interaction and market enlargement. It is important for regional networks of regulators, such as the Telecommunication Regulatory Association of Southern Africa (TRASA), the West African Telecommunication Regulators Association (WATRA), and the Association of African Regulators (AAR) to intensify their efforts to improve regulatory capacities at the national level to ensure universal access to improved telecommunications (see http://www3.sn.apc.org/africa/afstat.htm). Their efforts should enhance Africa's capacity to promote contacts between itself and outside partners wishing to do business on the continent. The various national telecommunications companies should also take appropriate measures to provide efficient services to internal users.

Though participation in outsourcing does not necessarily depend on a highly qualified workforce, the technical training of people to do ICT-related jobs must be supported by government and industry. The pace has already been set in South Africa and Ghana, and everything must be done to provide the labor pool needed for outsourcing. Obviously, public schools in Africa, whose funding continues to dwindle as the countries' economies weaken, do not have the capacity to single-handedly train the people. Private schools, colleges, and universities could also support this training, though there may be genuine fears among the people about the high cost of training. The African Virtual University (AVU), which is an initiative begun by the United Nations, is providing training in computer and Internet applications and programming languages to its 29 university campuses in 18 countries in Africa. The $60,000 annual fee per student for any of its online certificate, diploma, and degree programs in Business Communication in English is too high for those who need that training.

Governments, industry, and the private sector must collaborate in taking drastic measures to solve problems; local and regional institutions must also be supported to coordinate activities in ICT-related fields. For example, the African Information Society Initiative (AISI), which was adopted by the African Member States in 1995 and launched in 1996 under the sponsorship of the United Nations Economic Commission for Africa (ECA) as an action framework, can become the basis for information and communication activities in Africa. It can help initiate moves to support institutions willing to train people in ICTs. In any such venture, the ECA should join multilateral, bilateral, and nongovernmental partners as well as representatives of the private sector and African member-states in implementing the strategies of the AISI. Other existing institutions such as the African Regional Preparatory Conference for the World Summit on the Information Society (WSIS), the African Development Forum (ADF III), the African Learning Network (ALN), and the Information Technology Centre for Africa (ITCA) are already deeply involved in ICTs and should intensify efforts toward creating conditions for Africa to become a major participant in jobs requiring ICT expertise. It is important that Africans who have studied and practiced technical communication in other parts of the world seize the opportunity to establish networks for the technical communication training on the continent. Such a vocational and technical education should open new avenues for the labor pool needed to do outsourced jobs (see Hassan, 2003).

CONCLUSION

I have argued in this chapter that Africa has the potential to participate productively and meaningfully in large scale outsourcing and that the problems that hold back that depth of participation must be solved without further delay. It is my contention that the successes achieved through outsourcing in countries outside Africa depend on the availability of the requisite economic, human, political, technological, and technical resources. I have opined that Africa can also provide such resources if decisive action is taken to solve the "systemic" problems hindering the creation of an attractive environment for large-scale outsourcing. The low level of outsourcing currently taking place on the continent could be improved to make Africa an unavoidable destination in the future. Something is being done, but it is not enough. Over the past five years there has been a proliferation of Internet cafes and computer training in African schools, which makes it possible for Africans in most of the countries to become part of the dynamics of the information superhighway.

Companies considering Africa as their destination for outsourcing must also do some homework. Any effort to outsource jobs to Africa must involve an understanding of its sociocultural and linguistic diversity as well as technical, technological, and structural problems. These problems must be appreciated in their entirety because they could either make or mar business relationships in this era of globalization.

As the world continues to shrink into a global village and the search for new areas of economic activity intensifies, there are strong signals from the developed world that outsourcing will continue to influence the economic and political direction of most corporations there. For as long as this trend persists, Africa cannot continue to remain at the fringes without losing the opportunity to profit from outsourcing. Though outsourcing alone cannot rid the continent of its unemployment problem, its contributions could be substantial, and Africa should not pretend to be unaware of this fact. The truth is that the world is running fast toward new sources of economic practice and Africa must run fast too. If it continues to walk, the world will run away and leave it behind to continue wallowing in poverty.

REFERENCES

African Information Society Initiative (AISI). (1996). *Africa's digital agenda.* Retrieved October 29, 2004, from http://www.uneca.org/aisi/.

Cape Business News Online. (2003, March 19). Retrieved May 14, 2005, from http://www.cbn.co.za/issue/3180303.htm.

Cape Information Technology Initiative. (2002, March). *Cape information technology initiative sector scan 2001.* Retrieved March 11, 2005, from http://www.capegateway.gov.za/Text/2004/1/itc_sector_scan.pdf.

Coleman, M. (1954). Colonialism and the fate of Africa. In K. Kumar (Ed.), *Transnational enterprises: Their impact on third world societies and cultures.* Boulder, CO: Westview Press, 1980.

Datamonitor. (2004, November 9). *Research report. South Africa: An emerging offshore opportunity.* Retrieved June 18, 2005, from http://whitepaper.outsourcingpipeline.com/cmpoutsourcingpline/search/viewabstract /71644/index.jsp.

Earley, R. M. (2003). *Foreshore: A vision of CRM outsourcing.* Retrieved December 15, 2004, from http://www.tmcnet.com/cis/0703/Outsourcing1.htm.

Emeagwali, G. (1998, March 7). *Colonialism and science: The African case.* Paper presented at the conference on matrices of scientific knowledge, Oxford University, UK. Retrieved October 27, 2004, from http://www.africahistory.net/colonial.htm.

Foreign Dispatches Online. (2005, February 2). *Outsourcing reaches Africa.* Retrieved June 21, 2005, from http://foreigndispatches.typepad.com/dispatches/2005/02/outsourcing_rea.html.

Fortner, R. S. (1993). *International communication: History, conflict, and control of the global metropolis.* Belmont, CA: Wadsworth.

Ghana News Agency. (2003, February 9). Ghana opens West Africa's first ICT hub. Accra, Ghana.

Gupta, S. (2003). *Offshore call center outsourcing: International site selection strategies.* Retrieved December 12, 2004, from http://www.tmcnet.com/cis/0703/Outsourcing2.htm.

Hale, B. (2003a, May 20). *Ghana enters telesales era.* Retrieved October 10, 2004, from http://news.bbc.co.uk/2/hi/business/3039355.stm.

Hale, B. (2003b, June 9). *In search of profitable connections.* Retrieved October 11, 2004, from http://news.bbc.co.uk/2/hi/business/2974418.stm.

Hale, B. (2003c, June 3). *Ghana trumps mighty Microsoft.* Retrieved October 14, 2004, from http://news.bbc.co.uk/2/hi/business/2935210.stm.

Hassan, M. H. A. (2003). *Science and Africa's salvation.* Retrieved January 7, 2005, from http://www.project-syndicate.org/commentaries/commentary_text.php4?id=935&m=series.

India Daily Online. (2005a, February 22). *Media release. South Africa, another English-speaking nation moves ahead to challenge India in call center market.* Retrieved March 14, 2005, from http://www.indiadaily.com/editorial/1683.asp.

India Daily Online. (2005b, March 5). Retrieved June 16, 2005, from http://www.indiadaily.com/editorial/1798.asp.

Jensen, M. (2002, July). *African Internet connectivity.* Retrieved December 15, 2004 from http://www3.sn.apc.org/africa/partial.html.

Lacey, M. (2005, February 2). *New York Times Online.* Accents of Africa: A new outsourcing frontier. Retrieved June 20, 2005, from http://www.corpwatch.org/article.php?id=11824.

Mazrui, A. A. (1980). The impact of transnational corporations on educational processes and cultural change: An African perspective. In K. Kumar (Ed.), *Transnational enterprises: Their impact on third world societies and cultures* (pp. 207-229). Boulder, CO: Westview Press.

Michael, S. O., & Michael, Y. A. (1998). Multiculturalism in the context of Africa: The case of Nigeria. In K. Cushner (Ed.), *International perspectives of intercultural education* (pp. 186-208). Mahwah, NJ: Lawrence Erlbaum.

Odedra, M. (1992). Enforcement of foreign technology on Africa: Its effect on society, culture, and utilization of information technology. In C. Beardon & D. Whitehouse (Eds.), *Social citizenship in the information age* (pp. 143-154). London: Macmillan.

Offshore Outsourcing World Staff. (2005, April 7). *Offshore Outsourcing World Online.* South Africa: New call center hub. Retrieved June 15, 2005, from http://www.enterblog.com/200504070235.html.

Open Outsource. (2004, August 6). *Western European firms outsourcing to nearshore CEE call centers.* Retrieved March 13, 2005, from http://www.openoutsource.com/resource-dated9069-html.

Outsourcing Institute. (2004, Spring). Outsourcing essentials. *Online Newsletter, 2*(1), p. 1. Retrieved October 17, 2004, from http://www.outsourcing.com/content.asp?page=01b/other/oe/q104/smaller.htm/&non av=true.

Outsourcing Times Online. (2005, February 21). Africa enters outsourcing market. Retrieved June 20, 2005, from http://www.blogsource.org/2005/02/africa_enters_o.html.

Saha, S. (2004, July 9). Lack of English-speaking staff to blunt BPO edge. *India Business Standard Online.* Retrieved March 13, 2005, from http://www.openoutsource.com/resource-dated10572-phtml.

Siddharth, S. (2005, January 21). Could rising wages diminish India's outsourcing edge? *Siliconeer, New California Media Online.* Retrieved February 22, 2005, from http://news.ncmonline.com/news/view_article.html?article_id=167d1c86c1d28e760 7c942fd9891938e.

South Africa Department of Trade and Industry. (2004). *Department of trade and industry report.* Retrieved January 6, 2005, from http://www.thedti.gov.za/investing/howtodobusinessinsa.htm.

South African Broadcasting Corporation. (2002, June 19). *Employers hit by software skills gap.* Retrieved June 21, 2005, from http://www.sabcnews.com/economy/business/0,2172,89851,00.html.

South African Broadcasting Corporation. (2004, October 14). *$1m grant awarded for Western Cape ICT research.* Retrieved June 22, 2005, from http://www.sabcnews.com/sci_tech/computers/0,2172,36788,00.html.

Technews Online. (2003, October). Retrieved May 15, 2005, from http://estrategy.co.za/news.asp?pklNewsID=12476&pklIssueID=362&pklCategoryI D=134.

The African Internet—A status report. (1992, July). Retrieved October 18, 2004 from http://www3.sn.apc.org/africa/afstat.htm

Tillin, L. (2003, February12). Africa's development plan. *BBC News Online.* Retrieved January 6, 2005, from http://news.bbc.co.uk/1/hi/business/2062777.stm.

Zachary, P. G. (2004). The diversity advantage: Multicultural identity in the new world economy. *Daily Times of Pakistan Online.* (2004, June 24, p. 3). Retrieved February 20, 2005, from http://www.dailytimes.com.pk/default.asp?page=story_24-6-2004_pg3_6.

CHAPTER 4

Outsourcing of Technical Communication Tasks from German-Speaking Contexts

Petra Drewer and Charlotte Kaempf

For many years, worldwide expanding markets have challenged jobs in production and service arenas located in industrialized countries. With the present trend in globalization, we are witnessing the second phase of deindustrialization—outsourcing of white-collar jobs, including the research and development sector (R&D). Although the field of Technical Communication (TC) will benefit from the increased demand for multilingual documentation by global business, the trend to send TC jobs from a high-wage country to countries with a low-wage workforce that speaks the same language (in other words, offshoring) diminishes this benefit. With respect to globally important languages, exemplified by the six U.N. languages, the threat of offshoring applies foremost to English- and Spanish-speaking countries, on a limited scale to countries where Russian, French, and Arabic are official languages, but does not apply to Chinese-speaking countries. Currently, the phenomenon of outsourcing jobs to other countries poses an imminent threat to the TC profession in English-speaking countries; that is, jobs are sent from the United States, Canada, or Great Britain to low-wage, English-speaking countries such as India or China.

Our inquiry assesses how outsourcing affects and may affect the production of technical documentation in high-wage German-speaking countries and how the resulting effects are different from those in the high-wage English-speaking

United States. We will focus on issues related to production and documentation but not on problems encountered by virtual long-distance teams. We expect that answers to this inquiry will help professionals both in business and academe understand how the phenomenon of offshoring is experienced in national TC markets of industrialized countries whose main language is not English. To achieve this goal we will first look at the lexical field of outsourcing and technical communication to clarify potential differences in the meaning of English and German terms. A look at the economic frame condition in European countries, emphasizing the *status quo* in German-speaking countries, shall serve as a base for an up-to-date profile of the TC job situation in Austria, Germany, and Switzerland, with an emphasis on terminology management and multilingual documentation. Finally, we will analyze the present status of the TC degree and certificate programs in German-speaking countries.

LEXICAL FIELDS OF OUTSOURCING AND TECHNICAL COMMUNICATION IN ENGLISH AND GERMAN

We compared definitions for the GILT (Globalization, Internationalization, Localization, and Translation) community given in relevant American English and German encyclopedias, TC-relevant literature, and publicly accessible online sources such as the Localisation Industry Standards Association (LISA) Web site (www.lisa.org). For each of the terms discussed below, we will give definitions that are used in both English- and German-speaking contexts.

Globalization (business-related): An enterprise policy based on free trade to produce in the world market. The term globalization is a short form for "global economic liberalization." A networked global market implies, for example, an adaptive design of products and documentation as well as outsourcing and offshoring of jobs across continents; see below under "outsourcing" for a differentiation between outsourcing and offshoring.

Native-language support (NLS; product and service related): To enhance worldwide marketability, products and services have to be designed for use in various language contexts.

Internationalization is oriented to consider cultural and linguistic character-istics of a country or a group of countries during the production process. That is to say, developers will design products and documentation in a way that will allow for subsequent adaptation to national target markets (i.e., localization, details see below). Internationalization developers consider the following: (a) product-specific features such as the position of warning labels or switches, the form of power plugs, or requirement for voltage; and (b) language-specific features such as character sets, reading direction, and text length. White space for longer target-language texts is important as are standards for sorting order, date and time, cardinal numbers, and currency data (Sturz, 1998). In addition to these text-specific features, visuals (figures and symbols) have to be designed for easy adaptation. With respect to software development, LISA defines internationalization as "the process of generalizing a product so that it can handle multiple languages and cultural conventions without the need for redesign. Internationalization takes place at the level of program design and document development" (LISA, 2005).

Localization refers to the actual adaptation of a product and its documentation to a specific national target market. Localization includes the implementation of those cultural, linguistic, and technical features that have been planned out during the internationalization process. According to LISA, localization "involves taking a product and making it linguistically and culturally appropriate to the target locale (country/region and language) where it will be used and sold" (LISA, 2005). Strikingly, this definition lacks the aspect of technical appropriateness.

Members of the GILT community often use the acronyms I18N and L10N, referring to internationalization and localization respectively because there are 18 letters between the "I" and "N" in internationalization and there are 10 letters between the "L" and the "N" in localization.

Outsourcing (job and task related): The interdependent nature of the global economy forms a single global job market reflected by an increase of interdependence of global society—jobs transcend national borders.

Outsourcing. Originally, the English term is a collation of "outside + resource + using." It implies that specific tasks are handed to specialized service providers. In German-speaking countries, the English term has turned into the Anglicism *Outsourcing.* This Anglicism and its German equivalent *Auslagerung* mean subcontracting, thereby distinguishing between *outsourcing of production* and *outsourcing of services.* The subcontractor, whether delivering products or providing services, may be located in a non-German-speaking country. For example, jobs that localize product documentation are often (sub)contracted. A reasonable body of information is available on outsourcing. Relevant community portals offer specialized information: in March 2005, the EServer TC Library (www.tc.eserver.org) returned 20 hits and the database of *tekom* (www.tekom.de), Gesellschaft für Technische Kommunikation, the major German professional TC organization, 15 hits.

Offshoring. The English term meaning outsourcing to other countries is not readily translatable into German; the corresponding Anglicism has not yet become an established business term. A visit to relevant TC community portals in March 2005 confirms this fact: the EServer TC Library returned three hits and the *tekom* database zero hits.

Insourcing. In the United States insourcing describes the phenomenon by which foreign companies increase their investments and employment in the United States, such as Daimler's takeover of Chrysler. In German this term describes the return of internationally outsourced jobs back to their original company, hence it is not an antonym to the German outsourcing, meaning subcontracting.

After describing the lexical field of outsourcing, we will now turn to the lexical field of technical communication. Today developers of documentation often describe themselves with global terms such as publication manager, usability expert, information architect, information services coordinator, or knowledge manager. Tasks and expert's jobs involved in the creation and development of documentation for products and services in technical domains such as engineering, sciences, or medicine are represented through the following terms.

Technical documentation: This comprises all the written information that is produced in a publishing department. There is a distinction made between documentation that remains with the publishing department of a manufacturer or service provider (e.g., documentation on construction, assembly, and quality assurance) and documentation that is delivered for use by clients, users, or patent agents (e.g., installation manuals, operating instructions, directions for use, safety instructions). In view of a globalized environment, writers will have to take into account subsequent translation while crafting documents (for details see "Native-Language Support" in this section and the "Handling Language in a Multilingual Environment" section). In German, technical documentation translates to *Technische Dokumentation*.

Technical communication: The established term used by professional organizations in English-speaking countries such as the Society for Technical Communication (STC) in the United States or the Institute for Scientific and Technical Communicators (ISTC) in Great Britain. With the advent of the Internet, the spectrum of tasks has expanded over the past decade from traditional technical writing toward Web-based content development. As information engineers, technical communicators create and develop digital documents in close collaboration with subject matter experts (SMEs). Technical communicators are mediators between manufacturers or service providers and users. This definition of vocational tasks applies equally to technical communication jobs in German-speaking countries. Native German speakers interpret the term *Technische Kommunikation* as communication about technical subjects in general—written as well as oral communication. The direct, literal translation *Technischer Kommunikator* as occupational title does not exist, it is rather *Technischer Redakteur/Redaktor*.

Technische Redaktion: This is a term that is specific for German-speaking countries. It is an adaptation to the German *Redaktion* (editorial office of a newspaper or magazine publisher). Tasks of a *Technischer Redakteur* (Austria and Germany) or *Technischer Redaktor* (Switzerland) comprise writing as defined previously in "technical communication" and next in "technical writing" where emphasis is given to strategic tasks required for the management of a publication project.

Technical writing: This traditional term implies writing and editing a text that is useful for a target audience. Today, technical writing often is associated with basic formal requirements such as language correctness, factual accuracy, appropriateness of graphical design and layout, and legibility for existing texts (commodity writing). A direct literal translation to German does not exist The term most commonly used is *Technische Redaktion*. The English technical writing is geared toward meeting the readers' need for comprehensibility and readability. Thus, technical writing is considered a subset of both technical communication and *Technische Redaktion*.

Our overview on the lexical fields for outsourcing and technical communication shows that the meaning of globalization, internationalization, and localization is equal in the context of both languages, whereas some differences are obvious for the use of outsourcing and offshoring. The differences in meaning for terms in the lexical field of technical communication are substantial.

SOCIO-ECONOMIC SITUATION

Recently the economies of the countries in the European Union (EU) have been characterized by low productivity and stagnation of growth. In March 2000 EU statesmen adopted an action and development plan that is oriented to make the EU a dynamic and competitive knowledge-based economy ("Lisbon Strategy"; see Commission of the European Communities, 2005). The main objectives for reaching this goal are the establishment of innovative internal markets, a boost of research and innovation, and improvement of education. Economic, social, and environmental sustainability will create jobs, strengthen social networks, and protect ecological life-support systems. The goal seems attainable because the gross domestic product (GDP) of the EU is higher than that of the United States of America.

Why are some job tasks outsourced (subcontracted or offshored) while others are not? Stereotypical answers point to a lack of know-how or inefficient in-house operation for subcontracting and to the benefits of low wages, access to new markets, avoidance of high duties and taxes for offshoring. The practices of outsourcing jobs are often analyzed according to the example of an industrial sector in a distinct geographic region (automotive, computer software, or pharmaceutical industry in the United States, the EU, or southeast Asia). Today, quality products displaying first-class workmanship that were once uniquely German are manufactured in low-wage countries in eastern Europe or southeast Asia. For example, cars made in Germany contain components manufactured in dozens of other countries.

At present in low-wage countries, imported technology is applied or produced, meaning that there is little development of innovative technologies. This may change. There are indications that Germany is losing its reputation for innovation. Indeed, several German-based multinational corporations are about to offshore sections of their R&D departments from their headquarters. According to a recent survey among 1,554 companies, representing 60% of German investment in R&D departments, 15% offshored R&D sectors, and another 17% are planning this step within the next three years (Association of German Chambers of Commerce and Industry, *Deutscher Industrie und Handelskammertag*—DIHK, 2005). Companies invest foremost in European locations: about 50% of the companies invest in EU countries, and another 30% in Central and Eastern European countries; the remaining 20% invest overseas.

How easy is it to send jobs away from Germany? The legal situation for work contracts and trade unions' influence on tariffs is different than the prevalent situation in the United States. After a probationary period of several months, employees in Germany are protected against being laid off. This applies to both corporate industry and small businesses with more than five employees. Companies who want to outsource sectors to other countries must compensate local employees with adequate funding.

Within the supranational EU structure, borders between countries that have been members of the common European market and those that were part of former communist Eastern Europe have become transparent. Hence, it is expected that the competitive economic gradient will enhance the trend of outsourcing production of industrial goods toward the East; for example, from Germany and Austria to Poland, Czechia, and Hungary. Another problem is legal and illegal migrant workers undercutting German workers' wages. We observe a trend of wage dumping in Germany's labor market in blue-color job sectors (farming, building industry, meat packing) and also in service sectors such as nursing. Five million jobless citizens is an alarming number for a country with a population of 80 million; it is a clear indication that the era of full employment in Germany is in the past. Another factor to be considered in the context of the economic situation is the demographic change in EU countries, which is expected to show effects in 2020. Low birth rates and increased life expectancy will challenge workforce and social-pension systems.

STATUS OF TECHNICAL COMMUNICATION IN GERMAN-SPEAKING CONTEXTS

The major German professional TC organization, *tekom*, shows a constant increase in membership; for example, a 20% increase from 2003 to 2005, according to Michael Fritz, managing director of *tekom* (personal communication, January 3, 2005). Fritz ascribes this trend to a general economic pickup in the European service sector supporting industrial production. On the other hand, the Society for Technical Communication (STC), the worldwide leading U.S.-based professional TC organization, observed a decline in membership of 20% from 2001 to 2004 (Hayhoe, 2004). The numbers of technical communicators in German-speaking countries are shown in Table 1.

Table 1. Technical Communicators in German-Speaking Countries

	Population[a]		Technical communicators	Professional membership	
	Total [mio]	Ethnic German		National organizations	STC-TAC[b]
Austria (A)	8.2	88.5%	Total: 4–5,000[c]	*Tekom* (local group): 143[c] members	27
Germany (D)	82.5	91.5%	Total: 141,741 Professional training: 8,611 Continuous education: 15,858 Lateral hire: 117,272 (80%)	*Tekom* (founded 1978): 17 local groups: 5,100 members	66
Switzerland (CH)	7.4	65.0%	Total: 2–3,000[d]	*TECOM* (founded 1987): 320[d] members	18

[a]Data from *The World Factbook 2005* (U.S.A. CIA, 2005).
[b]Data from Vilma Zimboli, president of STC Transalpine Chapter (personal communication, March 13, 2005).
[c]Data from Maria Lanthaler, member of the Austrian chapter of *tekom* (personal communication, June 26, 2005).
[d]Data in Vernhein-Harren, 2005.

We will now shed some light on the national specifics of jobs and education in Austria, Germany, and Switzerland before turning to challenges and opportunities, and finally to issues of handling language such as terminology and translation.

Job Description and Occupational Education

In this section we will use the official German occupational titles *Technischer Redakteur/Redaktor* where the word *Redakteur* connotes editorial journalist (for the definition see section "Lexical Fields of Outsourcing and Technical Communication in English and German"). Next to the country's name we give the country's international code.

Austria (A), structured into nine provinces (*Bundesländer*), has been a member of the EU since 1995. German is the official language in Austria, while Hungarian, Slovenic, and Croatian constitute local minorities. Although the given number of 143 members in the Austrian *tekom* local group (see Table 1) represents foremost *Technische Redakteure,* it must be noted that an increasing number of translators is working in the field of technical communication (Maria Lanthaler, via e-mail June 26, 2005).

Two-semester certificates for vocational training in technical communication are offered by institutions of business development (*Wirtschaftsförderungs-institute*) in four provinces. Because the costs for these programs are considerably high, so far they are not widely accepted by students. The Donau-University at Krems specializing in continuing education offers a four-semester Master of Science program in cooperation with a German company in Dortmund (www.tecteam.de/d/bi/master_of_science.htm); here as well tuition fees are charged. This means that in Austria tuition-free academic TC education is not available.

Germany (D) is the largest of the German-speaking countries. The Federal Republic of Germany is a founding member of the EU. Expanding the task of writing to translation-supportive writing justifies the occupational title for a technical communicator in Germany: *Technischer Redakteur*. Furthermore, technical translators are in great demand for TC jobs. Although translators are not trained in information technology they are sought after due to their command of multiple languages and their competence in handling various technical documentation genres. The dividing line between writing and translating technical texts is blurred (Göpferich, 2002); the translator who writes ensures that the time to market for a product is minimal. Writing and translating had been strictly sequential tasks until the mid-1980s; today multithreaded writing is prevalent (Lanthaler & Hoppe, 2000).

Academic-certificate and degree programs (bachelor and master level), with nominal tuition fees (approximately 100 Euro per semester), are offered by an increasing number of Universities of Applied Sciences (*Fachhochschulen*; the first program was instated at FH Hannover in 1991; for an actual list see *tekom*) and one Technical University (*Technische Universität*; RWTH Aachen). In addition, the national professional society, *tekom*, offers a vocational certificate program for professionals (for details see the "Status of Technical Communication Programs in Germany" section). Although the meaning of the vocational title *Technischer Redakteur* implies journalism, by and large the curricula do not include newspaper and magazine management.

Switzerland (CH) has four official languages—French, German, Italian, and Rhaeto-Romanic. Although Switzerland is not a member of the EU, it has adapted to major EU-legislative frameworks because it is an export-oriented country. Annette Verhein-Jarren, president of *TECOM Schweiz* and professor of German and Communication at the University of Applied Sciences in Rapperswil, reviewed the status of the profession in Switzerland (Verhein-Jarren, 2005). She found that the professional organization *TECOM Schweiz-Suisse-Svizzera*, founded in 1987, had grown to 320 members in 2005, representing roughly one-tenth of the 2,500 people working in the field of technical communication, who are mostly technicians. In contrast to the situation in Austria and Germany, linguists rarely switch to working in the TC field. On the other hand, Verhein-Jarren indicates the importance of translation with her statement that computer-aided translation (CAT) will become a standard for this important branch. Process-data management (PDM) will close the gap between departments for research and development (R&D) and publishing. *TECOM Schweiz* members working in small companies are generalists with broad knowledge, whereas professionals working in international corporations are specialists with expertise in handling sophisticated software such as content management systems (CMS).

With respect to higher education, the three-year degree program *Technikkommunikation und Informationsmanagement* is presently under examination for accreditation at the University of Applied Sciences Zurich–Winterthur. The certificate program *Technischer Redaktor* is designed as a continuing-education program for professionals. This certificate program covers six study modules, which are partly overlapping: 1) defining, structuring, and writing subject content, 2) design of documentation, 3) legal aspects, security issues, and norms/standards, 4) instruction methodology, 5) production of documentation, and 6) organization and work processes (for details see www.tecom.ch/technikredaktor/).

Within the EU the status of certified national occupational standards for the TC profession is as follows: Great Britain was the first, establishing a "National Vocational Qualification Standard." The TC organizations in German-speaking countries, *tekom* in Germany and *TECOM* in Switzerland, offer vocational certificate programs. The umbrella organization representing TC professionals in eight EU countries is TCeurope in Brussels. To project the job situation for TC professionals in German-speaking countries, one has to factor in how the enlargement of the EU in May 2004 will affect production and service sectors.

Challenges and Opportunities for Technical Communicators

If outsourcing means subcontracting, and offshoring is understood as "outsourcing to other countries," then the trends in Germany are clear (see Table 2). Traditionally, companies have outsourced (subcontracted) translation jobs to service providers; offshoring is equally common for this TC-related activity. A study of key figures in the service sector confirmed this trend. Jörg Hennig and Marita Tjarks-Sobhani (2005) found that the translation of documents constitutes the bulk of subcontracted (outsourced) work, followed by image processing. Strategic tasks, such as the generation of concepts or conversion of data, are rarely outsourced.

Another important factor about outsourcing is EU product-liability legislation. Missing or defunct documentation is considered a product-related defect. Hence, technical communicators will always strive to comply with the relevant norms and standards. Whether companies invest additionally in serving the needs of the customer is a choice of compliance with the law and short-term benefit, rather than public relations and long-term benefit. The decisions that companies make about outsourcing jobs are guided by one principle: optimizing profit. This implies that those procedures that show high labor costs are outsourced, whereas complex and customized procedures such as project management or budgeting will stay in-house/on premises.

In this context, it is important to take a brief look at TC-related activities in the United States. Once geographic location became a major decision factor for contractors, TC professionals in the United States began to discuss whether offshoring affects all TC-related tasks equally (see, for example, Griffiths, 2001; Herr, 2004; Rosenberg, 2004). Rosenberg suggests that technical communicators should resist the urge to telecommute: "If you can do your job remotely, so can an employee in another country." One can't help but wonder if the tasks of a telecommuter are positively correlated to offshoring. In Germany the trend toward telecommuting is evident for part-time employed *Technische Redakteure*

Table 2. Outsourcing Trends in German Industry in Context with TC-Related Tasks and Activities (see for example Hennig, 2003)

	Subcontracting	Offshoring
Industrial production	+ for decades	+ for decades
Technical translation	+ for decades	+ for decades
Commodity writing	+ decades	+ slowly increasing
Text production	+ still growing due to the present economic situation in Germany	+ N.A. [there are no low-wage, German-speaking countries]

and translators (often women with small children). On the other hand, professionals who perform demanding superior tasks such as developing documentation in close cooperation with an R&D department, project management, translation management, marketing, or professional training typically would not be working at home.

The production of documentation is a demanding task that requires broad professional knowledge on issues such as the product, technical procedure, psychology and didactics, and, foremost, on language. These needs can be met only by in-house writers. As mentioned earlier, the production of documents is not restricted to writing a text with clarity, efficient organization, and appealing design, but involves handling of sophisticated software such as content management systems (CMS) for maintenance and update of modular texts and single-source publishing systems. Sending writers to workshops for handling these tools efficiently is expensive; therefore, most companies would invest in such training for in-house writers only and not for subcontractors.

The enlargement of the EU offers service providers better business opportunities. For example, the administrative sector can be considered a developing domain. An arena of interest is multilingual documentation for the management of the atmosphere or water bodies that extend across national boundaries. For instance, according to the Water Framework Directive (enacted 2000), all EU countries are challenged to establish local river basin management instruments by 2010. Among other things this requires the creation of instruments that will ensure transparent communication for public participation in decision making. According to Michael Fritz, it is assumed that the translation sector will benefit from the EU enlargement because multilingual documentation is mandatory for all major texts (personal communication, January 3, 2005).

Handling Subject-Specific Language (Terminology)

Documentation of terminology is well established in German-speaking countries because terminology science originated in Vienna. The most influential author was Eugen Wüster (1898–1977). In his seminal work *Internationale Sprachnormung in der Technik, besonders in der Elektrotechnik* (1931) Wüster postulates a system of interrelated terms as a base principle for the categorization of disciplinary terminology. The field of terminology science is expected to gain further momentum with the emergence of the Semantic Web, a project whose goal is to create a universal medium of information exchange by encoding meaning (semantics) contained in Web documents in standardized markup languages.

Effective management of product-specific terminology offers several benefits. Well-defined meaning of individual terms and thorough description of interrelationship among terms will ensure the following:

- lexical consistency;
- readability and translatability of documents, the latter with respect to computer-aided translation (CAT); and
- effective communication flow within a company where people in R&D, management, marketing, and publishing (technical documentation) need to understand each other.

A company that offers consistent, controlled terminology will be ahead of its competitors. For example, a new term assigned to a technology developed by *company A* becomes the common name for such technology. Thus for their request at a dealership of *company B*, customers will use the term created by *company A*. The competitive advantage will be similar to that which is derived from establishing standards for technical specifications. The main institution for standardization of terminology is the Deutsches Institut für Normung (DIN; http://www2.din.de), which is representative for German interests in supranational standardization.

An important tool supporting translation among official EU languages is the Eurodicautom, a multilingual terminology database maintained by the Commission of the European Union (http://europa.eu.int/eurodicautom/Controller). The currently listed 12 languages do not yet consider the 10 new assession countries; on the other hand, Latin is included for scientific and technical terms such as animal and plant species names.

Handling Language in a Multilingual Environment (Translation)

Most companies in Germany continue to produce their documentation texts in German and have them translated into several target languages as a second step, despite the fact that English is a simpler source language for subsequent localization translations. The demand for German-language texts is explained by the demand for quality in documentation. As an example, in traditional industrial branches such as mechanical engineering, companies continue to produce their documentation in German only. However, in the software industry, an increasing number of companies produce their documentation in English because their customers, used to reading English on the Web, accept English documentation. In short, the average German customer would not accept English documentation.

As long as German customers expect to read German documentation, German will remain the source language for translation. It would not be reasonable to produce in a first step a cheap, low-wage English documentation for German products in India or China and then translate this text in a second step into user-centered German in Germany. If a German company sends industrial production to Poland, then respective German documentation is written in

Germany and localized into target languages relevant for global marketing of these products.

International companies will produce documentation in two versions: one in German for the local German market, the other according to the Simplified Technical English specification of the Aerospace and Defense Industries Association of Europe (ASD) (www.simplifiedenglish-aecma.org/Simplified_English.htm), which is the most widespread controlled language as a translation source. Originally, Simplified English was developed to enhance interpersonal communication among professionals in large companies and research groups. Preedited texts in Simplified English would have to be modified for distribution in the U.S. or British markets. Simplified English as an auxiliary source language will prove beneficial when a document has to be translated into several target languages.

Two scenarios are prevalent: First, if the product's documentation has to be translated into a few target languages, then the source texts will be produced in German. Second, if a German global company needs their product's documentation translated into several languages, then dual documentation in German and simplified English as source languages is justified. In either scenario the translation service from German or English as source languages may be subcontracted.

State-of-the-art information and communication technologies (ICT) such as content management systems (CMS) ensure consistency for updates and facilitate the standardization of multiple-purpose texts. Hence, they add value to departments that engage in translation. A current trend needs some attention: the production of easily translatable texts (*Übersetzungsgerechtes Schreiben*). The continuum for controlling devices guiding the production of texts spans from using a simple style guide, which guarantees consistency in syntax, terminology, lexis, and semantics of the texts, to applying strict rules ("controlled language"). Texts in controlled languages (controlled texts) are easier to understand and can be translated more easily by using terminology databases and a translation memory system (Göpferich, 2002). Although machine translation was first considered a feasible technology for all stages of translation, at present it is used primarily for draft translations. So far only Translation Memory Systems allow efficient translation (see, for example, Ray & Ray, 1999).

Machine translation is applied successfully for highly structured texts that are characterized by limited vocabulary such as weather forecasts in Canada from English to French (Chandioux, 1976). The same restrictions of simple phrase structure and vocabulary apply for multipurpose text modules generated by single-source coding technology. Content management systems are used to compose complex documentation from texts that are structured hierarchically with SGML or XML code. Such structurally coded text modules contribute to consistency and increase both the effectiveness of text production and the rate of successful hits of translation through Translation Memory Systems. Consequently time and monetary resources used for translations will decrease.

The discussion on handling language would be incomplete without mentioning the reform of German orthography (*Rechtschreibreform*; enacted August 1998, amended August 2005) a unique challenge to text production in German-speaking countries (for details see Goethe-Institut, 2005).

STATUS OF TECHNICAL COMMUNICATION EDUCATION PROGRAMS

Is the ongoing change in TC's professional profile reflected in programs of higher education? Technical communicators in the United States are in the midst of global transformations and adapt their careers to this situation (see, for example, Ames, 2003; Hart-Davidson, 2001; Johnson-Eilola, 1996). This change reflects the overall transition in industrialized countries from industry-based to knowledge-based societies. Kelli Cargile Cook defined the following six layered teaching objectives for a pedagogy that prepares students effectively for the U.S. workplace: basic literacy, rhetorical literacy, social literacy, technological literacy, ethical literacy, and critical literacy (Cook, 2002). Recently, TCeurope published a guideline on professional education and training of technical communicators in Europe based on experiences in nine countries (TCeurope, 2005). Instead of six literacies, the authors define four areas of knowledge and capabilities: knowledge of product, service, or subject matter (applications and technical features of the product); knowledge of information types in the product life cycle; knowledge of the process chain in the creation of information; and knowledge of tools. Gerald Alred (2001) found in his overview of European study programs an emphasis on language proficiency and expertise in handling ICT software. In his overview of TC curricula in Germany, Herb Smith (2003) found the following three teaching goals emphasized: translation management and multilingual documentation, project management, and information technology.

The current reform in higher education in EU countries, known as the Bologna Process, strives for a system of academic grades that are easy to compare and, hence, implies a discontinuation of the traditional diploma degree in Germany. While the adaptation to the new degree system is still ongoing, a system of accumulation and transfer of credits has been instated (European credit transfer system, ECTS). The new degree system is based on a bachelor program (three years), geared to employment markets, and a subsequent master program (two years); the master degree programs usually include a one-semester thesis. This reform offers an opportunity for the adaptation of curricula to the global-market situation, because in general even minor modifications of curricula in Germany are long-term processes that require multiple administrative steps. The Bologna Process is part of the EU's Lisbon Strategy (for details see the "Socio-Economic Situation" section). At the same time, engineering departments are adapting their curricula to the communication-relevant accreditation criteria issued by the

U.S. American Accreditation Board of Engineering and Technology (Accreditation Board of Engineering and Technology (ABET), 2004), foremost to criterion 3g: "Engineering programs must demonstrate that their graduates have an ability to communicate effectively."

In this context, a comparative analysis of various TC certificate and degree programs seems helpful. We compared four programs that have been (re)designed within the past three years (for details see Table 3). It should be noted that the certificate programs of *tekom* and *TECOM* are modular, meaning that participants, mostly professionals, will customize their certificate plan according to previous expertise. Our overview revealed that subjects offered in TC study programs in German-speaking countries can be grouped according to four task-oriented study objectives:

- Text production for national and international audiences: theory and practice of basic competencies, document design, and communication within the respective legal framework.
- ICT proficiency (advanced programming): application of state-of-the-art software for structuring, administering, and reusing professional texts. For employment, proficiency in ICT is valuable. At present companies ask primarily for graduates with expertise in CMS.
- Technical and scientific subject-matter expertise: *Technische Redaktion* requires an understanding of publication as an interdisciplinary enterprise.
- Business practice: *Technische Redaktion* requires an understanding of communication occurring within and among nested sociotechnical for-profit organizations and communities.

The tabular overview reveals that in the curricula of TC programs in German-speaking countries, rhetoric is restricted to oral delivery of documentation. In contrast to TC programs in the United States, rhetoric is not explicitly considered as a disciplinary frame for *Technische Redaktion*. The uniqueness of German history in the first half of the twentieth century influences decisions of Germany's higher education officials to reinstate rhetoric as an academic discipline. It exists mostly as a subdiscipline in philosophy departments. At present there is one chair with the denomination of rhetoric at the University of Tübingen. Furthermore, the equivalent of composition studies as offered by English departments in the United States does not exist in departments of German studies. Communication studies belong to social-science departments. For example, Niklas Luhmann, the renowned communication scholar, had a chair in social sciences at the University of Bielefeld. In context with our inquiry, the Master of Science program *Technische Redaktion* at the University of Applied Sciences in Karlsruhe is presently affiliated with the social-sciences department.

Table 3. Task-Oriented Study Objectives as Reflected in Curricula of Degree and Certificate Programs in German-Speaking Countries

Study objectives (subjects)	A	D1	D2	CH
Text Production for National and International Audiences				
Basic competencies				
– research methods (audience analysis, data inquiry, interviews)	+	+	+	+
– argumentation, copy-/substantive editing (*Professionelles Deutsch*)	+	+	+	+
– terminology management and standardization of texts	+	+	+	+
– production of easily translatable texts	+	(+)	+	–
– translation management (internationalization and localization)	+	(+)	+	+
– (inter-)national security standards, technical norms, liability	+	+	+	+
Document design				
– state-of-the-art desktop publishing (typography, layout)	+	(+)	+	+
– visual design; image processing	+	(+)	+	+
– multimedia application	+	(+)	+	+
Communication				
– cognitive and psychological aspects (face-to-face and online)	+	–	+	+
– oral presentation; dialogue techniques (Rhetorik)	+	(+)	+	+
– (technical) training, teaching	–	–	+	+
– intercultural communication	+	+	+	+
– foreign-language proficiency (ESP, EST)	–	–	+	–
ICT Proficiency (Advanced Programming)				
– computer sciences (hardware, software)	+	(+)	+	–
– database management (SQL), content-management systems	+	(+)	+	+
– structuring texts (SGML, XML), single-source publishing	+	(+)	+	+
– Internet technology, online publishing, help systems	+	(+)	+	+
Technical and Scientific Subject-Matter Expertise				
– internal product-specific documentation	+	+	+	+
– usability testing of products (surveys, focus groups, usability lab)	+	(+)	+	–
– technical expertise (electrical or mechanical engineering)	–	–	+	–
Business Practice				
Publication process				
problem solving and decision making in complex networked teams				
– project management (scheduling, meetings; who does what when)	+	+	+	+
– quality management (usability testing of technical documentation)	+	(+)	+	+
– printing and distribution	–	(+)	+	+
Technische Redaktion *(TR)* as professional enterprise				
– marketing of TR products and services, business communication	+	(+)	+	+
– internship	–	–	+	–
– job profile (TR as service and market instrument)	+	+	+	+

Legend for columns. Austria (A): Donau University Krems/tecteam, 2y Master of Science. Germany (D): D1 *tekom*, certificate, and D2 University of Applied Sciences Karlsruhe, 3y B.A.+ 2y Master of Science. Switzerland (CH): *tecom*, certificate.
Acronyms and symbols: EST English for science and technology, ESP English for specific purposes; "+": mandatory; "(+)": optional, "–" not offered

CONCLUSIONS AND OUTLOOK

What does our study reveal with respect to outsourcing as subcontracting and offshoring from German-speaking countries? The offshoring trend that affects technical communicators in the United States is not yet noticeable in German-speaking countries. Nevertheless, it is expected to affect *Technische Redakteure* sooner or later, because R&D departments in international EU-based corporations are beginning to move overseas. Technical communication jobs offering commodity products and services (labor-intensive routine work) are increasingly outsourced; therefore superior tasks will secure jobs and advance the TC profession. In the United States a turn toward strategic tasks that are not susceptible to outsourcing has gained momentum.

Our overview on current curricula in German-speaking countries shows that study programs prepare *Technische Redakteure* for the present globalization trend. A distinct advantage in competitive markets will be preparedness for the production of texts for international audiences. Multilingual documentation production and international communication are pivotal study subjects. Equally useful will be a distinctive knowledge in terminology management, which is considered a basic competency. Proficiency in handling state-of-the-art ICT, such as database management and single sourcing, adds to professional expertise. All programs emphasize instruction in "business practice" such as project management, marketing of products and services, and business communication. Some programs offer courses in subject-matter expertise. Certainly subject-matter experts will value *Technische Redakteure* with a basic understanding of technical and scientific facts and concepts as competent partners in R&D projects. Noticeable gaps are public relations, service learning, and, in context with globalization, management of virtual-team projects.

Mutual acknowledgment of credits for courses among institutions of higher education in the United States, EU countries, and German-speaking countries would enrich students' studies on both continents. Online courses seem especially suitable for supplementary subjects. Furthermore, group activities in a virtual classroom offer a prime opportunity for intercultural experience. The credit-transfer system developed in the Bologna Process will be supportive of such initiatives.

ACKNOWLEDGMENTS

The authors thank Michael Fritz, Maria Lanthaler, and Annette Vernhein-Jarren for valuable discussion on the situation of the technical communication profession in Austria, Germany, and Switzerland.

REFERENCES

Accreditation Board of Engineering and Technology (ABET). (2004). *Guidelines for Criterion 3 of the Engineering Accreditation criteria* [White paper]. Retrieved February 25, 2006 from www.abet.org/Linked Documents-UPDATE/Program Docs/EAC Guidelines for Criterion3.pdf

Alred, G. (2001). A review of technical communication programs outside the United States. *Journal of Business and Technical Communication, 15*(1), 111-115.

Ames, A. (2003, May). *Transforming your career: Moving from commodity to strategic contributor*. Featured lecture at the Annual Conference Society Technical Communication, Dallas.

Chandioux, J. (1976). MÉTÉO: Un système opérationnel pour la traduction automatique des bulletins météreologiques destinés au grand public. *META, 21*(2) 127-133. Retrieved February 25, 2006 from www.erudit.org/revue/meta/1976/v21/n2/.

Commission of the European Communities (EU). (2005). *Working together for growth and jobs—A new start for the Lisbon Strategy*. Retrieved February 25, 2006 from http://europa.eu.int/growthandjobs/pdf/COM2005_024_en.pdf

Commission of the European Communities (EU). *The Bologna Process* (education policy) [Last update: October 5, 2005]. Retrieved February 25, 2006 from http://europa.eu.int/comm/education/policies/educ/bologna/bologna_en.html

Cook, K. C. (2002). Layered literacies: A theoretical frame for technical communication pedagogy. *Technical Communication Quarterly, 11*(1), 5-29.

Cox, K. (2003, November). Offshore outsourcing: What it is and why it's important to understand it. *The Willamette Galley, 6*(6). Retrieved February 25, 2006 from www.stcwvc.org/galley/0311/C02_OffshoreOutsourcing.html.

Davis, E. B., & Orchard, D. M. (1996). Outsourcing and virtual corporations: Implications for technical communication professionals and their employers. *Annual Conference Society Technical Communication, 43*, 82-85.

Deutscher Industrie- und Handelskammertag (DIHK). (2005, March 15). Deutsche Auslandsinvestitionen erreichen Rekordhoch [Press release by Georg Ludwig Braun, president of DIHK]. Retrieved February 25, 2005 from www.dihk.de/inhalt/informationen/news/meldungen/meldung007066.main.html.

Deutsche Auslandsinvestitionen erreichen Rekordhoch (2005, w/o date). Statement by Axel Nitschke to Braun's press release of March 15, 2005. Retrieved February 25, 2006 from www.dihk.de/inhalt/download/FuE_Statement_Nitschke.pdf.

Fritz, M. (2004). *Bedrohen Produktionsverlagerungen ins Ausland die Arbeitsplätze Technischer Redakteure?* tekom paper #948 [Is outsourcing to foreign countries a threat to the jobs of technical writers?]. Stuttgart, Germany: tekom Gesellschaft für Technische Kommunikation.

Göpferich, S. (2000). *Der technische Redakteur als Global Player: Dokumentation erstellen—übersetzen—managen*. Retrieved February 25, 2006 from www.doku.net/artikel/dertechnis.htm.

Göpferich, S. (2002). *Textproduktion im Zeitalter der Globalisierung—Entwicklung einer Didaktik des Wissenstransfers*. Tübingen, Germany: Stauffenberg.

Goethe-Institut. (2005, July). *Statement by Goethe-Institut on the introduction of the spelling reform*. Retrieved February 25, 2006 from www.goethe.de/kue/lit/dos/dds/en257045.htm.

Griffith, D. (2001). The theory and practice of outsourcing. *Annual Conference Society Technical Communication, 48,* 306-310.

Hart-Davidson, W. (2001). On writing, technical communication, and information technology: The core competencies of technical communication. *Technical Communication, 48*(2), 145-155.

Hayhoe, G. (2004). What's in store for 2004 And beyond? [Editorial]. *Technical Communication, 51*(1), 9-10.

Hennig, J. (2003). Tekom determines key figures in the sector. *Technische Kommunikation, 25*(2), 29 pp.

Hennig, J., & Tjarks-Sobhani, M. (2005). Technische Dokumentation in Deutschland. In J. Hennig & M. Tjarks-Sobhani (Eds.), *Technische Kommunikation International—Stand und Perspektiven* (pp. 11–25). Lübeck, Germany: Schmidt Römhild.

Herr, J. M. (2004, January). Trends in management: Observations of a SIG manager. *Intercom,* 14-15, 42.

Johnson-Eilola, J. (1996). Relocating the value of work: Technical communication in a post-industrial age. *Technical Communication Quarterly, 5*(3), 245-270.

Lanthaler, M., & Hoppe, B. M. (2000, November). *Multilinguale Dokumentation—Mehr als Übersetzung. Integration der Übersetzung in den Dokumentationsprozess.* Paper presented at the Annual Conference of tekom (Wiesbaden Germany, November 2000). Retrieved February 25, 2006 from www.itl.de/media/pdf/itl_multilinguale_doku.pdf.

Localisation Industry Standards Association (LISA). (2005). *Frequently asked questions about LISA and the localization industry.* Retrieved March 10, 2006 from http://www.lisa.org/info/faqs.html.

Ray, D., & Ray, E. J. (1999). Good, fast, cheap: Translation memory systems offer the potential for all three. *Technical Communication, 46*(2), 280-285. Retrieved February 25, 2006 from www.techwr-l.com/techwhirl/magazine/technical/translationmemory.html.

Rosenberg, N. (2004, July/August). Off shoring: What does it mean for us? *Intercom,* 22-23.

Smith, H. J. (2003). German academic programs in technical communication. *Journal of Technical Writing and Communication, 33*(4), 349-363.

Sturz, W. (1998, January). *Lokalisierung—Modewort oder aktuelle Herausforderung?* Retrieved February 25, 2006 from www.doculine.com/news/1998/01_98/Lokalisierung.htm.

TCeurope. (2005, April). Professional education and training of technical communicators in Europe—Guidelines (TecDoc-Net, version 1.0). Retrieved February 25, 2006 from www.tceurope.org/pdf/tecdoc.pdf

United States of America Central Intelligence Agency (CIA). (2005). *The World Factbook 2005.* Retrieved June 25, 2005 from www.cia.gov/cia/publications/factbook/.

Verhein-Jarren, A. (2005). Technische Dokumentation in der Schweiz. In J. Hennig & M. Tjarks-Sobhani (Eds.), *Technische Kommunikation International—Stand und Perspektiven* (pp. 26-36). Lübeck, Germany: Schmidt Römhild.

CHAPTER 5

Approaching Outsourcing in Rhetoric and Professional Communication: Lessons from U.S.-Owned Maquilas in Mexico

Barry Thatcher and Victoriano Garza-Almanza

COMPLEXITY OF OUTSOURCING'S RHETORICAL SITUATION

Although the two authors live in different countries with correspondingly distinct rhetorical and cultural systems, they also live just 40 miles from each other in perhaps one of the largest outsourcing economies in the world. The El Paso/ Ciudad Juárez area has a population of 2.3 million people and has over 1,000 maquilas or joint U.S.-Mexican manufacturing plants. In these plants, parts and materials are shipped into Juárez for assembly by Mexican personnel, and then the finished product is shipped back into the United States or exported elsewhere. Many of the shipping warehouses are located in the El Paso region. Thus, the cross-border, mutual influence is significant, with many U.S. maquila personnel living in El Paso and commuting to Juárez daily, and many Mexican personnel working side-by-side with U.S.-Americans and commuting to El Paso for shopping and recreation. Like many people in this border area, Thatcher and Garza-Almanza are in constant contact with each other. They can work together in the morning on a project in Juárez or Las Cruces, New Mexico and then cross the legal, geopolitical border and return in the afternoon to their own country.

Although this border region shares many values and is in constant contact, we are still amazed at the differences between the two populations and how these differences create complex rhetorical situations for technical communicators working in the outsourced manufacturing plants. Mexico and the United States have distinct legal and political systems, historical foundations, economic struc tures, social classes, and educational approaches, all of which profoundly reflect and reinforce distinct rhetorical traditions. How do these two major rhetorical traditions—combined with the influence of the border area and maquila manufacturing industry—work together in this outsourcing environment? What kinds of adaptations are needed for U.S.-sourced training materials and technical communications to be effective here?

This chapter explores the complex rhetorical situations of the maquilas along the U.S.-Mexico border. First, it compares the predominant rhetorical traditions in the United States and Mexico, contextualizing these traditions in the maquila situation. Next, it relates the complex outsourcing relationship of the maquilas between the United States and Mexico. Third, it summarizes findings from current research (Thatcher, 2006) about the technical communications patterns in Mexican maquilas. And fourth, it concludes by showing some adaptations U.S. technical communicators might consider when working in U.S.-Mexico outsourcing contexts.

HISTORY OF RHETORIC, TECHNOLOGY, AND OUTSOURCING IN MEXICO AND THE UNITED STATES

To understand the differences in rhetorical traditions, it is important to situate writing and technology in the United States and Mexico. Mexico and the United States were settled at about the same time: the fall of Tenochtitlán (central valley of Mexico) occurred in 1521, and Jamestown was founded in 1607. Although both areas attracted new colonizers, the motivations for colonialization and the ensuing social and cultural orders that evolved "could not be more different" (LaRosa & Mora, 1999, p. 1). The Spanish colonizers were motivated by economic and religious purposes, and they constructed their societies based on "Iberian institutions and priorities" (LaRosa & Mora, 1999, p. 1). The most important cultural and social mechanism of this institution was the *encomienda*, or labor grant. A Spanish soldier or colonist was granted a certain tract of land or village together with its native inhabitants. The Spaniards routinely set up a strict hierarchy over the land and its inhabitants, effectively creating an intricate caste system. An important part of this intricate caste system was intermarrying between races and social classes, effectively creating innumerable levels of social hierarchy. The encomienda also allowed for the establishment of the Catholic Church, which tended to dominate education and social life. Many of the Spaniards amassed great fortunes and were able to return to Spain as nobleman (LaRosa & Mora, 1999).

The United States had a remarkably different historical formation and corresponding social, cultural, and political organization. Many of the original colonies were settled by Dutch and English religious dissidents. They were escaping the religious persecution in Europe and had little desire to return there. Unlike the situation in Latin America, these religious dissidents were automatically skeptical of authority, especially traditional religious authority mixed with state government. They tended to set up small, highly independent communities of "like-minded individuals" (LaRosa & Mora, 1999, p. 2). Significantly, the U.S. colonizers did not intermarry with the indigenous populations; they just exterminated them or forced them onto reservations. The U.S. colonizers had much weaker ties to their mother countries than did their Latin American counterparts; U.S. independence was much shorter and easier to carry out; and breaking with the cultural, religious, and social order of the mother countries was relatively easy and abrupt. In distinction, the Latin American journey to independence was much more ambiguous and complex, and most importantly, the independence gained by the Latin American countries did little to change the cultural, religious, and social order that existed in the preindependence society. Latin American independence has been characterized as "same mule, different rider" (LaRosa & Mora, 1999, p. 3).

These two different foundations eventually yielded strikingly contrastive cultural and rhetorical traditions. In Latin America, the result of the encomienda foundation is collective, yet highly stratified cultures. Collective means that personal identity, seeing the world, and dealing with the world are based on the person's kinship or social group. Mexico consistently ranks high in collective values according to most intercultural theories (see Hofstede, 1997; Trompenaars & Hampden-Turner, 1998). Osland, de Franco, and Osland (1999) argue that the high collectivity in this region is different from the horizontal, often harmonious, collectivity common in other parts of the world such as Japan. Latin American collectivity is often hierarchized, creating strict observance of in and out groups.

The cultural and rhetorical differences also correlate strongly with organizational management approaches. According to many theorists, management in Mexico valorizes dependency, hierarchy, and close overseeing of subordinates' activities, while management in the United States tends to emphasize more independence and equality, leaving a reasoned amount of problem solving to the subordinates (Hofstede, 1997; Kras, 1989; Trompenaars & Hampden-Turner, 1999). Closely related to this distinction is the concept of *power distance*, which measures the ability of two people with different power and authority to influence the other (Hofstede, 1997). In Hofstede's measure, Mexico has the second-highest power-distance score, which means that the subordinate has very little influence on the superior, but the superior significantly influences the subordinate. The United States generally has much lower scores, indicating more mutual influence. Thus, both manager and subordinate in Mexico prefer that the superior closely oversee the work of the subordinate, while the U.S. style is more consultative. The communication patterns associated with high power-distance cultures are usually one-way, exact, and to be followed literally. In Mexico, these patterns reflect authoritative relationships that are often setup in the home, church, and school and then are carried to the workplace (Kras, 1989). Communication in lower power-distance cultures is often more consultative, involving more feedback, creativity, and flexibility in interpretation and application.

These cultural differences are also compounded by two different legal systems, both of which encourage distinct rhetorical strategies. Civil law is the basic legal system in all the countries in Latin America, although some are developing some tenets of common law (Alcalde, 1991). Civil law in Latin America is based on a long tradition that dates back at least to the Roman Empire when Justinian developed a remarkable set of codes (Rosenn, 1991). The United States developed its legal tradition from the common law of England, which begun as unwritten assumptions about appropriate conventions and behaviors.

In the civil-law tradition, the legislature is responsible for creating deductive legal frameworks or comprehensive codes that are to be applied by judges to each case at hand, independent of previous cases. The system is also designed to be judge-proof. "Latin America inherited from Spain a lack of confidence in the judiciary. It is for that reason that its hands are tied . . . by the rigid formalism of the Codes of Procedure" (Eder, 1950, p. 145). Thus, judges in Latin America have historically been subordinated to the legislature in creating laws (Rosenn, 1991). On the other hand, the common-law tradition is an inductive system based on case- or common-law precedence. Legal interpretations were based on previous cases of similar situations or what was commonly accepted as proper or legal conduct. Judges tend to have significant creative power in linking the case at hand with previous precedents, thereby continually extending and refining the law, case by case.

These different legal approaches imply different expectations about certainty and ambiguity, especially as they relate to written communications. One principal purpose of the civil law is to obtain certainty in judicial decisions. Merryman (1969) explains that "there is a great emphasis in the literature of the civil law tradition on the importance of certainty in the law. . . it has come to be a kind of supreme value, an unquestioned dogma, a fundamental goal" (p. 50). In this search for certainty then, the codes or legal frameworks developed for judges have become exceedingly complex and ostensibly comprehensive, trying to cover as many contingencies as possible. As a result, most Latin American countries actually have many more laws than the United States (comparatively) (Alcalde, 1991; Rosenn, 1991). They are also unwieldy and difficult to adapt to new situations. The U.S. legal tradition is best characterized as a loose framework of principles and guidelines (Alcalde, 1991). Ambiguity can be good because it can invite effective interpretation and application of laws. The U.S. legal system, however, has become just as unwieldy because it has fostered a very litigious culture (Alcalde, 1991). This difference is because the Latin American approach is not based on precedence, which assumes a continuous building of law based on one decision; rather, the continuation of law is based on developing codes to meeting changing circumstances in society.

The final crucial difference in the legal traditions is the paradoxical uses of writing and orality. Because of the fear of corruption and interpersonal relationships, historically, orality or oral testimony is not used in Mexican legal proceedings (Eder, 1950), although this trend is now changing. Rather, most evidence gathering and presentation is paper or document based, which the judge or panel of judges must evaluate. Juries of peers are also much less common or nonexistent in most Latin American legal systems. Conversely, oral testimony is central to evidence gathering and presentation in the U.S. legal tradition. And a major purpose of this oral strategy is to convince a jury of peers of the desired judicial outcome. This is a contradictory use of orality and writing because the predominant cultural values in the United States correlate much more strongly with writing, while the predominant values in Latin America correlate much more strongly with orality (see Thatcher, 1999).

RELATIONSHIPS OF RHETORICAL TRADITIONS TO TECHNOLOGIES AND WRITING

These two different cultural and legal systems exemplify and reinforce different rhetorical traditions, which significantly influence technical communications in outsourcing contexts. First, when colonizing Mexico, the Spaniards conveniently drew upon the rhetorical traditions of the native populations (Maya, Aztec, Mixtec, and Zapotec) for their colonizing purposes (see Marcus, 1992). Marcus (1992) explains that all four indigenous populations used writing as a colonizing tool: as a way to rewrite history for the benefit of their group; for developing propaganda to pursue their own interests; for instilling myths appropriate to their positions of power; and as a class marker. Thus, when the Spaniards arrived in Mexico, it was easy to use writing and written discourse the same way, and many researchers have argued that they did (see León-Portilla, 1996). For example, Kellog (1995) explains that the Spanish used the legal system and legal documents "as a powerful tool of acculturation, profoundly altering Mexico and Nahua conceptions of family, property, and gender." And it played "a critical role in establishing and maintaining Spanish cultural hegemony" (p. xxix). As a result, writing became associated with all the elements of colonialization, serving what Kellog (1995) calls notary-like functions.

This rhetorical tradition of writing as a colonizing and notary-like mechanism contrasts remarkably with U.S. traditions such as the signing of the U.S. Declaration of Independence. According to many comparative legal scholars (Alcalde, 1991; Rosenn, 1991), the signers of the Declaration and the U.S. Constitution were able to rely on a cultural and rhetorical context that enabled such a use of written communication. This is why these documents have worked so well in the United States, but comparable documents have had significantly less influence on Latin American countries (Alcalde, 1991). In the U.S. tradition, writing reflected and reinforced traditions of individuality, universalism, equality, and common-law reasoning (Thatcher, 2000). On the other hand, the Mexican rhetorical traditions reflect and reinforce an in- and out-group orientation that is common in collective cultures, hierarchical social organizations, and particular or relational thinking patterns (Thatcher, 2000).

Consequently, outsourced technologies meet different cultural and rhetorical assumptions when they are deployed in Mexico and the United States. In Mexico there is probably a much stronger association of the new technology with colonialism and hegemonic cultural and economic structures, especially when that technology comes from a colonial power such as the United States. This association of colonialism and hegemony is probably compounded if that new technology is deployed using written documentation, another traditional tool of hegemony.

Maquilas and Outsourcing Along the U.S.-Mexico Border

These complexly different U.S. and Mexican rhetorical traditions come together in the maquila outsourcing contexts in U.S.-Mexican border areas. Maquilas are manufacturing plants that are mostly located in Mexican cities that border the United States. The maquilas are the assembly portion of the manufacturing process. Materials are imported into Mexico and assembled or manufactured using lower-wage Mexican workers. The finished products are then returned to the United States or other countries. The history of the maquila situation is important for understanding the current outsourcing context.

Origins and Development of the Maquila Outsourcing Industry in Mexico

The migratory movements between Mexico and the United States have existed since the origin of the last binational border in the nineteenth century. The motives that initiated the mobilization of Mexican groups to the north include the blood bond that existed among families that stayed on each of the sides during the demarcation of the territories, the search for peace during the country's war periods, and most of all, the need for jobs among the people in the countryside.

During the 1930s, when the Great Depression of 1929 in North America started to relent, the migratory flow to the United States increased. The owners of agricultural fields were in urgent need of labor that they could not find in their country or that was too expensive. At this time Mexican laborers would enter the United States without any difficulty and find employment wherever it was most convenient for them. Even though there were migratory regulations, there were no controls that would impose order on the entrance of legal or illegal migrants.

Also at this time Europe was living its last moments of peace, which would end with the German expansion and the beginning of a new war in September 1939. Two years later, when the United States entered the war, it initiated a warfare program that required all the civilian support available. It made good use of the industrial infrastructure and created numerous factories for the manufacture of war supplies. The Army recruited a considerable number of male citizens; therefore, thousands of women took their place in factories.

There was not enough personnel to perform the work in U.S. agricultural fields and for the construction of roads and railroads. Consequently, President Franklin D. Roosevelt, under emergency circumstances, expressed the United States' need for human resources to Mexican President Manuel Avila Camacho. In July 1942 the United States and Mexican governments signed an agreement through which Mexican agricultural laborers, who voluntarily chose to seek work in the neighbor country, could do it legally. Under these circumstances, the Bracero Program was created. This program covered the period from 1942 to 1963; and even in 1964 Mexicans were still crossing the borders until the definitive termination of the agreement. During this period, and as part of the program, approximately five million Mexicans crossed the border legally, many of who settled in the United States indefinitely.

Since the Bracero Program allowed workers to enter the United States, then go back to Mexico during different periods of time, and then return again to their work in the fields, many Braceros were living in Mexico at the time that the North American authorities closed the borders and could not go back to their work or for their belongings. But given that "bracerismo" had become a tradition among laborers for as long as 21 years, the termination of the program was hard for them to accept. As a consequence, thousands of agricultural workers traveled toward the United Stated during harvest time, with the hope that the United States would withdraw the veto, allowing them to enter once again. However, this never happened, and thousands of Mexican laborers accumulated at the Mexican frontier.

To address this situation, in 1961 Mexican President Adolfo Lopez Mateos created a plan to develop the communities settled on the north border of the country and called it Programa Nacional Fronterizo (PRONAF). The first stage of the program focused on gathering information about the economic and urban situation of each of the cities, as well as the needs of the region. The fundamental objective was to identify the climate for the capitalization of industrial growth and the exploitation of potential North American tourists; from this information, important international commerce centers would be designed. These places would serve as nodes to store, exhibit, and distribute consumer products from Mexico and Latin America.

Between 1961 and 1964 several actions were taken by the Mexican government to further this plan, such as the acquisition of territory and the construction of local headquarters. In this fashion, the formation of PRONAF and the
termination of the Bracero Program coincided in time and marked a turning
point for the plan that the Mexican Federal government had for the border region
Due to the entrenched habit that led them to the north, which had been blocked
by legal barriers, the Braceros, who quickly changed from being migrant workers
to unemployed people in their country, did not return to their places of origin;
instead, they settled in great numbers in the cities on Mexico's northern border
(Carillo, 1989; Garza-Almanza, 1999; Lowery, 1990).

The Beginnings of Maquila Industry

The plans of PRONAF had not contemplated the abrupt demographic growth
that took place in the border region; neither did it foresee the problems that this
would cause. Without having considered the impact of the Bracero program once
it was terminated, the local management in Mexican border cities found that
their facilities were insufficient. The accumulation of people in the border cities
quickly resulted in complaints directed to authorities on higher government
levels. Thus, PRONAF was chosen to become the instrument to respond to this
emergency (Carillo, 1989; Garza-Almanza, 1999; Lowery, 1990).

D. Antonio J. Bermúdez, director of the PRONAF, coordinated actions and
appointed an international private company (Arthur D. Little) to evaluate the case
and find a viable solution to the situation. The investigator in charge of the study
reported that some U.S. manufacturing companies had a keen interest on the
border. He recommended that, in order to attract them, a zone of guaranteed
manufacture should be created in the border region, in which the factories would
be settled in pairs with the purpose of keeping a parallel and comparative pursuit.
The investigator also recommended that the raw materials or semiprocessed
products needed for the manufacture could be imported free of taxes. For the rest,
the companies had the advantage of offering low wages, paying low taxes,
creating labor sources for both sides of the frontier, and the control of the
operations would be exclusively by the owners of the companies (Carillo, 1989;
Garza-Almanza, 1999; Lowery, 1990).

In 1966, two years after the conclusion of the Bracero Program, the first twelve
companies of this kind were established in Ciudad Juarez, a northern city across
the border from El Paso, Texas. In the beginning, the companies were settled in
pairs; in other words, one factory was settled in a Mexican city, and the other one
in the American city right next to it. Consequently, these companies were called
twin plants. Even though the advantages were in favor of the investors (low
wages, the opportunity to import tax-free raw material, absolute control over
their companies, etc.), the twin plants were designed in such a way that the North

American plant could monitor the Mexican plant, in order to determine if it was convenient to settle in Mexico.

In a short period of time the people of Ciudad Juarez started referring to the foreign plants as "maquiladoras" or the shorter term, "maquila." It remains unknown who introduced the use of this term, which comes from the old Castilian that defined "maquila" as the "fare paid to the miller or owner of a farm to grind grains or flower" (from the hisp. n. *makíla*, and this from the Castilian n. *makílah*, measured object) (Carillo, 1989; Lowery, 1990).

In relation to these industries, the term indicates the manufacturing labor and the services offered; likewise, the same term is used to denote the factory where the assembly of the imported parts takes place. Another of the characteristics is that the final product of the industries is not sold in the country; instead, it is exported. From there it takes its final name "industria maquiladora de exportación" (manufacture industry of exportation) or simply "maquiladora."

The system of twin plants was discontinued by many companies, the main reason being that in 1990 less than 10% of the companies still had their twin in the United States. Another of the schemes that also changed, with the arrival of German, British, Japanese, Dutch, and French companies, was the hegemony of North American corporations (Lowery, 1990).

The producers of electronic components were the first industries to enter the country. Following them, plastic, automobile parts, metal, and textile industries started to arrive. Usually, from the beginning of their operations and due to the nature of the manual labor, the industry exclusively hired women—something that seems paradoxical given that the industry emerged as a response to the unemployment among the Braceros, who were predominantly males. As the industry diversified, the laborer population became varied as well; however, this did not happen until the mid 1980s (Lowery, 1990). Today the female population is still predominant (www.CANACINTRA.org.mx).

It took some time for the manufacturing project to mature. According to official Mexican government data, four years after having started in 1970, there were already 120 companies registered on the border. In 1980 there were 620. In 1990 there were 1,920 factories, half of which were settled in Ciudad Juarez and Tijuana (Lowery, 1990).

Tratado de Libre Comercio (Free Commerce Treaty)

The negotiation and signing of the Tratado de Libre Comercio de América del Norte (NAFTA—North American Free Trade Agreement) between Mexico, the United States, and Canada gave investors in this border region a unique opportunity in history; and by the thousands they jumped into the exploration of the area to invest in. The manufacturing sector in particular grew from fewer than 2000 industries that existed in 1990 to more than 3,700 within ten years (www.canacintra.org.mx). Its impact on the development of the national economy has been of great importance; next to the national petroleum industry (PEMEX), manufacturing has reached the second place as a source of income.

In 2000, as a consequence of the optimism caused by the NAFTA (Tratado de Libre Comercio) and the euphoria generated by the democratic opening in the Mexican political system, the number of registered companies according to CANACINTRA (Mexico's National Association of Manufacturers) was of 3,793 "maquiladoras," and just over a million employees. Nevertheless, ever since the September 11 terrorist attacks in the United States in 2001, and due to questionable political and economical decisions made by Mexican authorities, hundreds of industries left the country. At the beginning of 2004 the number of manufacturers in Mexico had been reduced to fewer than 3,000, and the number of lost jobs was over 250,000. In addition, many of the maquilas left Mexico in favor of lower wages and operating costs in Asia, most notably China, the Philippines, and Korea. As a result, many of the maquila leaders are looking to develop more complex or "value-added" processes that could draw on Mexico's educated—or educatable—population. In 2006 the maquila industry rebounded, again expanding its bases, but also looking for long-term development of more value-added processes.

The next section describes issues that develop specifically in outsourced technical communications at a variety of maquilas. A more detailed version of this study is published elsewhere (Thatcher, 2006). This section highlights the most common features of this outsourcing context.

TECHNICAL COMMUNICATION ISSUES IN MEXICAN MAQUILAS

Most maquilas in the U.S.-Mexico border area are U.S. owned but managed by Mexican personnel. Except for some of the larger maquilas such as Delphi, where a great many patents have been awarded, most research and development of technology takes place in the United States and then is transferred to Mexico for manufacturing. Thus, there exists a great need for effective communication in technology transfer—of implementing U.S.-developed technologies in the Mexican context. As detailed next, a number of important cultural and rhetorical factors influence effective technology transfer and technical communication. These include management and organizational behavior; documentation, hierarchy, and information control; turnover; problem solving; training; and profiles of technical communicators.

Organizational Culture and Communicating Outsourced Technologies

One key issue when communicating with maquilas in Mexico is to understand that U.S. and Mexican management strategies will most likely assign different purposes to technical communications. This difference is due in large part to high and low power differences and work and communication strategies encouraged by civil- and common-law legal traditions. As detailed elsewhere (Kras, 1989; Thatcher, 1999, 2006), most U.S. leadership and management assume that technical communications serve more as a guide to appropriate behavior, to be modified according to the contextual restraints and creativity of the staff. However, Mexican managers often see much more authority in technical communications, giving them legal and technical authority far beyond that of the end users. Thus, in maquila outsourcing situations, U.S. personnel will often expect their Mexican colleagues to take more initiative from the content delivered by the communication; and U.S. personnel might easily characterize their Mexican colleagues as unmotivated or lacking creativity because they did not move beyond the technical communications. However, U.S. personnel are most likely unaware that it is their low-power-distance management expectations and common-law legal traditions that encourage such a view. In essence, technical communications become much like legal precedence to guide current behavior but only roughly; and it is assumed that standard operating procedures will continuously evolve from what was laid out in the technical document.

Mexican personnel, on the other hand, will likely see technical communication as a deductive blueprint that should clearly delineate most processes and policies with great authority. In this sense, the technical communication is much like the deductive codes developed by legislation that form part of Mexican civil-law tradition. Consequently, Mexican personnel often feel that the technical communications developed for them by U.S.-Americans are too general and not tailored to their individual contexts, and consequently, that U.S.-Americans are not sensitive to the Mexican situation. Therefore, it is not surprising that in many maquilas, Mexican personnel believe the technical communications are inadequate in technical detail, and thus, many maquilas develop their own manuals, written by their own engineers (Thatcher, 2006). This tendency was also apparent in Thatcher's work with Ecuadorian accountants (Thatcher, 1999) who were implementing accounting software changes. They too threw out the translated software manuals and instead learned the software on their own and on their own terms and then wrote their own set of instructions. In addition to the management and legal issues, much of the resistance to U.S.-American manuals might derive from the colonialism associated with official documentation coming from the outside into Mexico and Latin America.

Documentation, Hierarchy, and Information Control

Clearly linked to these different purposes for technical communications are the different roles of writing and orality. As described earlier, writing in Mexico has strong overtones of official authority and power. However, one problem with granting such power to writing is that a document or technical communication also needs to be comprehensive in its normative power. In other words, because a technical document is much like a legal code—rather than a legal precedent—an effective technical document has to cover all bases, not allowing for loopholes. Developing such effective documents is a difficult task, just as developing new legal codes for civil law in Latin America is mostly exhausting and usually not entirely effective (Alcalde, 1991). Consequently, most Latin American and Mexican organizations rely on "personalismo" (Kras, 1989; Osland et al., 1999) to mediate organizational behavior. Personalismo is strong interpersonal relations mediated by clear lines of authority and motivated by loyalty. Not surprisingly, in four maquilas studied in Juárez (Thatcher, 2006) and two organizations in Ecuador (Thatcher, 1999), very little written policies and procedures actually existed. Rather, the policies and procedures of the organizations were directed interpersonally and orally by leadership. As Thatcher (2000) describes elsewhere, U.S. personnel are used to written documents as a normalizing force for everyday organizational behavior, while Latin Americans are most likely used to a person in authority.

This difference resituates the roles of documentation and information control in the organizational hierarchy in outsourced maquilas. As Thatcher describes in greater detail (2006), Garza-Almanza and Thatcher actually debated this point with 15 maquila engineers in a group interview. Many of the Mexican maquila engineers did not want to communicate through the documentation of work procedures because they felt that oral training was best. However, it was brought up that relying on oral training had many drawbacks, including maintaining problems of hierarchical management systems and constant need of training because of the high turnover rate at most maquilas. Some engineers also understood that relying on oral training fostered an inability to solve problems and shirking of responsibilities. Other engineers, however, maintained that traditional lines of authority and decision making needed to be in place to effectively manage personnel. A few engineers strongly asserted their right to limit the amount of documentation so as to maintain "their control" of the manufacturing processes.

Garza-Almanza listened to the debate and then asked Thatcher specifically what he thought. Thatcher told them that the issues of high turnover and low problem-solving skills (to be discussed later) could be addressed by better-written documentation. Two engineers vehemently disagreed with him, never linking problem-solving and effective training to written documentation. From their perspective, the best training was to have the engineer on-site to oversee all functions at all times. Written documentation brought lineworker independence, which could "introduce errors into the manufacturing process." Another maquila "environmental engineer," who actually had an M.D. but served as the health and environmental specialist for a small maquila, immediately saw the link between high power-distance modes of management and problem solving at her maquila. She quickly challenged the two engineers (coincidentally male) about their high power-distance methods. Garza-Almanza then explored his general frustration that hierarchical management styles produce passivity in Mexican lineworkers, a passivity that he sees in Mexican culture in general, regarding the integration of new technologies. From his perspective, there was resistance to empowering employees to solve problems or influence policy, procedures, or workplace practices. This high-power distance relationship was not isolated to this group interview. Lines of authority in all four maquilas were very clear and rarely were subordinates in positions to influence training (Thatcher, 2006).

Turnover, Problem-Solving, and Documentation

The combination of high-power organizational cultures and high turnover was an important factor working against written technical communications for training in the maquila contexts. Because managers or superiors at Mexican maquilas tend to favor maintaining control through interpersonal power relationships, this type of training method takes much time to develop in order to function well (see Victor, 1992). However, the maquila industry is consistently plagued by a high turnover rate and poor training budgets. In good times with plenty of job opportunities, many employees job hop; that is, move from job to job looking for the best wages and situations. However, in the leaner years when employees actually stay long enough for significant training, there is not much budget for training, even though the Mexican government mandates 40 hours of training yearly for full-time maquila employees. Thus, there is a tradition and culture for training at the maquilas, and many personnel sought for as much training as they could.

Using technical communications in this training environment is complicated by Mexican organizational culture. As Victor (1992) explains, management in high power-distance cultures requires a capable person at the top orchestrating all relationships. When this person is capable and functions as expected, the organization runs well (pp. 138-158). However, there is considerable lag time when personnel change. Thus, despite the desire of many maquila engineers to tightly control the operations on an oral basis, many Mexican personnel see a need to change the organizational culture through more written documentation. This desire was sparked by what these Mexican personnel saw as a lack of initiative and problem solving at the lineworker level. Most Mexican engineers and managers link "effective" written documentation to taking initiative and problem solving, which is a connection that Thatcher observed in Ecuador as well (Thatcher, 1999). According to some Mexican engineers, oral and hierarchical management mode produces workers that did not have initiative or responsibility. Thus, they were not valued as much as those who combined initiative and responsibility that was facilitated by good written documentation (Thatcher, 2006). Further, many maquila lineworkers wanted the "independence" and "time" that written documentation afforded when learning new procedures.

One of the difficulties, however, in implementing written documentation in Mexico is the strongly correlated cultural values of personalismo, orality, writing, relatively low salaries, and the already-mentioned high power-distance modes of management. The other two variables have been discussed, but the economic variable is most illuminating. Put simply, most of maquila engineers made US$600–$1,500 a month, a salary above Mexico's minimum wage but below U.S. averages. This is an important factor because developing effective documentation is actually more expensive than simply hiring another engineer to explain the processes that documentation would have explained in a U.S. context, for example. Thus, these three variables (interpersonal orientation, dislike of writing, and greater cost of developing written documentation) strongly encourage an oral and high power-distance approach to training in new technologies. Consequently, using technical communications in Mexican maquilas as a medium of training faces significant obstacles that require, perhaps, key changes in predominant cultural values.

One force for change, however, seems to be the desire to obtain ISO certifications, which require standardized and written documentations of work processes. The ISO 9000 Management certification has forced an increasing number of maquilas to rethink their views of written documentation. This change included the use of written documentation to encourage some openness and desire for change in traditional Mexican cultural and rhetorical traditions. It seems, however, that without these kinds of "outside forces," many Mexican maquilas will continue with high power-distance and oral methods of training their personnel in new technologies.

Profiles of Technical Communicators in a Mexican Maquila

It is important for U.S. technical communicators to understand that the field of technical communication is well developed only in the United States and Western Europe. Although Mexico has a long history of research and university curriculum in communication media, advertising, and organizational communication, it has very little in technical communication (Garza-Almanza, 2004). In fact, only one university, the Monterrey Institute of Technology and Higher Studies (Instituto Tecnológico y de Estudios Superiores de Monterrey or ITESM) has technical communication as a well-developed subject and curriculum. The UNAM (Autonomous University of Mexico), the very large state university in Mexico City, has well-developed curriculum and pedagogy in composition, and some in basic business and technical writing, but little in what the United States and Western Europe have defined as technical communication.

Although technical writing (as a profession or academic field) is uncommon in Mexico, there are technical writers of training materials at most maquilas. Who, therefore, is doing the technical writing and how is it being done and what is it like? At four maquilas studied by Thatcher (2006), the engineers did most of the writing—when they had time and felt the necessity. The writing situation in one maquila is perhaps most revelatory in situating the profiles and roles of technical communication in Mexican maquilas (see Thatcher, 2006 for a fuller explanation). At this maquila, there were three employees who did the technical writing, specifically, the procedures manuals for manufacturing the cruise controls. These three writers (all young women), however, were not called writers; rather, they were trainers in the human resource department; and as a way to improve their training effectiveness, they worked with the manufacturing engineers to create short manuals on the line operations. The profiles of the three writers are the following:

Ana Maria (pseudonym) had worked for this maquila for four years, two years as an instructor/trainer and two years writing manuals. Like all the other personnel in the human-resource departments, Ana Maria started her work at the maquila as a lineworker, but was "promoted" to human resources as a trainer because she demonstrated an ability to master the line operations quickly and was able to teach others effectively. Ana Maria was about 25 years old at the time of the interview, was from Chihuahua, and finished only her secondary (middle school) education. She remembers receiving some instruction in her schooling on orthography (grammar/syntax) but no formal instruction in writing. She actually became a writer because she likes to write.

Lourdes (pseudonym) was the second of three manual writers at this maquila. She was born in a small "pueblo" in the state of Chihuahua, just south of Chihuahua City. Lourdes was forced to quit school after the fourth grade and work. She had worked at this maquila for eight years and before that had worked at another U.S.-owned maquila in Chihuahua for three years. Like Ana Maria, she was also in her middle twenties. She was hired as one of the first lineworkers at this maquila and had been there "since the beginning." She was also one of the first to "create" (generar) the job of writer/trainer at this maquila. She also liked to write and enjoyed her job.

The third writer was Belén (pseudonym), who had recently graduated from a local university as an industrial engineer and was in her middle twenties. She had been working for this maquila for six years and had studied part-time throughout her college degree process. Belén was also from Chihuahua City, and like Ana Maria, was one of the first to develop the role as a technical writer. Belén wanted to continue her studies in an MS program in manufacturing engineering as soon as she could. She also liked to write, but her heart was in engineering, and so she was also looking for a job as an engineer that designed and managed engineering manufacturing, rather than as a trainer and writer.

All three writers had a lot in common: they were trainers first and used writing to improve their training effectiveness. They were all young female workers from the surrounding area, and none had received any explicit training in technical writing. The profiles of these three writers are not surprising given the cultural and rhetorical traditions of Mexico and maquila workers. Most technical communications at maquilas carry with them strong rhetorical elements associated with the legal tradition, colonialism, and high power-distance modes of management. In other words, technical communicators serve a notary-like function, legitimizing the official standard operating procedures but offering little to guide everyday practical activities, which were governed by oral interpersonal means. This tradition, however, seems to be changing, due in part to the roles of writing in ISO processes. For example, in one maquila studied by Thatcher (2006), written manuals were beginning to be used as "criteria for judging engineering acceptability" and "reason" in the manufacturing process, something far beyond notary-like functions.

CONCLUSION: STRATEGIES FOR U.S. TECHNICAL COMMUNICATORS WORKING IN MEXICAN MAQUILAS

Many of the rhetorical patterns explored throughout this article will help U.S. technical communicators adapt to the Mexican outsourcing context. In summary, the following section briefly describes only four adaptations that are perhaps the most crucial when working in U.S.-Mexican intercultural contexts (see Thatcher, 2006).

Universal-Particular: The U.S. rhetorical tradition encourages writing as a precedent-setting form of expression. Thus, universal precedence and processes (or "due process," as it's known in the legal field) are highly valued in the United States. Hence, many U.S. technical communicators believe their documents will have the same kinds of normalizing power in other contexts, which is simply ethnocentrism. On the other hand, the Mexican tradition favors a particular approach, focusing on the specific relationships, uniqueness of the situation, and the impossibility of universal approaches. This pattern often gets played out in a tendency to make writing patterns either as parallel as possible in the United States, or not parallel—and therefore unique and novel—in Mexico. Consequently, it is important for U.S. technical communicators to particularize the documents as much as possible to the Mexican situation. This includes eliminating as much as possible universal references, standardized situations, and apersonal roles and responsibilities.

High and Low Context: The United States tradition tends to favor low-context writing, which focuses on the accuracy of the explicitly coded text, strong adherence to written protocols, great attention to details, and low attention to intention. The Mexican tradition looks for meaning more in the surrounding context rather than in the written text. Thus, the Mexican tradition tends to favor concrete sensory stimuli that evoke the context; more focus is given to interpersonal relations rather than written guidelines; less attention to detail; and more attention to intention. U.S. technical communicators will probably have to contextualize and narrate much more than they are used to when working in Mexican contexts.

Individual-Collective: U.S. rhetorical traditions generally favor directness to situate the communication topic, great precision in flow of events, and what has been called "read-friendly writing"—overt signposting for the guiding of readers. Mexico has a less-direct tradition, often involving subtle invocations of social networks and interpersonal relations. Mexican traditions are often called "writer friendly" because they reflect the writer's thought processes rather than overtly guiding the reader through the materials. This tradition is actually interesting from a border perspective because many of the U.S. values of individualism are also strongly present in northern Mexican border cities. If U.S. technical communicators are working in northern Mexican border cities and with Mexican personnel who are used to U.S. styles of direct communication, it is customary to use direct and reader-friendly writing patterns. However, other parts of Mexico, especially southern areas and Mexico City, still use more writer-friendly, indirect, and collective approaches. U.S. technical communicators need to be aware of this intracultural difference in Mexico.

High and Low Power-Distance: In high power-distance cultures such as Mexico, there is unequal, centralized distribution of power, acceptance of authority, high levels of overseeing, and top-down communication styles. This is perhaps one of the most difficult adjustments for North Americans working in Mexico (see Albert, 1996; Kras, 1989). In lower power-distance cultures such as the United States, there is more participatory decision making and power distribution. U.S. technical communicators must understand and situate their technical communications in the appropriate power structures in Mexican maquilas. Otherwise, their documents will be ignored or appropriated for unintended purposes.

Understanding these cultural and communicative differences, especially as related to written instructions, is critical for developing effective technical communications in border populations. U.S. technical communications will most likely exemplify U.S. rhetorical traditions, including what the materials are used for, how one learns from them, and what they actually empower the reader to do in a specific context. Those not familiar with these U.S. traditions will probably not understand, learn from, or be capable of doing what the U.S. authors intend.

REFERENCES

Albert, R. (1996). A framework and model for understanding Latin American and Latino/Hispaniccultural patterns. In D. Landis & R. Bhagat (Eds.), *Handbook of intercultural training* (2nd ed., pp. 27-48). Thousand Oaks, CA: Sage Publications.

Alcalde, J. (1991). Differential impact of American political and economic institutions on Latin America. In K. W. Thompson (Ed.), *The U.S. Constitution and the Constitutions of Latin America* (pp. 97-123). Lanham, MD: University Press of America.

Carrillo, J. (1989) Transformaciones en la industria maquiladora de exportación. In B. González & R. Barajas (Ed.), *Las maquiladoras*. Ciudad Juárez, Mexico: El Colegio de La Frontera Norte.

Dealy, G. C. (1992). *The Latin Americans: Spirit and ethos*. Boulder, CO: Westview Press.

Eder, P. (1950). *A comparative survey of Anglo-American and Latin-American law*. New York: New York University Press

Garza-Almanza, V. (2004). La divulgación de la ciencia en México. *Cultura científica y tecnológica*, *1*(5), 3-16. Ciudad Juárez, México: Universidad Autónoma de Ciudad Juárez.

Garza-Almanza, V. (1999). Comercios regionales y ambiente: Integración del desarrollo y el ambiente en el tratado de libre comercio de América del Norte. *Ambiente Sin Fronteras, 2,* 6-7. Ciudad Juárez, México: Universidad Autónoma de Ciudad Juárez.

Hawisher, G., & Selfe, C. (Eds). (2000). *Global literacies and the world-wide web*. New York: Routledge.

Hofstede, G. (1997). *Cultures and organizations: Software of the mind*. New York: McGraw-Hill.

Kaufer, D., & Carley, K. (1993). *Communication at a distance: The influence of print on sociocultural organization and change*. Hillsdale, NJ: Lawrence Erlbaum.

Kellog, S. (1995). *Law and the transformation of Aztec culture, 1500-1700*. Norman, OK: University of Oklahoma Press.

Kras, E. (1989). *Management in two cultures*. Yarmouth, ME: Intercultural Press, Inc.

LaRosa, M., & Mora, F. (1999). Introduction: Contentious friends in the western hemisphere. In M. LaRosa & F. Mora (Eds.), *Neighborly adversaries: Reading in U.S.-Latin American relations* (pp. 2-18). Lanham, MD: Rowman & Littlefield Publishers.

Leon-Portilla, M. (1996). *El destino de la palabra. De la oralidad y los códices mesoamericanos a la escritura alfabética*. México City: El Colegio Nacional Fondo de Cultura Económica.

Lowery, S. (1990). A look back: The birth of the maquiladora industry. *Twin Plant News, 6*(1).

Marcus, J. (1992). *Mesoamerican writing systems: Propaganda, myth, and history in four ancient civilizations*. Princeton, NJ: Princeton University Press.

Martin-Barbero, J. (1993). *Communication, culture and hegemony: From the media to mediations*. E. Fox & R. A. White (Trans.). Newbury Park, CA: Sage Publications.

Merryman, J. H. (1969). *The civil law tradition: An introduction to the legal systems of western Europe and Latin America*. Stanford, CA: Stanford University Press.

Osland, J., de Franco, S., & Osland, A. (1999). Organizational implications of Latin American culture: Lessons for the expatriate manager. *Journal of Management Inquiry, 8*(2), 219-237.

Rosenn, K. (1988). A comparison of Latin American and North American legal traditions. In L. Tavis (Ed.), *Multinational managers and host government interactions* (pp. 127-152). South Bend, IN: University of Notre Dame Press.

Stewart, E., & Bennett, M. (1991). *American cultural patterns: A cross-cultural perspective* (Rev. Ed.). Yarmouth, ME: Intercultural Press, Inc.

Sullivan, P., & Porter, J. (1997). *Opening spaces: Writing technologies and critical research practices*. Greenwich, CT: Ablex.

Thatcher, B. L. (2006). Intercultural rhetoric, technology transfer, and writing in U.S.-Mexico border maquilas. *Technical Communication Quarterly, 15*(3): 383.

Thatcher, B. L. (2000). L2 professional writing in a U.S. and South American context. *Journal of Second Language Writing, 9*(1), 41-69.

Thatcher, B. L. (1999). Cultural and rhetorical adaptations for South American audiences. *Technical Communication, 46*(2), 177-195.

Trompenaars, F., & C. Hampden-Turner, C. (1998). *Riding the waves of culture: Understanding diversity in global business* (2nd ed.). New York: McGraw Hill.

Victor, D. (1992). *International business communication.* New York: HarperCollins Publishers.

PART II

Management and Cross-Cultural Communication Issues

CHAPTER 6

The Information Developer's Dilemma

JoAnn T. Hackos and
William Hackos, Jr.

The technical communication profession in the United States (and, for that matter, in Western Europe) is in the midst of an attack coming from low-cost economies around the world. As a whole, technical writing is not at risk, but technical-communication jobs in the developed world are. We contend that this attack is real and serious. At its source is a process called disruptive innovation, explored by Harvard professor Clayton M. Christensen first in *The Innovator's Dilemma* (1997) and most recently in *The Innovator's Solution* with Michael E. Raynor, researcher, (2003). In applying the observations, conclusions, and recommendations reached by Christensen, we demonstrate how Americans and Europeans can protect their long-term investment in the discipline.

Christensen and his coauthor Raynor point to two kinds of innovation that spark the development of profit-making companies—sustaining and disruptive innovation. Their work is based on many years of in-depth analysis of the progress of technology and business competition. They trace the history of companies that have survived over long periods and those that have been overcome by relentless competitive pressures.

Throughout the past twenty years, roughly since the introduction of consumer electronics, technical communicators in the United States and Western Europe have pursued a program of sustaining innovations. Sustaining innovations are the kinds we all strive to make. Can we find new technology or other ways to make our products better? Can we improve our processes of developing products to make them better or less expensive? Big companies are generally masters of sustaining innovation.

In the field of information development, we are constantly finding ways to improve the effectiveness of our information-product development. We study our consumers; test our information products for usability; and improve our processes of planning, editing, and document design. In fact, we have ourselves prospered by helping technical communicators find the best ways to make sustaining innovations. Our colleagues in document design, usability, user-centered design, and process innovation have spent twenty years or more improving the information products we deliver to customers.

Christensen's work is about a different kind of innovation—disruptive innovation. Unlike sustaining innovations, large market-leading companies (incumbents) do not have a natural advantage over small startups (entrants). Instead, they are at a disadvantage and may even be destroyed by the entrants. If you have worked for a startup that is dedicated to developing and marketing a cheaper, more efficient, sometimes better version of established products, you have participated in the process of disruptive innovation.

Technical communication in the United States and Western Europe is today in the midst of a disruptive innovation in the form of competition from technical writers in countries where the salaries are markedly lower. Before we give a detailed description of disruptive innovation, we'd like to explain the four principles of disruptive innovation described by Christensen.

Principle #1: Companies Depend on Customers and Investors for Resources.

We think of companies and their management as being in control of their destinies. We tend to believe that companies succeed because management is brave and smart. Companies fail because of management mistakes. Christensen claims these notions are completely wrong. Instead, companies are completely at the mercy of their customers and investors, even when management is doing all the right things. If a company doesn't satisfy customers, it doesn't generate the revenue that is crucial to company operations. Similarly, if a company doesn't satisfy stockholders' demands for continued growth, it doesn't get the investment it needs for sustained growth. No matter how hard companies try to violate the first principle, all they can do without customers or investors is go out of business. In fact, companies that produce products with features that customers want and growth that investors demand do thrive. The best performing companies market products or services with features that exactly match what customers want and will pay for, and no more.

Technical communicators who work for customer-centered companies are generally encouraged to produce information products that are superior and help to sustain long-term customer satisfaction.

Principle #2: Small Markets Don't Solve the Growth Needs of Large Companies.

Disruptive innovators find small markets that are ignored by large companies. In every case, these disruptors pursue new technology, developing suites of products for underserved small or nonexistent markets. Generally, the disruptive products or services are not quite as good for existing upscale customers, but they are cheap and convenient. They precisely meet the needs of small companies just beginning to find a place for technological innovations.

Because the disruptive innovators succeed in small markets with low-cost products and lower profit margins, their markets are not generally attractive to the large incumbent companies. After all, why should large companies fool with products that have small markets and low profitability? Isn't it better for them to improve existing products for their large, high-markup customers? Their stockholders don't want them to pursue unprofitable markets either. If large companies try to move into the disruptive product's market niche, they are likely to slow rather than accelerate their growth. At the same time, small disruptive companies can thrive on revenue that is of little value to established companies. Technical communicators who have worked on information development for company products that are not especially profitable often find they are seriously underfunded.

Principle #3: Markets That Don't Exist Can't Be Analyzed.

Large incumbent companies are typically experts at market research. They do not assign resources to capture not-yet-existent markets because they have no way to do research on these markets. Small companies can afford to aim toward these markets in the hope and expectation that their disruptive products will create a market. Of course, many small companies aim wrong and go out of business before we know they ever existed. Among the companies that succeed, as we saw through the 1990s, are those that will eventually completely take over the markets of the incumbent companies.

Principle #4: Technology Supply May Not Equal Market Demand.

Most companies, large and small, make continuing improvements in products because their sustaining innovations allow them to enter new, more upscale markets. By taking advantage of the greater markup in these markets, they increase revenues as well as profit margins.

Unfortunately, as many technical communicators know from their own experience, the large incumbent companies may improve or add features and functions to their products to the point that the improvements are of no additional value to any customer group. Technical communicators typically refer to this process as "feature creep." Christensen calls it "over-serving" the customer. When feature creep sets in, technical communicators are often faced with the difficult task of explaining features that make little sense to the customers.

Small entrant companies take the same route in moving upscale, but their improvements enable their disruptive products to serve at a lower cost in some of the same markets as the incumbent's products. As the low-cost disruptive products gain market share, they become commodities, and entrant company begins to erode the incumbent's market based on price. Once this process begins, it may not be possible for the incumbent to recover. Christensen goes through case study after case study to show how these four principles explain disruptive innovation in the real world. To be brief, we will give a single hypothetical scenario of a disruptive innovation event.

A TYPICAL INNOVATOR'S DILEMMA SCENARIO

We begin with an incumbent company that has achieved considerable success in a technology and maintains a large market share. The company continues to make improvements in its products based on customer and end-user research. Customers are happy and seemingly loyal. Out of nowhere, or so it seems, a new technology emerges, not necessarily high-tech, but perhaps based on a new process or business model. An entrant company seizes on the new technology and creates a product that is at the low end of the market or even serves a previously nonexistent market. Its low price, improved simplicity, and convenience create a new market or possibly make inroads into the lowest-margin market of the incumbent.

Both the entrant company and the incumbent company are thrilled. The entrant is finally producing some revenue. The incumbent is happy because it is getting rid of its low-end market, which has the lowest profitability. In fact, its average profitability has increased. "Good riddance!" The incumbent's marketing department does a thorough market analysis and concludes it is not worth getting into a technology to compete with the entrant. The entrant's products will never be as good as the incumbent's, the markup potential is small, and the market is not large enough to bother with.

After a time, the entrant company starts using its technology to improve its disruptive product and begins eroding some of the high-quality market of the incumbent. At first, it's just pesky. The incumbent continues to improve its product by adding features that the customer likes but is less and less willing to pay for. But the entrant continues to erode the market. Marketing is flabbergasted. "What is wrong with our customers?" "Why don't they understand that our quality is better?" Eventually, things get bad enough for the incumbent that management decides to act to protect its customers from this competitive onslaught. "We must produce that low-end product and compete directly!" But it's too late. Try as it may, the incumbent just can't compete with the entrant. It doesn't have the same expertise in the technology as the entrant. It is not as efficient, not willing to accept a lower profit margin, and has lost its brand advantage. It's convinced that its products are still much better. But why are customers not loyal? You probably can think of many well-known companies that are no longer with us or are only skeletons of their former selves. In fact, you may work for one of the incumbents.

What, then, is the Innovator's Dilemma? The dilemma occurs because incumbent companies react to the threat by pursuing sustaining innovations in their products that raise the price and possibly make the product more complex and less usable. The more market they lose, the more they try to compete by improving their product. It's a dilemma because they lose if they don't compete by improving their product and they lose if they compete by improving their product. The customer really wants a simpler, cheaper, more convenient product, but the incumbent is unable to produce it. What does this situation have to do with information developers?

THE INFORMATION DEVELOPER'S DILEMMA

The U.S. information-development community and many other high-tech professions are currently under attack from a disruptive innovation. The new technology is high-speed, inexpensive, worldwide communications. The competing organizations are technical communicators and other high-tech disciplines in third-world, low-cost economies.

Because of the new communications technology, technical writers no longer need to be in close proximity to developers or end-users. In fact, unless direct physical contact is essential or heavy equipment or products are involved, jobs can be performed anywhere as long as workers have sufficient skills. Recall that we have proved this point through telecommuting arrangements here at home.

We didn't notice the onset of this competition in the 1990s because we were too busy making money. In fact, in the beginning, only the less-desirable "grunt" jobs were offshored, such as maintaining legacy documentation, data entry, format conversion, and so on. "Good riddance!" We could do all the fun stuff. Then, somewhere around the year 2000 or 2001, we began to notice that, because of the economic slowdown and because the offshoring had already made a beachhead with the grunt work, a lot of technical communicators were losing their jobs.

We reacted. "We need to improve our documentation products." "Management will see that we are better than those pesky third-world writers." Now we are asking, "Why don't they realize that our information products are better than theirs?" We are on the horns of the dilemma. No matter how hard we try to improve our information products, management doesn't seem to care. They think of technical communication as a commodity and prefer the least expensive option.

WHAT SHOULD WE DO?

First, **what will not work.** Government, no matter which party is in control, will not be able to stop the disruptive competition. We have to do it ourselves. We may have considerable difficulty convincing management that third-world writers can't produce information products as well as we can, particularly when we appear to focus our time and effort on quality measures that don't affect the customers. In today's environment, upper management is generally trying to save money on information development or even on product development in an effort to increase profits and raise stock prices.

What will work. Technical communicators need to make a direct attack against the disruptive innovation. At present, the primary advantage that the third-world has is lower salaries. Information development in the United States must become more efficient and less costly than the third-world competition. Technical communicators in the United States have many advantages. They reside in the world's largest market—the United States. They use the products they write about. They have a direct relationship with the culture of the potential buyers and users of the product. They have considerable technology available to help lower costs. They are innovative and practical.

RESPONDING TO DISRUPTIVE INNOVATION IN INFORMATION DEVELOPMENT

To succeed among disruptive market forces, technical communicators need to step up to serious business-management challenges. They need to take an aggressive position that includes understanding market forces as well as setting and pursuing tough business objectives. They need to concentrate on learning how to save money and avoid adding costs that have little measurable value to the customer. As a starting point, we recommend that the following actions be pursued. We'll begin with a brief overview of possible responses and then consider each in more detail.

Understanding Management Goals

First, understand the goals of upper management with respect to information development. After all, as employees of the organization, your primary customer is your own management. Recognize that upper management rarely sees technical communication as the creative, artistic pursuit that you do. You must be efficient as well as creative.

Focusing on Cost Savings

Next, be diligent in tracking and analyzing your current costs of operation. Without knowing your current costs, you cannot adequately and persuasively evaluate the costs of outsourcing and offshoring.

As a critical part of your cost analysis, educate yourselves about the hidden costs of outsourcing. Despite lower salaries, the real savings from offshoring appear to be closer to 20% than to the vaunted 80%. Communicate the real costs to upper management.

Find innovative ways to save your own 20% through process improvements such as minimalism, prioritization of projects, single sourcing, and content management. Look realistically at the salaries you are paying. Can you find your own lower-cost help? Are the salaries you are now paying left over from the dotcom boom? Are inflated salaries in the United States helping to make the third world's case?

Reconsider Telecommuting

Consider the dangers of working at home. Certainly, telecommuting may reduce costs if companies spend less for office space; but much telecommuting is for the benefit of individuals and creates an atmosphere that fosters offshoring. Offshoring is a kind of telecommuting. If you can do your job from home with little contact with products, users, developers, or colleagues, perhaps the same job can be done in Africa, Asia, or South America.

Find ways to increase your need to have close and continuous contact with your users, developers, and products. Become the knowledge-management organization. Become the user- and task-analysis group. Make information development as visible as possible in your organization and across the corporation.

Consider the role of information development in your organization. Be careful about making assumptions. You may be well compensated and respected today, but the tables can turn quickly. Disruptive innovators are at the door. If you want to survive professionally, you need to take immediate action. Remember that it isn't enough to produce high quality work. You must consider how much quality is needed, how it affects customers, and how you can reduce costs. It is your job and the future of the profession that is on the line. Now let us consider each of these responses in more detail.

ALIGNING WITH CORPORATE STRATEGIES

Critical to the process of combating disruptive innovations is to understand clearly what management's goals are with regard to cost controls, profitability, and quality. These goals are often products of the company's positioning as either incumbents or entrant disruptors. If your management represents the incumbent in your industry, they may be staving off a disruptive attack of their own. If your management represents an entrant disruptor, they are trying hard to keep costs under control while at the same time moving up the scale into more profitable and larger markets. If you work for an incumbent who is not being attacked, you may have some remaining time to focus on quality in your information product. Your company may have customers who are still not adequately served by the product. They may be experiencing significant usability issues that could be addressed by better user and task analysis or better delivery of quality information products. However, it is very dangerous to become complacent in this environment. If the disruptive innovators are not already nipping at the heels of your company's products, they will be soon.

If your company is the incumbent and is being attacked by the entrant disruptors, your job will be to gain efficiency and reduce costs to stay in business. If your company is the entrant disruptor, you were probably hired at a lower cost in the first place. Your job is to drive down costs and remain efficient. The only time you will be given explicit resources to increase customer quality is when your company is working hard to capture upscale markets that demand more quality in the product and its information. Be aware that it may not be easy to discover your management's strategies. You need to understand the market forces on the company, pay attention to demands for increased stockholder value, recognize the signs of customers unhappy about the quality of the product, and know when customers are really not interested in spending more money for more functionality or information.

We suggest that you review both of Christensen's books and consider reading Geoffrey Moore's two earlier works, *Crossing the Chasm* (2002) and *Inside the Tornado* (1995). Moore provides insight into the problems of introducing new products into mainstream and highly demanding markets. Use Moore to better understand how to use individual product life cycles to decide on the level of information required by customers.

MEASURING YOUR OWN DEVELOPMENT COSTS

Exactly how much does it cost your organization to produce each information-product deliverable? If you don't know precisely, then you are not ready to combat disruptive innovators who promise lower costs for equal or nearly equal quality.

To measure your own costs, you need to keep track of the current resources used to produce your information, including project management, writing, editing, translation, and production, and other areas that may apply to your operations. You must ask staff to track their exact hours worked, including time in addition to the standard 40-hour week that they devote to all of their information-development activities. Don't forget information gathering, meetings with developers and among team members, validation, and all other associated costs.

If staff members balk at tracking their time, explain that it is in their own best interests to know their real costs. You cannot argue against proposed offshore or outsourced costs unless you know your own. For information about cost tracking, consult *Managing your Documentation Projects* (Hackos, 1994).

DEMONSTRATING COST SAVINGS

As soon as you know your operation costs precisely, you have the capacity to examine them for opportunities to save. Cost-savings opportunities can come through several types of innovation.

Single Sourcing

Single sourcing your content and using the same content in multiple deliverables can lead to significant operational savings. Most information developers are fully aware of content that is repeated or almost the same in multiple deliverables. For example, an organization may produce many varieties of the same product for which the technical documentation may be nearly the same. By authoring stand-alone topics and using these topics in all the related documentation, information-development organizations save authoring time. In some organizations, reusable content may account for as much as 80% of the content of a documentation library.

Content Management

Content-management systems enhance an organization's ability to manage and reuse content, thus reducing development costs. By storing stand-alone topics in a repository, an organization may be able to automate the final assembly of topics into a variety of deliverables and media. For example, from a repository rich in topic-based content, an organization can automate the production of print, PDF, HTML, help, and other deliverables simply by applying the appropriate style sheets. In addition, if the topics are carefully labeled with customized metadata, it may be possible to filter the content so that custom deliverables are automatically produced to serve the needs of a range of users from expert to novice or end-user to professional. With both single sourcing and content management, the assembly and final production processes of information development can be automated, reducing staff time and increasing the quality of the information delivered.

Controlled Language and Writing for Translation

Controlled language refers to the process of writing with a set, limited vocabulary; writing for translation refers to writing with an awareness of the needs of a non-U.S. audience. Both of these activities will help to reduce translation costs. As you are well aware, U.S. companies are under competitive pressure to provide technical information in more languages than ever before, at substantial cost. In fact, the cost of translation may exceed the cost of producing the information in the source language. Information developers can actively pursue reducing translation costs by writing more carefully and consistently and by being trained to avoid expressions that are difficult to translate. Our research has shown that translation costs can be reduced by 25% to 30% through controlled language and translation-aware writing.

At the same time, multilanguage content-management systems can add to the cost savings. By storing topics in parallel in multiple languages, content-management systems enable organizations to translate only new or changed content, rather than sending all content to the translators. Translation memory systems can also be employed to store previously translated words and phrases so that the translation of minimally revised content can be largely automated. Automated production of final deliverables in multiple languages can eliminate the cost of desktop publishing, which often represents as much as 50% of the total translation costs today.

Collaborative, Team-Centric Development

Much information-development work has been conducted by technical writers working independently, even when they are housed in the same departments. As a result, we find considerable duplication of effort, from writing topics that have already been written by other team members, interviewing the same developers and other subject-matter experts, mastering the same content, and producing multiple deliverables by individual handcrafting of desktop-published documents. Team-centric development, in which technical writers work together from the beginning of projects, can significantly reduce development costs.

Working in a collaborative information-development team means planning the content and distributing the content-creation responsibilities to avoid duplication. It means using a repository to store team-developed content so that the content is always accessible to all team members. It means developing final deliverables using automation rather than handcrafting. Although a collaborative development environment in which team members share content resources may take time and resources to develop, the efficiencies gained benefit the entire organization and are difficult to outsource.

Technology to Reduce Production and Deployment Costs, Including Web-Based Delivery

The more that information-development organization can use technology to automate processes, the more time is available to produce high-quality content for customers. For too long, technical communication has been a cottage industry in which individual contributors work independently, handling all aspects of the content-development and production process, a situation fostered by the desktop-publishing technology of the past 20 years. With topic-based authoring, enhanced by XML-based structured writing, and content-management technology, we have an opportunity for the first time to automate a significant portion of the information-development life cycle.

In addition, we have available to us the means to deliver better, more integrated content through the Web than we could ever deliver in print. We have the ability to quickly and easily receive customer feedback and deliver continuous updates to content online.

Each of the cost-reduction methods mentioned above is discussed in detail in *Managing your Documentation Projects* (Hackos, 1994) and *Content Management for Dynamic Web Delivery* (Hackos, 2002). See also Bob Boiko's, *The Content Management Bible* (2004), for additional perspectives on the cost savings possible through creative content management.

Addition of Interns or Lower Cost Staff to Decrease the Average Compensation

We recognize that, in the past, information-development managers may have preferred to hire only experienced staff members. They tend to require less supervision and training and can often be immediately productive. In light of low-cost disruptors, managers may want to rethink their hiring practices. By employing interns in the midst of their educations, staff members get help with more mundane tasks, freeing experienced members to focus on content development. By hiring lower-cost staff to handle repetitive activities, such as the assembly and production of deliverables, proofreading, style-sheet maintenance, and so on, organizations reduce the average salary levels and increase productivity.

Note that productivity is measured by dividing revenue by the total cost of employees. Lower-cost employees immediately result in a productivity gain. In fact, one of the reasons that U.S. corporations have increased productivity in the last 5 to 10 years is the employment of low-cost labor in third-world economies.

Controlling High Level Salary Increases

In certain areas of the country, such as Silicon Valley in California, technical communicators may have priced themselves out of the market. By some reports, the employment of writers in high-tech industries in Northern California may have declined by 50% or more since 2000. Managers must of course attract talented individuals with adequate financial packages, but in general, salaries for direct-employed technical communicators have apparently decreased since 2000 because of the pressures a more competitive buyer's market.

COMMUNICATING ABOUT OUTSOURCING WITH MANAGEMENT

All the methods discussed above should be examined carefully. Some will require initial investments in time and technology, but these may produce the greatest savings. Carefully track the effects of your cost-control efforts and communicate clearly and frequently with senior management.

Investigating the Hidden Costs of Outsourcing

The experience of U.S. publications organizations with offshore outsourcing is often very negative. Many of the advantages that appear to be gained through much lower salaries are offset by increased costs to produce acceptable products. One organization must spend large amounts of senior-writer and project-manager time to create detailed specifications and service-level agreements to ensure that the offshore writers produce acceptable products.

Hiring and training costs increase significantly, including the cost of travel between the United States and the offshore sites. Often, managers must be assigned to the offshore locations for extended periods of time to ensure that operations follow company procedures. In many cases, we find that high turnover significantly increases the cost of hiring and training. Remember that to be viable, an offshore operation must be in existence for 3 or 4 years. Because salary levels in many high-tech-oriented developing countries are increasing rapidly, the initial cost savings may erode quickly.

Consider also the loss of intellectual capital. Knowledge once clearly in the hands of long-term employees is transferred to temporary or short-term staff. We have learned of cases in which basic product knowledge is used to start local companies in competition (disruptive innovation) with your own organization.

Increasing Visibility

No one in the rest of the company is going to come to you and inquire about your work. You have to market your organization and its capabilities to the larger organization. That means acting more like extroverted salespeople than introverted writers.

Make presentations to other departments about your work. Communicate to stakeholders throughout company about your cost savings initiatives. Show the data you've collected frequently and explain how peer organizations can themselves contribute to the cost-savings efforts. Remember that product developers are also at risk for outsourcing and offshoring.

Be certain that your work produces unique results. Know your customers better than anyone else. Customer knowledge is the least likely capacity to be outsourced. The better you respond to customers' real information needs, the stronger your contributions to the bottom line will be.

Don't become commodity writers. Anyone can be hired to format developers' notes. Become experts in the product and the customers. Be able to point out deficiencies in the product workflow and inconsistencies in interface design that will improve the customers' satisfaction. Decrease the costs of low-value activities in your workflow and reserve time for high value.

Christensen points out over and over again in his work that if we understand the process of disruptive innovation, we can fight it on its own terms and win. Remember that management prefers to use local professionals for information development if it perceives that costs are acceptable.

REFERENCES

Boiko, B. (2004). *The content management bible* (2nd ed.). New York: John Wiley & Sons.

Christensen, C. M., & Raynor, M. E. (1997). *The innovator's dilemma: When new technologies cause great firms to fail.* Cambridge, MA: Harvard Business School Press.

Christensen, C. M., & Raynor, M. E. (2003). *The innovator's solution: Creating and sustaining successful growth.* Cambridge, MA: Harvard Business School Press.

Hackos, J. T. (1994). *Managing your documentation projects.* New York: John Wiley & Sons.

Hackos, J. T. (2002). *Content management for dynamic web delivery.* New York: John Wiley & Sons.

Moore, G. M. (1995). *Inside the tornado: Marketing strategies from Silicon Valley's cutting edge.* New York: HarperCollins.

Moore, G. M. (2002). *Crossing the chasm: Marketing and selling high-tech products to mainstream customers.* New York: HarperCollins.

CHAPTER 7

Language, Culture, and Collaboration in Offshore Outsourcing: A Case Study of International Training Team Communication Competencies

Jim Melton

The large-scale movement of jobs caused by offshore outsourcing affects both nations and industries, as shown by other chapters in this volume. While technical communicators may be able to influence these macrotrends in some ways, as individuals they are often left to adapt to conditions rather than drive them. Thus, an awareness of global currents and an understanding of the kinds of abilities required to navigate them is vital for individuals seeking to remain competitive in the field, as well as for the programs seeking to prepare them.

International training is an appealing area where technical communicators can contribute their abilities because of the increasing integration between oral, written, and online training, and because training adds value to technical communication products. However, technical communicators will be able to take advantage of these opportunities only if they can cultivate the competencies used in international training. This chapter will first discuss opportunities for technical communicators in the area of training, then describe a case study of an international training team based in Hawaii who regularly delivers training in Japan, and finally sketch an outline of related competencies.

TRENDS AND OPPORTUNITIES IN
OFFSHORE OUTSOURCING

Kalakota and Robinson (2004) argue that outsourcing is a long-term trend that will be adopted by more organizations at almost all stages of the product life cycle. Technical communication work or products at each stage are also prime candidates for offshore outsourcing. Although these trends are a potential threat to the livelihood of the profession, they are also an opportunity for technical communicators to redefine themselves and find new applications for their abilities. Demand is increasing for project managers who can collaborate from remote distances and across languages and cultures: "Companies that don't have these skills will look internally for people to enhance their knowledge, or hire people to supplement their teams" (Kalakota & Robinson, 2004). The silver lining for technical communicators is that global organizations need individuals who are capable of dealing with both the technical and cultural obstacles of communication across distances. Those who can help organizations solve the communication challenges of outsourcing will be highly valued, whether they come from within the organization or are hired from the outside.

Training is a particularly important communication challenge within the context of outsourcing for two main reasons:

1. As organizations become more "flat," multinational, and outsourced, both the necessity and complexity of organizational learning increases (Buckman, 2004; Iles & Hayers, 1997; Prahalad, 1997).
2. As the competitive edge moves from making the best product to helping others find ways to adapt and use knowledge to solve their problems (Reich, 2001), the demand for specialized learning paralleling documentation will increase (Faber & Johnson-Eilola, 2002).

Faber and Johnson-Eilola (2002) argue that the most desirable future for technical communicators is not merely to turn out information products but to "find ways to leverage our knowledge and build new knowledge to create and add value in a business culture that is increasingly agnostic to physical products" (p. 141). They give an example: "Our task is not to make clear why a group of technical communicators can build a better Web site. Our task is to add value to that software by teaching people and companies how to use it to solve their problems" (p. 141). Training can be a vital part of this value-added process, where technical communicators who have inside, tacit knowledge as well as technical expertise can make unique contributions. Their role will be "not merely to learn and teach new technologies, but also to provide creative and innovative solutions to unique and specialized business problems" (p. 143).

The practical benefits of combining technical communication and training have already been noted by Hackos (1994), who states, "As a strategic-planning consultant, I strongly recommend, in fact, that training and publications be closely aligned in the development of documents and job aids" (p. 124). She notes that key to both functions is an accurate analysis of audience, which is, in many cases, the same audience. Carliner (2001) adds that technical communication is evolving toward a "campaign-like approach more typical of marketing than of traditional documentation libraries. We can no longer tell users something once—we must use a variety of media and methods to reach them" (p. 156). Customized training can be one of these methods, delivered in a traditional face-to-face setting or through online media, interactive video, print documents, or, increasingly, using a blended combination of these (Armstrong, 2002; Bridges, Baily, Hiatt, Timmerman, & Gibson, 2002).

As markets become global, products in any of these media will have to effectively cross national, cultural, linguistic, and technical boundaries or be severely limited in their application and marketability. For this reason, internationalization consultant Marcia Sweezey recommends that training be included as one of four parts of a coordinated information strategy to solve localization and translation problems common in international technical communication (Hoft, 1995). These four parts are printed information products, user interface, online information products, and training.

As with all kinds of technical communication, trainers need to make content accessible to their audiences, which may require not only translation but comprehensive cultural adaptation as well (Huang, 1996; Marquardt, 1995; Thornhill, 1993). Cultural expectations about methods, objectives, and content of training will need to be considered, as well as assumptions about age, gender, and ethnicity. Choice of training media and methods must be considered in light of linguistic and cultural factors (Connor, 1996; Thatcher, 1999, 2000).

It is also highly possible that linguistic or cultural backgrounds will differ between trainers and audience as well as between training-team members themselves. A training team might consist of a curriculum developer in the United States, a multimedia specialist in India, and a face-to-face presenter from Singapore, with an audience in Shanghai. Increased diversity among training-team members may enhance potential reach across cultures and overall effectiveness; but it may also pose intercultural communication challenges within the team (Hampden-Turner & Trompenaars, 2004; Iles & Hayers, 1997; Lazear, 1998; McDermott, Waite, & Brawley, 1999).

PURPOSE OF THIS STUDY

Among those best equipped to contribute to emerging offshore training projects may be technical communicators, because ideally they already possess many of the abilities needed, including bridging communication gaps between disparate groups, negotiating different communication genres, and facilitating remote communication technology (Earley & Gibson, 2002; Iles & Hayers, 1997;

McDermott et al., 1999). These abilities match up with many of those identified by Rainey, Turner, and Dayton (2004) in their study of key competencies for technical communication and also fit with the technical-communication-competency frameworks proposed by Hart-Davidson (2001) and Carliner (2001).

However, if technical communicators are to contribute to offshore training projects, they will need to retool their present abilities and gain others. Thus, information is needed about the competencies used by members of international training teams. Such knowledge may not only help individuals refine and adapt their skills, but also guide technical communication curriculum planners and programs. Yet a review of literature shows that this area has not been fully explored, as shown in the following sections.

Recent studies have identified what core competencies technical communicators need, but more research is required to find out how these competencies apply in the context of international training. As the following sections will show, a large body of research exists on intercultural competencies, but it is fragmentary and focuses mostly on long-term, lived experience in foreign countries. International training literature is somewhat useful but lacks the rhetorical approach that would be most helpful to technical communicators. It also focuses mostly on individual trainers, not the intensive team training situation that will probably be most common for technical communicators.

A competency model or framework to fill this gap would be useful for technical communicators interested in international training because it would integrate previous findings and act as a platform for inquiry both for scholars pursuing research and practitioners interested in honing their abilities.

Technical Communication Competencies

Recent efforts to identify the core competencies of technical communicators provide general guidance but require further research for application in the specific area of international training. Rainey, Turner, and Dayton (2004) identified several broad-based competencies in a survey of 67 managers of technical communicators in the United States and around the world:

- Collaboration with subject-matter experts and co-workers
- Writing clearly for specific audiences
- Assessing and learning to use technologies
- Taking initiative as a self-starter
- Evaluating one's own work and the work of others

They also identified secondary competencies:

- Creating documentation in various media using technologies
- Writing, editing, and testing documents

Tertiary competencies included usability testing, single-sourcing and content management, instructional design, budgeting, oral presentations, research, multimedia, and awareness of cultural differences.

The question for technical communicators interested in the particular context of international training is this: how do these competencies apply in the context of international training, and are there any other competencies that are necessary? Indeed, Rainey, Turner, and Dayton (2004) and others (Carliner, 2001; Hart-Davidson, 2001; Whiteside, 2003) have called for this kind of exploration of specific contexts for technical communication competencies.

Intercultural Competencies

Rigorous studies have been conducted on almost every conceivable aspect of intercultural competence, ranging from the abstract, such as such as "tolerance for ambiguity" (Ruben, 1976) to the concrete, such as interaction management, or the ability to begin, end, and take turns in conversation (Chen, 1989; Olebe & Koester, 1989; Ruben & Kealey, 1979). However, this range of information is difficult to use because specific findings are scattered across different contexts and produced in different disciplines. Chen and Starosta (1996) explain:

> This literature is fragmentary and lacks a holistic view. Conceptually, scholars in the area of intercultural communication competence have been unable to provide a consistent framework for an understanding of the notion of interdependence and interconnectedness of the complex multicultural dynamics in the contemporary age (p. 370).

Much of the problem lies in differing assumptions. For technical communicators and trainers, many competence models prove unworkable because their purpose is to prepare people for extended lived experience in a foreign country rather than preparing people to produce documentation and training across cultures. Behavior is assumed to be the basis of intercultural interaction rather than language, communication, or rhetoric, making the model hard for technical communicators to use. Do printed words on a page or illuminated words on a screen constitute behavior? Is writing behavior? Conversely, is interpreting written or spoken words behavior? Can't behavior be viewed as a form of nonverbal communication (Hall, 1976)?

From the perspective of many technical communication scholars, what technical communicators are engaged in is not just behavior or communication, but rhetoric (Spilka, 1993; MacKinnon, 1993; Mirel & Spilka, 2002; Winsor, 1996, 2003), and thus, crossing cultural borders in technical communication is intercultural rhetoric (Thatcher, 1999, 2000; Yuan, 1997). Models of intercultural competence for technical communication should reflect that perspective, while still using a multidisciplinary approach to draw on knowledge from other fields.

Training Competencies

Several studies have been done on the competencies required for training across cultures (for example, see Burba, Petrosko, & Boyle, 2001; Marquardt, 1995; Thornhill, 1993). Using surveys, interviews, and observation, these studies have identified a range of competencies for international trainers, including flexibility, sense of humor, respect, tolerance for ambiguity, cultural knowledge, presentation skills, communication skills, and speaking skills. Such studies provide a good basis for further research on the competencies used by members of international training teams, but, as with intercultural competency research, they assume behavior as the basis of interaction. Again, a rhetorical perspective would add to their usefulness for technical communicators.

Most of these studies also assume an individual rather than a team basis for the operation of intercultural training competencies. This is a notable gap because most training is conducted by teams (Larson & LaFasto, 2001) and because each individual team member might not need the full range of competencies if team members could collaborate and each contribute their own strengths to the project. Context-based, qualitative research could explore how competencies relate to one another in a team situation and how team members use competencies in collaboration with one another.

Research Gap and Competence Models

Taking into account previous research in the areas of technical communication, intercultural competence, and training, the research gap for technical communicators who want to contribute in international training teams is this: what communication competencies do members of an international training team use, and how do they use them?

A competency model for international training might be the most valuable response to this gap because it can bring together previous findings and act as a platform from which to extend future research (Lucia & Lepsinger, 1999; Spencer & Spencer, 1993). Competency models can be oriented to a specific job within an organization or constitute a general outline. General models do not address particular jobs or purposes, but building a job-specific model from scratch can be time-consuming and cost-prohibitive (Lucia & Lepsinger, 1999; Spencer & Spencer, 1993). Perhaps most useful for technical communicators who want to contribute to international training would be a midrange model that, while not oriented to a specific job, is directed at the particular context of international training.

A good starting point for this effort is a model proposed by second-language teaching scholar Byram (1997), which encompasses six aspects of intercultural competence: linguistic, sociolinguistic, discourse, strategic, sociocultural, and social. The framework is practical for technical communicators because it focuses on communicative competencies and assumes communication (and specifically language) as the basis of human interaction, a grounding that is much closer to rhetoric than are behavior or perception. In this study, I use qualitative research methods to test how the framework applies to international training.

METHODS

During the summer of 2004 I conducted research on an international project team based in Honolulu, Hawaii, that regularly delivers training to Japanese salespeople working for a health-food company that is based in the United States. Using Bryam's (1997) framework as a starting point, I wanted to find out (1) What competencies the members of the team used in creating and delivering a training seminar across US-Japanese national, cultural, and linguistic boundaries; (2) how these competencies related to each other; and (3) how the participants used these competencies in collaboration with each other.

Case Study

Qualitative research and, specifically, case study was the best approach for answering these questions. Competencies are complex and rooted in particular situations (Lucia & Lepsinger, 1999; Spencer & Spencer, 1993), most predominantly in team situations (Iles & Hayers, 1997). Although survey research might provide a broad view of the competencies individuals believe they and others are using, case study allows for in-depth, observation-based examination of these competencies while maintaining the context within which they are used (Flick, 2002; Yin, 1994). Case study is also well suited to exploratory research, because its data gathering and analysis is an iterative process that takes place both during and after fieldwork (Flick, 2002; Miles & Huberman, 1994; Yin, 1994).

This particular case study was selected because it was relevant to the research questions and because the team shared several similarities with other international training teams that technical communicators may be a part of. First, the team had a deadline: a training date in Japan including with the reservation of hotels, meeting rooms, and company facilities. Second, the work was cyclical. The project team had created and delivered similar training programs three or four times a year for the previous five years, allowing me to place the project in the context of the team's evolution of working with each other. Third, the participants were providing training on how to do something—sales knowledge and techniques in this case. Finally, and most cogent for offshore outsourcing and associated international training, the process was richly intercultural: training content was originally created for an American context but adapted for Japanese personnel, and the project team itself was multicultural.

Participants

The training team leader, Branford (pseudonyms are used for all participants), was a Chinese-American man in his late fifties who spoke English as a first language and Mandarin Chinese as a second language. The second participant was a Japanese man named Okito in his late thirties who was not only bilingual but also bicultural, having grown up in both Japan and the United States. The third participant, Emi, was a Japanese woman in her mid to late thirties who moved to the United States as an adult, where she operated her own English-Japanese translation company for several years. Branford and Okito had been developing and delivering training seminars for Japanese audiences together for about five years, and Emi had been a part of the team for four years.

Data Gathering

Before the study began, I adapted Byram's (1997) framework to fit the field of technical communication by renaming some of the terms and merging some of the categories that seemed redundant for the purposes of the study. Beneath each area of competence, I included the competencies listed on Byram's original framework and added others drawn from intercultural competence literature. This revised preliminary framework acted as a guide for data gathering and analysis and was gradually revised throughout the process to reflect the findings described in the results section.

Using the team's three-month training cycle as the boundary of the case, I observed the development of a sales-training seminar over a period of two-and-a-half months, from the planning phase in Honolulu to the delivery of the training in Japan (four full days). The participants understood training as a holistic process that, in addition to communicating information, was also aimed at building and maintaining relationships, which they recognized as particularly important in Japan (Yamada, 1997). Thus, it was not enough to look at the training seminar only; all of the participants' efforts related to the training also had to be considered, including gathering feedback about what training topics were needed, planning social events and recognition awards, and meeting with individuals to answer questions.

My primary means of data gathering were observing planning meetings, interviewing participants, collecting documents such as PowerPoint presentation slides, and observing training seminars and social events. Planning meetings took place primarily at the beginning of data gathering; training seminars and related events toward the end. Throughout the process, I also conducted a total of ten formal interviews, many of them in a group format. My main purpose in these interviews was to check what I thought I was observing in the planning meetings and learn more about it. I also observed the delivery of training in Hawaii—where English and Japanese were used side-by-side throughout—and in Japan. The seminar in Japan was conducted only in Japanese except for Branford's portion, which Okito and Emi interpreted from English to Japanese.

Having only a rudimentary knowledge of Japanese, I was in a linguistic position similar to that of Branford. I was able to understand what was going on in the seminar in Japan because I had already seen the hybrid version in Hawaii and because the team had been reviewing the content with each other in English for several months beforehand.

ANALYSIS AND FINDINGS

Using the preliminary framework discussed in the methods section, I did a rhetorical analysis of each interview, meeting, training seminar, and social event, as well as the overall process of creating and delivering the training. My analysis focused on identifying patterns that would show (1) what competencies the members of the team used, (2) how these competencies related to each other, and (3) how the participants used these competencies in collaboration with each other. Patterns fell into five main areas: linguistic competence, translation competence, intercultural communication competence, collaborative competence, and adaptive competence—around which I organize my findings.

Linguistic Competence

Linguistic competence is defined as "the ability to produce meaningful utterances" with respect to a given language through speaking or writing (Byram, 1997, p. 10). The case study revealed two important findings for technical communicators entering the context of international training:

1. Using the host language was not just a way to transfer information but a rhetorical act with the potential to connect the identities of the audience and the presenter.
2. The participants' ability to use the host language rhetorically was both constrained and enabled by the cultural expectations of the audience.

Participants' use of the language as a rhetorical strategy ran throughout the case study. One example was Branford's use of Japanese writing to build rapport with the audience. Japanese written characters, or *kanji*, are borrowed from Chinese and have similar meanings. Thus, as a Mandarin speaker, Branford was able to write *kanji* impromptu on a white board, usually as Okito or Emi were interpreting his spoken English into Japanese. This act did not serve a practical function beyond the few characters that were written; instead, it served a larger symbolic function by creating a cultural connection between Branford and the audience. Branford explained, "When I *write* in Chinese [they say] this guy is smart or this guy relates to me . . . [so] although I don't do the spoken language well . . . I can do the written and . . . it just closes the cultural gap." All three participants said this ability was a key reason Branford was able to build rapport quickly, which they believed made the audience much more willing to accept and value what he said in his training presentation.

Significantly, participants were aware that cultural expectations influenced how they could use the language rhetorically. With regard to the above example, the participants noted that Branford's use of spoken Japanese would not be perceived in the same positive way. His lack of spoken Japanese fluency, combined with cultural expectations about his appearance, would make such a strategy counterproductive. The participants explained that although Branford is Chinese-American, many audience members in Japan think he looks Japanese or at least familiar, often commenting, "He looks like my uncle." This perception puts limits on Branford's use of spoken Japanese. Okito explained, "If you're a foreigner that speaks Japanese, that'd be awesome; but in Branford's case . . . if he spoke Japanese people would feel like, 'Oh he talks real bad.'" He added, "But because he's talking in English, people perceive, 'Oh that's right, he's American.'" The research participants believed that Branford had a certain ethos as a Western foreigner (Yamada, 1997) and that for this reason the audience was more attentive to his ideas.

From this perspective, then, writing Chinese characters allowed Branford to be simultaneously foreign and familiar: "He's from abroad, yes, but you know there's a connection there, something strong, some of it words," Okito said. "They always thought he was American—Chinese-American, yes—but when he writes [the *kanji*], it goes to a different dimension you see." Thus, three rhetorical strands worked together: (1) physical appearance, which marked Branford as familiar; (2) spoken language in English, which marked him as foreign; and 3) competency with written language, which invented a unique identity for him as both foreign and familiar. According to Okito, this identity created a rhetorically transformative power: "Before Branford wrote the Chinese characters, when he said something, some people might have got offended. The same person after he wrote that might say, 'Maybe it's me that's not thinking hard enough . . . Let me pause a little bit and try to see what he's trying to say.'"

This illustrative example is just one of many in the case study wherein the participants used linguistic competence as a rhetorical strategy within a particular context. Implications of these findings for technical communicators include the following:

• Linguistic competence can have great rhetorical value for international trainers who wish to build ethos with their audiences.
• The value of *limited* linguistic competence to build rapport should not be ignored or underestimated.
• To realize the rhetorical benefits from using linguistic competence, trainers must be aware of cultural expectations that constrain or enable their use of the language.

These findings and related implications are just a new iteration of social-rhetorical theories widely accepted in the field of technical communication, now in an international training context. For example, Berlin's (1987) social-epistemic theory of rhetoric asserts that communities are built around language peculiar to themselves, and membership in a group is determined by the ability to use language competently (pp. 166-167).

Most technical communicators would likely agree with this statement and reject the notion that rhetoric is merely a device for transferring information cleanly. However, gaining foreign-language competence can be such a daunting task that technical communicators may focus only on the practice of "getting it right," or, alternatively, not attempt to learn or speak a foreign language at all. They may overlook the *rhetorical* value of speaking a language, including opportunities to build rapport through limited linguistic competence. Not recognizing these opportunities, they may also fail to consider cultural expectations that shape the way they are perceived as speakers of a language, either constraining or enabling certain kinds of language use.

Translation Competence

I expected translation to be an important area of competence for the Japanese-speaking team members because they do most of the written translation as well as the real-time, oral interpretation of the training presentation. (In this chapter, I use "translation" as a default term for both written translation and oral interpretation.) However, the whole process of translation turned out to be much more rhetorically-grounded and collaborative than I had imagined and required each member of the team, whether translator or translatee, to be competent. I found that the quality and efficiency of the team's translation was enhanced by

1. team member-translators (Okito and Emi) who were familiar with the context and audience of the training presentation,
2. the long-term relationship between translator and translatee,
3. a team member, Okito, who was bicultural in addition to being bilingual, and
4. team members who were able to collaborate in both the "big picture" process and the technical aspects of translation and interpretation.

First, a key to Okito's and Emi's effectiveness as translators was their familiarity with the context of the training—including the industry, company, and products—a familiarity the participants stressed had developed over a period of five years. In addition to allowing for a more precise, contextually-based vocabulary to develop, participants said this grounding was necessary to understand the overall direction and purpose of the training.

At the team's beginning, Branford, who had been a professional trainer for about twenty years and was already familiar with the company and products, presented the training content, and Okito and Emi acted primarily as on-the-spot, rote interpreters. Over time, these roles shifted, as the participants explained in a group interview:

BRANFORD: Now remember, they [Okito and Emi] didn't know what they were doing [at the beginning], so they were hearing a lot of the stuff for the first time.

OKITO: Yeah, that's true.

BRANFORD: So we just went to Japan and went at it slowly. Between what we did there and what we did here [in Hawaii], they started to understand all of the training. That was a big breakthrough because they could anticipate the direction that we were going in and knew the information.

Second, over the period of five years, the three team members also built a relationship with one another. A recurring theme in my conversations with the participants was the distinction between being able to "translate words" and being able to interpret thoughts, feelings, ideas, and intent. Okito explained, "Giving them a translation of what Branford says is not enough. You've got to become Branford."

At the time I observed the team, Emi and Okito had become active contributors throughout the creation and delivery of training. Because of the integration of their roles as translators and trainers, they could represent not only the message but the messenger; indeed, they were messengers themselves. The familiarity they had developed with the training content and audience allowed them to collaborate fully and actively not only on translation, but also on content invention and delivery.

Hoft (1995) recognizes the importance of a translator's familiarity with both context and collaborators, noting that "many companies now invest in training translators, even if the translators work for a translation company" (p. 195). The purpose of this training is usually to introduce translators to the project team and help them learn about the products. In the case study, Okito and Emi were already part of the project team, so they had gained a built-in, on-the-job familiarity with each other and with the training content and context.

A third important factor was something that all three participants noted: having Okito as a bicultural member of the team greatly increased the quality of translation. Emi, who was uniquely qualified to evaluate this ability because she had previously operated her own translation company, said Okito was an excellent translator because, in addition to speaking both languages, "he knows both cultures [and] both mentalities," and so was able to translate words with full comprehension of cultural context. Branford added, "I could be a terrific Japanese speaker, but unless I know Japanese culture I'm not going to be effective. That's why the key is someone like Okito if you're working in a foreign market."

As an expert on both the company and cultural contexts, Okito was able to take an informed, rhetorical approach to translation. While much of the translation of training content such as PowerPoint slides was, in Okito's words, "just straight translation," some phrases were modified to fit the cultural values of the audience. For example, at one point in the English version of the training, the presenters talk about focus and why it is necessary for success in sales. Okito explained that he and Emi had instead chosen to use a Japanese phrase that, translated directly, means "drench head," with a connotation of being deeply devoted and immersed. In English, such a phrase might be seen as too strong. However, Okito and Emi believed this emphasis would be appropriately received by the audience members in Japan. Similar kinds of adaptations were made in other parts of the presentation.

A fourth factor in effective translation was that, in addition to having contextual familiarity and cultural fluency, team members collaborated with one another and with outsiders on translation. Okito and Emi often consulted with each other and with other Japanese speakers to get a consensus opinion on the best translation for the slides. Branford also used subtle but essential competencies as a translatee, including technical aspects of working with interpreters, such as adequate pausing, as well as understanding the overall process of translation and how he fit into it.

These findings should not be surprising to technical communicators trained in rhetoric. If language and rhetoric are social, then translation is not merely a mechanical or informational process but a social, rhetorical process connected to social and cultural values (Byram, 1997). Yet, as technical communicators, we may forget our own foundations when approaching translation in international training. We may harbor concepts of literal translation rather than valuing appropriateness or the overall process of translation (Flint, Van Slyke, Starke-Meyerring, & Thompson, 1999; Hoft, 1995; Walmer, 1999). As with the writing process, translation of international training content often requires the observance of certain prescribed conventions as well as a much broader negotiation of social and cultural expectations and values to create shared knowledge (Walmer, 1999; Flint, Van Slyke, Starke-Meyerring, & Thompson, 1999).

Technical communicators will have an advantage in international training contexts if they approach translation not just as a mechanical process but as a *rhetorical* process, complete with audience, author, and message, all filtered through cultural values and expectations (Bazerman, 2004; Cross, 2001; Winsor, 2003). In fact, the rhetorical dimension of written, oral, and written-oral hybrid professional communication may become even more apparent to international trainers as they are forced to choose a translation strategy (Hoft, 1995), build relationships with translators (Walmer, 1999), and view their own expectations and values about communication in light of other cultures (Connor, 1996; Thatcher, 2000).

Intercultural Communication Competence

Intercultural communication competence is the ability to negotiate divergent cultural values and their corresponding influences on communication (Byram,

1997; Hampden-Turner & Trompenaars, 2001). Participants used intercultural communication competence in two ways: adapting the training seminar to fit the cultural values and expectations of the Japanese's audience and managing the context surrounding the training seminar.

To evaluate the participants' rhetorical adaptation of the seminar, I compared the texts of two training presentations the participants made: one a presentation in Hawaii for a mixed audience of Americans and Japanese in both English and Japanese, and one in Japan for a Japanese audience only. I found that the participants made two main rhetorical adaptations between the presentations: first, they used more detail in the Japanese version; and second, they used graphics more heavily in the Japanese version.

I had expected the texts of the PowerPoint presentations to differ according to the theory of contrastive rhetoric (Connor, 1996; Kaplan, 1966, 1987), in which arrangement would cater to the language and cultural background of the audience. For the Japanese audience, I expected a more delayed introduction of purpose, or quasi-inductive arrangement (Hinds, 1990) than for the hybrid audience. However, I was surprised to find that the arrangement of both presentations was quite similar. The major difference was that the Japanese seminar contained more information on sales strategies (16 slides versus only 12 slides for the hybrid presentation) and a ten-minute role-play sales demonstration in Japan versus none in Hawaii. When asked why, the participants responded that Japanese audience members generally want more detail than Americans, who are often content with a broad overview (Yamada, 1997).

The use of graphics was also heavier in the Japan seminar, although information in both seminars was depicted visually, with several slides using stand-alone graphics, including cartoons, to illustrate the presenters' points. One indicator of the difference in use of graphics was that the Japanese presentation had ten graphics-only slides while the hybrid seminar had just five. When asked about this difference, Okito and Emi said they were catering to the Japanese preference for visual over written information (Kohl, Barclay, Pinelli, Keene, & Kennedy, 1993; Yamada, 1997). They added that graphics tend to lighten the mood of the presentation in Japan, which might become too serious otherwise: "We try to insert some [graphics] in to make it not so intense but understandable." Participants were aware of these differing audience expectations about the text and responded accordingly.

Perhaps more importantly, the participants used an intercultural approach to manage the context surrounding the training seminar. They were highly sensitive to what Hall (1976) defines as high-context communication, or communication that comes primarily through the *context* of a message rather than the content. For example, all of the Japan meetings included a dinner or banquet afterwards, which the participants said was standard practice for the team there but not in the United States. The participants said these functions were more important than the training seminar itself because in an informal setting, audience members could ask questions or raise concerns that they would be reluctant to mention in the meetings (Hall, 1990; Yamada, 1997). Okito said the tendency of Japanese audience members to ask questions only in an informal setting stemmed either from the concern that they might lose face by asking an unintelligent question in front of everyone or that they might make the presenter lose face by asking a question he or she couldn't answer. The fact that the training team planned and sponsored a social event after the training session was an unspoken message that they were personally committed to helping the audience members become better salespeople.

Beyond the expertise required to recognize the importance of social events, the posttraining banquets and dinners were themselves infused with nonverbal communication, requiring cultural expertise on the part of the team members. For example, it was important that people be seated in their proper places at the table; this nonverbal cue, defined according to a culturally defined hierarchy, maintained the cohesion of the group and helped everyone feel there was a proper place for them, both at the table and in the organization (Hall, 1990; Yamada, 1997). The Japanese team members were able to navigate these kinds of cultural protocols seemingly without effort. The American team member was also able to negotiate these events, an ability the research participants said he had gained through experience and by seeking feedback from others, particularly his teammates. Overall, team members adapted not only the content and delivery of the presentation for their Japanese audience, but also took an intercultural approach to the surrounding events, treating the entire training effort as an integrated whole.

Implications of these findings for technical communicators include the following:

- In international training, communicative expertise cannot be limited to just speaking or writing (Spilka, 1993; Thatcher, 1999). Trainers must recognize what Hall (1976) calls "the total communication framework," which includes "words, actions, postures, gestures, tones of voice, facial expressions, the way [a person] handles time, space, and materials, and the way he works, plays, makes love, and defends himself." As Hall explains, "All these things and more are complete communication systems with meanings that can be read correctly only if one is familiar with the behavior in its historical, social, and cultural context" (p. 42).
- Because of the complexity of intercultural communication, extensive personal and team preparation is essential (Hoft, 1995). International trainers can't assume that international audiences will respond in the same way as domestic audiences. As a first step, they might develop "localization cookbooks," which provide "cultural, linguistic, technical, marketing, sales, training, and legal information about a specific target country and the users

who live and work there" (Hoft, 1995). Even more important, international trainers should not overlook the necessity of building strong relationships with cultural insiders who can help them adapt to situational nuances.

To meet these new challenges, technical communicators can work to gain expertise through study or international internships. At the same time, they should not forget that they can compensate for competency gaps by collaborating with others, an ability that is discussed in the next section.

Collaborative Competence

Collaborative competence refers to the ability of individuals to adapt to new environments in collaboration with team members. In the case study, if team members could collaborate with one another, it wasn't necessary for each individual to have all of the competencies necessary. However, this collaboration did require the participants to have two main abilities: giving and receiving feedback along with recognizing and using individual competencies to compensate for gaps in team members' abilities.

With regard to the first ability, feedback was given both by team members and by outside associates. During team meetings, Okito and Emi gave feedback on what would be culturally appropriate. For example, Branford wanted the audience of salespeople to fill out a worksheet on financial goals, but Okito and Emi were skittish about it:

> BRANFORD: I got a work sheet for them where they can actually be involved.
> OKITO: Do you have that worksheet [with you]?
> BRANFORD: Um, I didn't bring it with me. I was just gonna, you know, savings you know, federal retirement, what you need to retire, and . . . take 'em through each of the steps.
> OKITO & EMI: [speaking to each other in Japanese]
> OKITO: Yeah we can't let it because that won't be appropriate.

Okito later explained that their concern was based on Japanese cultural values: that asking people to write down information involving personal finances in a meeting, especially if they thought they would have to show their goals to a supervisor, might cause them to lose face. Branford still wanted to include the sheet in the meeting, reasoning, "You need to get them somehow thinking about it. If they don't think about it they don't do something." He added that the sheet wouldn't have to be completed at the meeting but could be taken home. The team resolved the dilemma by passing out the worksheet in the meeting and making it clear that if the audience members wanted to, they could take it home and set voluntary goals. Audience members also had the option of showing their goals to a supervisor but did not have to.

Similar reconciliations between cultural values were made in other planning meetings. Branford explained, "I understand [some things], but there are other things that are very hard for me to understand, so sometimes [Emi and Okito] spend hours trying to help me understand. If you understand the situation then you can correct [your errors.]" At the same time, participants recognized the value of an outside perspective. Okito said, "Sometimes the unusual happens too. Sometimes we talk to Branford, we might take an hour or so, [and] Branford will come up with this totally western version of what a Japanese might be able to do, which becomes very good because it's a new idea."

Team members also sought feedback from associates in Japan, both before and after the training. Getting this feedback required intercultural expertise beyond the ability to speak Japanese. Okito and Emi stated that because they were geographically separated from their Japanese associates, they often had to encourage the use of e-mail for questions or concerns. In Japan, the more important the communication is, the more likely it will be face-to-face (Yamada, 1997). Thus, there is often a tendency to put off discussion until a face-to-face meeting can be arranged. Since the training team traveled to Japan only three or four times a year, a face-to-face meeting might not happen for months. Not only would it be more difficult to resolve questions and concerns at such infrequent intervals, but it would be difficult to create training that met real needs. As Emi noted, "To know the feedback from people after the training is very important, sometimes more important than the training."

Thus, a subtle but vital part of the training for Okito and Emi was encouraging Japanese associates to use remote communications technology in ways they were not accustomed to. In so doing, the participants emphasized the long-term nature of their relationship with associates in Japan. Over time, trust had become strong enough to support more remote communication, and associates felt comfortable sharing questions and concerns through phone or e-mail rather than reserving them for face-to-face communication. As with translation competence, giving and receiving useful feedback both within and outside the team was enhanced by long-term relationships.

A second important collaborative ability was using one's individual competencies to compensate for gaps in team members' competencies, and allowing them to do the same. This chapter has already reviewed how team members combined their individual competencies in the areas of linguistic and translation competence. In another example, team members collaborated to reconcile culturally defined expectations about age and gender. Referring to himself and Emi, Okito noted, "Certain things we cannot say that Branford can say," and cited an example: "I cannot tell a guy in his sixties, 'You'd better prepare [for] retirement.'" Such a statement would be offensive coming from a man in his late thirties or early forties, given the Japanese cultural value of respect for elders (Yamada, 1997). Okito added that "certain directions have more weight" when coming from someone with "higher seniority and more status," which in Japan is often defined by age (Yamada, 1997). He noted, "In some cases we repeat it too. Certain people—younger people—might relate more to us, middle-aged people might relate to Branford and us, but the older generation might only respect what Branford says."

Another important collaboration between team members involved gender roles. Traditional Japanese gender roles limit how women are able to act in relation to men in the business world (Hall, 1990; Yamada, 1997). However, this limitation also poses a barrier to men who are in positions of authority; women are less likely to voice opinions or concerns (Hall, 1990; Yamada, 1997). Because over half of the salespeople in the organization were women, Emi's role as listener and confidant was important. It was to her that much of the feedback from female personnel was directed. Emi met with female salespeople individually and, during group events, prepared the way for more open interaction between the male training team members and female salespeople.

These examples illustrate how the team acted as an integrated whole, requiring each member to recognize strengths and weaknesses and rely on others' unique abilities. In this way, the team could accomplish things none of the participants could do alone. Each had to be willing to draw upon and contribute strengths throughout the process (Larson & LaFasto, 2001). Participants were careful to note that building their relationship as a team was at least as important as developing the content of the training. On several occasions team members reminded me that they had been working with each other and some of their associates in Japan for five years. They saw this process and the training itself as a long adaptation—an evolving, "living thing." Team members needed to be familiar with the way each other thought, especially since Okito and Emi would be interpreting Branford's portion of the seminar. They emphasized that developing such a connection took time and often happened in indirect ways.

Implications for international trainers include the following:

- Collaborative competence is important in any team situation, but in an intercultural context requires an even stronger and more long-term collaboration among team members.
- Giving and receiving feedback is key to successful intercultural collaboration.
- Cultural outsiders need to rely on teammates for cultural expertise; at the same time, outsiders may add a valuable perspective to the team.
- Intercultural collaboration abilities are required for collaboration with diverse team members and outside associates. International trainers can adapt to the cultural expectations of others; they can also help others reconcile their cultural values and expectations with the demands of the situation (Hampden-Turner & Trompenaars, 2004). As the e-mail example demonstrates, intercultural collaboration is intercultural for all collaborators, not just for the "sojourner" (Byram, 1997).

While collaboration has long been recognized as vital to successful technical communication projects (Dicks, 2004; Hackos, 1994), technical communicators must be flexible about what collaboration means in different international training contexts. As cultural expectations vary, so does the cultural expression of collaboration. Hierarchy versus egalitarianism, high- versus low-context communication, individualism versus collectivism, and gender roles are all areas where cultural expectations about collaboration might diverge (Hall, 1976; Hofstede, 1996; Hampden-Turner & Trompenaars, 2004). By integrating intercultural communication competence and collaborative competence, technical communicators can work successfully with training-team members and audiences from diverse cultural backgrounds.

Adaptive Competence

Implicit in the four areas of competence reviewed above is an ability that can be added as an umbrella competence: adaptation. Also called fundamental competence (Spitzberg & Cupach, 1984), adaptive competence is the ability to adapt in order to meet changing conditions. In sum, it is "knowing what you don't know" and how to get it. International training-team members must be able to recognize what skills and knowledge are needed, discover ways to obtain them, decide when to collaborate, assess the success of their communication strategies, and adjust accordingly.

Technical communicators often approach problems in terms of adaptation (audience analysis and usability testing being two examples of this tendency) and can apply these abilities to international training situations. However, adaptation that is useful in a domestic context may find different expression in an intercultural context, requiring a different approach than technical communicators might be used to. Cultures may have differing views of such basic concepts as time, leadership, collaboration, and communication, requiring an openness to new learning and ways of doing things (Hoft, 1995). Ways for technical communicators to gain perspective on adaptation may include foreign language learning (Byram, 1997), international internships (Smith, 2003), and classroom instruction with international interaction and an intercultural focus (Connor, Davis, De Rycker, Philips, & Verkens, 1997; Sapp, 2004), including project management, planning, collaboration, and rhetoric.

CONCLUSION

International training holds promise for technical communicators who want to stay competitive in the outsourcing environment. As Faber and Johnson-Eilola (2002) argue, "If technical communicators hope to influence their (or another) company's strategic missions, they must leverage their knowledge and skills to add value to the company through new knowledge which, in turn, creates new revenue-generating products or processes" (p. 142). Customized international training is one such process that adds value when integrated with other technical communication products.

Full competence in all areas is not always necessary for success in international training as long as team members can adapt and collaborate with others who are competent in these areas, including team members with different linguistic and cultural backgrounds. By developing the necessary linguistic, translation, inter-cultural communication, collaboration, and adaptive competencies, technical communicators can leverage their knowledge and skills as members of inter-national training teams. These abilities will position technical communicators to find new applications for their abilities and add value to global projects and organizations.

REFERENCES

Armstrong, A. (2002). Applying instructional design principles and adult learning theory in the development of training for business and industry. In P. Rogers (Ed.), *Designing instruction for technology-enhanced learning* (pp. 209-227). Hershey, PA: Idea Group Publishing.

Bazerman, C. (2004). Speech acts, genres, and activity systems. In C. Bazerman & M. Prior (Eds.), *What writing does and how it does it* (pp. 309-339). Mahwah, NJ: Erlbaum.

Berlin, J. A. (1987). *Rhetoric and reality: Writing instruction in American colleges, 1900-1985*. Urbana, IL: CCCC.

Bridges, B., Baily, M., Hiatt, M., Timmerman, D., & Gibson, S. (2002). A blended technologies learning community: From theory to practice. In P. Rogers (Ed.), *Designing instruction for technology-enhanced learning* (pp. 209-227). Hershey, PA: Idea Group Publishing.

Burba, F. J., Petrosko, J. M., & Boyle, M. A. (2001). Appropriate and inappropriate instructional behaviors for international training. *Human Resource Development Quarterly, 12*, 267-283.

Buckman, R. H. (2004). *Building a knowledge-driven organization*. New York: McGraw-Hill.

Byram, M. (1997). *Teaching and assessing intercultural competence*. Cambridge, UK: Multilingual Matters.

Carliner, S. (2001). Emerging skills in technical communication: The information designer's place in a new career path for technical communicators. *Technical Communication, 48*(2), 156-175.

Chen, G.-M. (1989). Relationships of dimensions of intercultural communication competence. *Communication Quarterly, 37*, 118-133.

Chen, G.-M., & Starosta, W. J. (1996). Intercultural communication competence: A synthesis. *Communication Yearbook, 19*, 353-383.

Connor, U. (1996). *Contrastive rhetoric: Cross-cultural aspects of second-language writing*. Cambridge, UK: Cambridge University Press.

Connor, U., Davis, K. W., De Rycker, T., Philips, E. M., & Verkens, J. P. (1997). An international course in international business writing: Belgium, Finland, and the United States. *Business Communication Quarterly, 60*(4), 63-74.

Cross, G. A. (2001). *Forming the collective mind: A contextual exploration of large-scale collaborative writing in industry*. Creeskill, NJ: Hampton Press.

Dicks, R. S. (2004). *Management principles and practices for technical communicators*. New York: Pearson.

Earley, P. C., & Gibson, C. B. (2002). *Multinational work teams*. Mahwah, NJ: Erlbaum.

Faber, B., & Johnson-Eilola, J. (2002). Migrations. Strategic thinking about the future(s) of technical communication. In B. Mirel & R. Spilka (Eds.), *Reshaping technical communication: New directions and challenges for the 21st century* (pp. 135-148). Mahwah, NJ: Lawrence Erlbaum.

Flick, U. (2002). *An introduction to qualitative research*. London: Sage.

Flint, P., Van Slyke, M. L., Starke-Meyerring, D., & Thompson, A. (1999). Going online: Helping technical communicators help translators. *Technical Communication, 46*, 238-248.

Hackos, J. (1994). *Managing your documentation projects*. New York: Wiley.

Hall, E. T. (1976). *Beyond culture*. Garden City, NY: Anchor.

Hall, M. (1990). *Hidden differences: Doing business with the Japanese*. Garden City, NY: Anchor.

Hampden-Turner, C., & Trompenaars, A. (2001). *Building cross-cultural competence*. New York: John Wiley and Sons.

Hampden-Turner, C., & Trompenaars, A. (2004). *Managing people across cultures*. West Sussex, UK: Capstone.

Hart-Davidson, W. (2001). On writing, technical communication, and information technology: The core competencies of technical communication. *Technical Communication, 48*, 145-155.

Hinds, J. (1990). Inductive, deductive, quasi-inductive: expository writing in Japanese, Korean, Chinese and Thai. In U. Connor & A. Johns (Eds.), *Coherence in writing: Research and pedagogical perspectives* (pp. 91-110). Alexandria, VA: TESOL.

Hoft, N. (1995). *International technical communication: How to export information about high technology*. New York: Wiley.

Hofstede, G. (1996). *Cultures and organizations: Software of the mind*. New York: McGraw-Hill.

Huang, Z. (1996). Making training friendly to other cultures. *Training and Development, 50*(9), 13-14.

Iles, P., & Hayers, P. (1997). Managing diversity in transnational project teams: A tentative model and case study. *Journal of Managerial Psychology, 12*(2): 95-117.

Kalakota, R., & Robinson, M. (2004, February 27). Offshore outsourcing: Will your job disappear in 2004? *Addison Wesley*. Retrieved Oct 28, 2004 from the World Wide Web: http://www.awprofessional.com/articles/article.asp?p=169548.

Kaplan, R. B. (1987). Cultural thought patterns revisited. In U. Connor & R. B. Kaplan (Eds.), *Writing across languages: Analysis of L2 text*. Reading, MA: Addison-Wesley.

Kaplan, R. B. (1966). Cultural thought patterns in intercultural education. *Language Learning, 16*, 1-20.

Kohl, J., Barclay, R., Pinelli, T., Keene, M., & Kennedy, J. (1993). The impact of language and culture on technical communication in Japan. *Technical Communication, 40*, 62-73.

LaFasto, F., & Larson, C. (2001). *When teams work best*. Thousand Oaks, CA: Sage.

Lazear, E. P. (1998). Globalization and the market for teammates. *Working Paper Series: National Bureau of Economic Research*. Cambridge, MA: NBER.

Lucia, A. D., & Lepsinger, R. (1999). *The art and science of competency models: Pinpointing critical success factors in organizations*. San Francisco: Pfeiffer.

MacKinnon, J. (1993). Becoming a rhetor: Developing writing ability in a mature, writing-intensive organization. In R. Spilka (Ed.), *Writing in the workplace: New research perspectives*. Carbondale, IL: Southern Illinois University Press.

Marquardt, M. (1995, May). How to globalize your training. INFO-LINE. Alexandria, VA: ASTD.

McDermott, L., Waite, B., & Brawley, N. (1999). Putting together a world-class team. *Training & Development, 53*(1), 46

Miles, M., & Huberman, M. (1994). *Qualitative data analysis: An expanded sourcebook*. Thousand Oaks: Sage Publications.

Mirel, B., & Spilka, R. (2002). Introduction. In B. Mirel & R. Spilka (Eds.), *Reshaping technical communication: New directions and challenges for the 21st century*. Mahwah, NJ: Lawrence Erlbaum.

Olebe, M., & Koester, J. (1989). Exploring the cross-cultural equivalence of the behavioural assessment scale for intercultural communication. *International Journal of Intercultural Relations, 13*, 333-347.

Prahalad, C. K. (1997). The work of the new age managers in the emerging competitive landscape. In F. Hesselbein, M. Goldsmith, & R. Beckhard (Eds.), *The organization of the future*. San Francisco, CA: Jossey-Bass.

Rainey, K., Turner, R., & Dayton, D. (2004). *Report of a survey of managers about core competencies*. Presented at the annual meeting of The Council for Programs in Technical and Scientific Communication, West Lafayette, IN, October 7, 2004. Retrieved from http://www.english.vt.edu/~dubinsky/CPTSC_04/program_links.htm.

Reich, R. B. (2001). *The future of success*. New York: Knopf.

Ruben, B. D. (1976). Assessing communication competency for intercultural adaptation. *Group and Organization Studies, 2,* 470-479.

Ruben, B. D., & Kealey, D. J. (1979). Behavioral assessment of communication competency and the prediction of cross-cultural adaptation. *International Journal of Intercultural Relations, 3*, 15-47.

Sapp, D. A. (2004). Global partnerships in business communication: An institutional collaboration between the United States and Cuba. *Business Communication Quarterly, 67*, 267-280.

Smith, H. J. (2003). German academic programs in technical communication. *Journal of Technical Writing & Communication, 33*, 349-363

Spencer, L. M., & Spencer, S. M. (1993). *Competence at work: Models for superior performance*. New York: Wiley.

Spilka, R. (1993). Moving between oral and written discourse to fulfill rhetorical and social goals. In R. Spilka (Ed.), *Writing in the workplace: New research perspectives*. Carbondale, IL: Southern Illinois University Press.

Spitzberg, B. H., & Cupach, W. R. (1984) *Interpersonal communication competence*. Beverly Hills, CA: Sage.

Thatcher, B. (2000). Writing policies and procedures in a U.S. and South American context. *Technical Communication Quarterly, 94*, 365-400.

Thatcher, B. (1999). Cultural and rhetorical adaptations for South American audiences. *Technical Communication*, *46*, 177-195.

Thornhill, A. R. (1993). Management training across cultures: The challenge for trainers. *Journal of European Industrial Training*, *17*(10), 43-51.

Walmer, D. (1999). One company's efforts to improve translation and localization. *Technical Communication*, *46*, 230-237.

Whiteside, A. L. (2003). The skills that technical communicators need: An investigation of technical communication graduates, managers, and curricula. *Journal of Technical Writing and Communication*, *33*, 303-318.

Winsor, D. A. (1996). *Writing like an engineer: A rhetorical education*. Mahwah, NJ: Lawrence Erlbaum.

Winsor, D. A. (2003). *Writing power: Communication in an engineering center*. Ithaca, NY: SUNY Press.

Yamada, H. (1997). *Different games, different rules: Why Americans and Japanese misunderstand each other*. Oxford, UK: Oxford University Press.

Yuan, R. (1997). Yin/yang principle and the relevance of externalism and paralogic rhetoric to intercultural communication. *Journal of Business & Technical Communication*, *11*, 297-320.

Yin, R. (1994). *Case study research: Design and methods*. Thousand Oaks, CA: Sage.

CHAPTER 8

The Implications of Outsourcing for Technical Editing

Clinton R. Lanier

Technical editing is an important part of technical communication and perhaps even more important for the outsourcing environment. With regard to technical communication in general, it is an essential element in the creation and delivery of information units, such as documents, Web pages, and help files. Rather than being responsible for developing the information in the documents, technical editors serve as designers of the information and of the information units themselves (Rude, 2003). Within this broad position, editors have such roles as basic copyeditor, document coordinator, or overseer of the information within the document, including "the focus, organization, depth of coverage, language and supporting material" (Turpin & Bronson, 1997, p. 222). Rude calls this type of editing "comprehensive" (p. 13).

Functionally, Rude (2003) describes the technical editor as having two primary duties, that of "link[ing] between writing and publishing" and that of making the text "complete, accurate, comprehensible, and usable" (p. 12). In each it is clear that the responsibility of the technical editor in a documentation project is both important and substantive. Although the writer investigates and documents the content of the information unit itself, that writer depends on the technical editor for expertise in the standards and conventions defined by the publishing organization and for the user's needs and goals.

Because of the value of their duties, technical editors may become even more important than they were in the past. As companies increasingly choose to outsource their technical-publication tasks, editors may be needed to bridge a gap between an organization and the outsourced writers creating the organization's documents. They may become so important, in fact, that in the summary of a roundtable discussion about offshoring technical writing, it was suggested that "technical writers should retrain into editors" (Ramos & O'Maley, 2003). The roundtable participants made this suggestion because they foresaw a growing reliance on a group of documentation experts who locally managed projects to be completed by an outsourced group of writers working offshore.

In one scenario that was discussed, the local documentation experts included, among others, editors who checked the "completion, quality, accuracy, (and) style compliance" of the products being written offshore (Ramos & O'Maley, 2003). This documentation project relied on technical editors to bridge the gap between the organization and the outsourced writers. These editors became quality-assurance experts in the documentation project, using their skills to ensure that the documents received from offshore writers measured up to the quality demanded by the organization.

Though, as the roundtable suggests, technical editing may see a progressively greater demand because of offshoring (Ramos & O'Maley, 2003), there has been no literature attending to how the profession may be impacted by outsourcing in general. This is an important subject, especially if technical writers are expected to retrain to technical editing: they should know what to expect with this transition. What implications does outsourcing hold for a technical editor? What new skills (if any) should a technical editor have when working in an outsourced environment? How is the relationship different between editor and writer due to outsourcing?

In an attempt to answer the above questions, this chapter reports on the issues raised in a focus-group discussion with professional technical editors. These issues reflect the ways in which the traditional tasks, roles, and responsibilities of the technical editor will evolve due to outsourcing. The specific points raised by these editors inform new considerations and implications that outsourcing will have for technical editing.

FOCUS-GROUP DISCUSSION

To gain information about some of the principal issues, and attempt to answer the above questions concerning technical editing and outsourcing, I formed a virtual focus group to discuss broad issues of technical editing in general (such as collaboration with writers or the technology used) and asked participants to ground their responses on outsourcing specifically. I chose to use a focus group because research has shown that they are more flexible than surveys and can provide a greater amount of information when used to explore a topic (Flick, 1998; MacNealy, 1999).

Rather than simply answering a question, focus-group participants use the group itself to shape the conversation in ways that clarify, specify, and stimulate further responses. Therefore, unlike one-on-one interviews, focus groups allow participants to interact with each other in order to elicit even more information. Focus groups have commonly been used in marketing and usability research, but have also been used in exploratory research in technical communication to establish considerations in new fields (see, for example, Farkas, 1987). The primary goal in using a focus group is to gain issues for further research or to further explore known issues through the content of the discussions.

In my particular case, I chose to use e-mail to conduct the focus-group discussion. Using e-mail as a tool for facilitating interviewing, rather than face-to-face meetings, has been found to have some very significant advantages, such as creating a sense of safety that may make a participant more willing to answer questions. After studying the use of group discussions utilizing electronic technologies such as e-mail, Tse (1999) concluded that there was "an increased level of participation and interaction among participants in an online focus-group-discussion environment, which subsequently leads to a higher level of openness on the part of participants, and a higher level of satisfaction with the group discussion experience" (p. 410).

Sproull and Kiesler (1991) agree with Tse and indicate that because of the use of e-mail in group discussions, there is increased decision making, a higher likelihood of participants responding, and a lessened chance of a discussion being dominated by only one or a few individuals. In my case, and also pointed out by Sproull and Kiesler, an e-mail discussion was further desirable due to the physical separation between participants.

Those included in the electronic focus group were respondents to my request for participants posted to the e-mail discussion list of the Technical Editing Special Interest Group of the Society for Technical Communication. There were five professional technical editors who chose to participate in the focus group. The editors who participated were each familiar with technical communication projects that had been outsourced, and were either currently working or had in the past worked with outsourced writers. Three of the editors were collaborating with writers who worked outside of the United States and Canada, and two of those consistently worked with non-native English (L2) writers. At the time of the focus group three of the editors worked as in-house editors for high-tech organizations, and two were outsourced technical editors. Following is a list of the technical editors who participated (whose names were changed to assure anonymity) and brief demographic information:

- John: An outsourced technical editor from Canada who currently resides and works in Europe. He has over ten years of experience as a freelance writer and editor and has worked both locally and at a distance with writers and editors. With the exception of one writer, John is presently collaborating with native English-speaking writers.

- Brad: An in-house technical editor from the United States who currently resides and works in the United States, but is working for a high-tech firm located in Israel. He has worked as an in-house technical writer and editor as well as freelance writer and editor for over twenty years. Brad is editing documents prepared by L2 writers.
- Janet: An in-house technical editor who works for a high-tech firm that is located in the United States, and contracts out technical writing. Janet has been a professional technical writer and editor for nearly twenty years. She is currently editing for writers who speak English natively and who were physically located close to her firm.
- Liz: An outsourced technical editor working and residing in Canada. Liz has been working as technical editor in the aerospace industry for ten years and has worked with both in-house and outsourced writers. She has edited for both native English and L2 writers when editing for a large international aircraft manufacturer.
- Donna: An in-house technical editor for a high-tech firm that has outsourced their writing department to India within the last two years. Donna has over seven years experience as a technical editor and over twenty years as a technical communicator. She is currently editing documents written by L2 writers.

The discussion lasted five days. On each day, I sent a discussion prompt and asked the participants to respond to the prompt and to reply to everyone when doing so. Table 1 summarizes the prompt that was sent for each day.

Respondents were free to reply whenever they chose and could respond to the prompt or to an issue raised by another participant. Throughout the day, I would send follow-up or clarification questions to elicit further information from each of the respondents.

The rest of this chapter focuses on the issues raised by the participants and on additional research conducted—post-focus group—into each of these issues. The issues that the participants raised fell into three broad categories. The first considers the tools that the participants felt would be important to editors in an outsourced environment. The second deals with the many collaborative factors that an editor should be aware of, and the last category focuses on the issues of culture that were raised.

TOOLS, SKILL SETS, AND TECHNOLOGIES

The focus group participants pointed to three main themes when discussing what tools, skill sets or technologies may be important to editors in an outsourced environment. These skill sets or tools included style guides, the insider's knowledge held by an editor, and electronic editing tools.

Table 1. Summaries for Each Prompt That was Sent
to Start a Day's Discussion

	Summary of discussion prompt
Day 1	What is the role of the editor when working with outsourced writers: Does it change and how? Does it stay the same?
Day 2	How might the relationship between the editor and author change due to an outsourced environment? How do editors and writers collaborate in an outsourced environment? How does an editor establish a rapport with writers in an outsourced environment (is that important)?
Day 3	What type of tools do you use to solve problems you may have encountered? How do these tools help you (if at all)? How do you normally communicate with those you collaborate with? What have you found that supports your communication needs (or have you)?
Day 4	How much editing for content do you normally do? Do you edit for technical accuracy as well as format? What type of understanding do you have with the writers about what you will edit and how?
Day 5	What impediments (if any) to collaboration might exist between you and writers in an outsourced environment? What specific obstacles have you encountered and what were some ways you have found to solve these problems?

Style Guides

Style guides were often brought up in the focus-group discussions. Janet stated that "a style guide and approved templates are a must," and that "without a style guide, I think you would be likely to have a mess." The participants specified three uses for style guides, all of which were important to them as editors. Brad noted that he formatted and edited "according to a lengthy checklist," indicating that he was concerned with his own consistency as an editor. According to literature, this is one of the traditional uses of style guides. Rude (2003), for example, writes that it is essential for an editor to have some type of reference to turn to when making decisions about elements within a document. With this reference—the checklist that Brad relies on and the style guide that Janet sees as essential—the editor can make consistent choices throughout the document's review.

From the point of view of an editor who is outsourced, however, this guide for consistency is even more important. If the organization for which the editor is working does not provide the style guide or checklist, the editor will have no way of knowing their expectations. Liz pointed to this problem when she stated that "one difficulty that can arise, however, is when the client does not have adequate guidelines (such as a house style guide, etc.)." Not only does she feel that she needs the written guidance for her own consistency, but also to agree on writing styles with writers, because "much time can be wasted going back and forth on seemingly simple [editing] issues."

Those who worked with prepared style guides in fact also used them to back up their own reviews of a writer's work. John stated that he created and updates a "style guide for the writers where I list guidelines and give the reasoning for the guideline." That way, he feels, when discussing with a writer changes that he made during a review, he "always [has] backup reasoning." Liz stated that she often needed to be able to do the same, especially when she "has to explain to newer writers that a specific style is used for client X, but client Y wants it the other way." Not having the style guide to point to lowers Liz's credibility (which she indicates by way of explaining to a fictional writer: "Really! I'm not crazy").

Further, Liz indicates in the above quote that a style guide is useful for explaining issues or conventions to "newer writers", a third possible use of style guide as indicated by literature. Magyar (1994), and Perkins and Maloney (1998) suggest that training writers could be done through a style guide, something that may be especially important for editors working with outsourced writers. As the outsourced writers begin a project, editors can relay much of how to write specific documents through their style guides. In any case, having a style guide on which to base the "rules" of a review brings consistency to the project and allows editors to justify their editorial decisions while at the same time training writers with whom they work.

Insider's Knowledge

The importance of an insider's knowledge was also stressed in the focus group. Janet suggested that having insight into the publishing organization is a resource when discussing editorial decisions with a writer. She feels confident when writers disagree with her because, as she stated, "I know the company." This insider knowledge is significant for Coggin and Porter (1993), who point out that "the editor, with a personal interest in the company's documents and a thorough understanding of the company's audience(s) and specs, focuses on the text and graphics and tries to ensure that the highest quality product possible is produced by the company" (p. 12).

As an editor reviews documents, she draws on insider's knowledge about the project, including the history of the company, the document's subject matter, or the document itself. Janet indicated that this same insight was useful when "the editor needs to earn the respect of the writers." "In my case," she said, "I have more knowledge of the company, the process, and the products we're documenting." This knowledge could be especially important when a document discusses the context of the subject matter: such as when it was created, or why it was created.

An outsourced writer will not have this "big picture" of the company—its history or context—so will not be able to call upon the implicit contextual knowledge that an insider will have. Donna pointed out that the level of knowledge the writers have about the subject matter shows in the documentation, and that this level of knowledge is a result of how long they write for an organization. The same can be said for editors. Note that both Donna and Janet are in-house editors with a history of the organization. Just as Liz suggested that a style guide is a must for an outsourced editor, so might the ability to learn about the organization be essential to gain some form of insider's knowledge. Janet points to this when she stated that "overall, I think the editor-writer relationship is easier to manage when the writers are outsourced. It makes the editor an automatic 'inside expert'."

Electronic Editing Technologies

With the exception of Janet, all of the writers used some form of electronic editing technology. Donna, Brad, and John used Microsoft Word's Track Changes and Comments features when reviewing and editing a document. Liz primarily used FrameMaker to review documents, and Janet edited hard copies of the documents. Donna, Brad, and John all agreed that the important features of an electronic editing tool included allowing them to highlight changes without changing the actual file, embed comments directly to areas in the text, and transfer the files electronically via the Internet. All of these features are important to electronic editing technologies because they facilitate faster review and transfer procedures (Dayton, 1998), allow for easier review of the edited document (Lanier, 2004), and allow collaborators to work through a document via the embedded comments (Miles, McCarthy, Dix, Harrison, & Monk, 1993).

With the above features in mind, however, Donna explicitly stated that she would "prefer performing hard copy edits," and Brad stated that in his former job he reviewed and edited printed documents. These comments confirm surveys that have shown not all editors prefer using electronic editing technologies and would rather hand edit printed documents (Dayton, 2003; Duffy, 1995; Rude & Smith, 1992). Though Brad and Donna may have preferred something else, they (as well as Alice) edited electronically because, as Donna put it, "it is so much more convenient and cost efficient to be able to provide edits in electronic form."

Janet was the only one who was still able to edit printed hard-copy documents—the method she preferred. However, Janet herself pointed out that the only reason she could do so was because of her writers' close proximity to her, which allowed them to meet frequently to discuss an edit and to exchange hard-copy versions of the document without concern for lengthy time in transit. The implication of this is that editors who prefer to edit printed versions of documents may need to become familiar with the electronic editing technologies that allow editors to more easily negotiate dimensions required by certain outsourced environments, such as long distances and short turnaround times.

COLLABORATIVE DYNAMICS

Collaboration was another broad theme that participants were concerned with. All felt, as Janet did, that "it helps to have a casual/friendly relationship with the writers." Brad agreed, saying that "developing this rapport is very important in an author-editor relationship." These opinions are not surprising, because a good collaborative relationship between an editor and a writer (regardless of whether either or any are outsourced) is essential when the two are mutually responsible for the documents being produced (Deaton, 1990; Edmands, 1988; Rude, 2003; Stocker, 1990). With this in mind, however, the participants indicated that outsourcing introduced a number of dimensions to this collaborative relationship.

Collaboration at a Distance

One problematic factor that some participants spoke at length about was the distance separating them from the writers. Specifically, as Liz stated, "the problem is that it is much more difficult to communicate over long distances." She also said that "the nuances (good and bad) of body language, tone, etc are lost in e-mail and even on the phone." In Liz's case she was editing for only one writer not located at her office. For Brad, however, who was editing for writers all located outside of the United States, the problems were more difficult: "working for developers (authors) in another hemisphere can be challenging because e-mails and occasional phone calls (which are seldom, because of time-zone differences) hinder rapport building."

Most authors agree that personal contact factors into the success of a document (Coggin & Porter, 1993; Rude, 2003), and that using, for example, the telephone or e-mail without meeting personally may prove difficult to a documentation project. Brad indicated that many of the writers with whom he works used to be located in the United States, and at the time it was easier to collaborate with them: "it was much easier to do when most of the writers for whom I edited worked here in the same building with me." Now Brad finds himself negotiating problems over long distances. He stated that "if a disagreement develops between me and a developer I've never met who is working in Israel, I'm more inclined to adopt an adversarial mindset." He also stated that meeting people face-to-face before working with them at a distance is important: "attempts at building rapport through e-mail with someone I've never met while I'm trying to tactfully criticize his or her writing can be stressful and certainly more challenging than sitting at a desk with a writer where we can exchange nonverbal cues along with the normal pleasantries of face-to-face conversation."

Donna, who also worked with a group of writers located offshore, did not mention the same problems as Brad, precisely *because* her company allowed them to build personal rapport before they worked apart. She stated that "all of our offshore writers began their work with us by staying here at our corporate headquarters for 3 to 4 months," and that doing this "helped us get to know each other and work with each other." Donna further suggested that while together, time was spent developing a collaborative relationship to be continued later: "it allowed us the time to establish relationships with them and get to know the nature of our work, culture, [and] environment."

Once the writers were offshore, however, editors were still faced with communicating over long distances. Brad, especially, felt that personal contact made a difference to the relationship between an editor and a writer, and he missed being in the same building as the writers, because "just running into people in the elevator or kitchen or lobby enables some personal interchange and communication," thereby allowing exchanges of ideas or the strengthening of the relationship. One solution that may help in Brad's situation is used by Alice, who said that when communicating with writers, she uses "telephone and instant messenger more than anything." As Pascal (2003) points out, instant messaging software can often take the place of the "chance interactions" that Brad was missing. Also, Alice pointed out that "messenger is good for rapid-fire discussions." Instant messaging software facilitates real-time dialogue between users about quick or simple questions or commentaries. If an editor has a question about an area in the text, it is often easier to "fire" a query to the writer about it than to send an e-mail message or make a phone call.

The discussion of this topic seems to imply that technology alone cannot facilitate the type of relationship needed or wanted by the editors. Their points suggest that meeting with writers before a project (at the very least) is important to the collaboration in which the two are involved. Donna and Brad, especially, stated that they had stronger relationships and therefore, better working relationships with the writers that they had previously met before they went overseas. All of the editors agreed that it takes a strong collaborative relationship to successfully create technical documents, and that personal contact of some sort is essential to this relationship.

High Turnover of Writers

Another obstacle to collaboration, which was pointed out by Donna, was the high turnover rate of outsourced writers. Donna said that this turnover rate particularly affected the amount of knowledge each writer had about the product they were documenting: "I assume that if we had long-term relationships with the offshore writers and they stayed with [our] company for a long period of time, they would become familiar with the software they document as well as the [subject-matter experts] for the product. But, we have had high turnover."

Additionally, Janet suggested that "short term relationships are an obstacle to collaboration," and that "outsourcing is a problem for collaborating, unless you can build stable relationships that last over time." Liz noted, agreeing with Coggin and Porter (1993), that when given time to form a relationship, "the editor and writer become used to each other's methods, strengths, weaknesses and quirks." Brad had been working with the same writers for a number of years and was used to their styles and personalities. He indicated that this—having known the writer for a long time—helped in their working relationship.

Ultimately, all of the editors implied that the length of the relationship (and the longer the editor and writer work together the better that relationship will be) could be more important than where the partners in the relationship are located. Therefore, ensuring that writers do not depart from the relationship is a significant factor in the success of a documentation project.

Different Time Zones

Working in vastly different time zones, however, was indicated as especially restrictive for the editor and writer's communication. Donna, specifically, mentioned the "complications caused by a 10.5 hour time lapse." She said that it created delays because "[the editors] were not available when [the writers] had questions, and [the writers] were not available when [the editors] gave them answers—causing a day lag time in most cases." Brad, who works with writers in Israel, also stated that the time-zone difference was difficult and that phone calls were seldom made because of this difference. However, he did state that "even though our time zones are 7 to 8 hours apart . . . we usually have a few hours overlap each day because of varying work schedules."

The need for this overlap was addressed by Hoft (1995) in her discussion about management issues in building an international technical communication team. She suggested that organizations "stagger work hours to accommodate time differences if real-time communication is required on a regular basis" (p. 39). In other words, a technical editor who is collaborating with outsourced writers in another country may come in later (or earlier), and leave later (or earlier) than normal so that some overlap in work hours occurs with those outsourced writers, thereby facilitating synchronous communication (such as a telephone conversation).

Interestingly, Brad suggested that the staggered work schedule—caused by the writers being located offshore—was *useful* in some cases:

> Sometimes when a particularly hot project comes up, such as a [request for proposal] response that has a particularly short turn-around time, several technical [editors] in different countries will hand off the editing of the response matrix as their relative work days come to an end. I sometimes share work with writers in Israel and Australia to keep the job in work continually so that we can meet severe deadlines.

INTERCULTURAL DIFFERENCES

With the exception of Janet, the editors regularly worked closely with people from different countries and from different cultures. Liz had in the past worked for a corporation with writers located globally, and Brad and Donna both (at the time of the focus group) worked directly with writers located offshore and native to another country. John, meanwhile, is himself outsourced and regularly works immersed in cultures different from his own. All of these experiences provided wonderful insight to the type of intercultural dimensions that outsourcing may bring.

Cultural Differences

When the issue of culture was introduced, John simply stated that "cultural differences always impact a project significantly, in my experience." This impact is something that, according to Liz, technical editors *must* expect. To facilitate these differences, the editors who work with L2 writers first suggest that fellow editors approach the situation with an open mind. Brad stated that he must remember at times that the writers he collaborates with are "limited in English skills," especially when the writer's e-mails "come across with a very brusque or even rude tone." Liz merely suggested that "an editor working with outsourced writers (especially offshore) would benefit greatly from strong cross-cultural skills."

In her discussion of these skills, Liz pointed to several specific factors that could affect the relationship between an editor and writer. She stated that "the overall social framework can be high context or low context, power dynamics can be either democratic or hierarchical, relationship dynamics within cultures can be individual or collective, [and] the concept of time can be linear, or cyclical." These factors, she said, "in addition to extreme distance, can add to the level of 'communication' effort."

Although it is important not to generalize or stereotype, one of the first things an editor could do when beginning a project with a writer from another country is research the prominent cultural values of the writer's country to develop the cross-cultural skills that Liz recommends. Prominent researchers such as Trompenaars and Hampden-Turner (1998), Hall (1998), and Hofstede (2001) have conducted significant studies into the factors described above.

Writing Differences

The difference between the editor's and writer's cultural values could also have an enormous impact on how the documents are written. Thatcher (1999), for example, has identified specific ways in which writers express cultural values in their writing. Although these cultural values are important when writing for audiences who share them, the document may fail when read by another audience that does not share them. An editor would do well to understand what values a writer may express in the document, because as Brad points out, "the editor must constantly filter what is written through an awareness of the writer's cultural background, watching for culture-related idiosyncrasies and tendencies."

Technical editors must also be aware of potential problems caused by language differences. Brad stated that "in general, the writing of nonnative English-speaking writers differs TREMENDOUSLY from that of native English speakers." Brad said that these differences effectively increased the volume of editing that he must do on a regular basis. Donna, who edits L2 writers, commented on the quality of the end result those writers produced: "when we are talking about writing American English documentation that is supposed to read like it came from the same American English source, this was a huge issue." She too indicated an increased amount of work because of language differences: "by the time I edited the documentation, communicated my comments, returned markup to the offshore writer, and edited it again to make sure the changes were incorporated, I could have done the work myself."

Brad noted that the writers he regularly edited had particular errors that they made often. His list of common mistakes included small problems, such as "confusion of terms (compliant vs. complaint, then vs. than, filed vs. field, and so on), misapplication of prepositions (especially "until"), and confusion and mixture of tenses." Brad also pointed out larger issues, like "excessive wordiness," which "occurs frequently because the limited vocabulary often results in very long phrases to 'write around' the lack of the appropriate word."

Like learning about the predominant values of a writer's culture, learning about specific language differences may also help an editor. Grove (1988) points out that the many problems found in the writing of a Japanese L2 writer stem from differences between the English and Japanese languages. Specifically, she mentions that the Japanese language does not recognize differences in the plural or singular form of a noun, does not have definite or indefinite articles, and does not include punctuation marks similar to those used in English. As Grove makes clear, if editors who are reviewing documents from L2 writers can study the differences between the writer's native language and English, they will be better prepared for the type of problems the writer may have, and will therefore be better able to help the writer solve those problems. In the end, as Brad notes, "the more familiar the editor becomes with the peculiarities of the cultures represented by the writers, the more effective and accurate will be the edit."

Language differences aside, Brad, Donna, and Liz all made it clear that the L2 writers with whom they worked were very receptive to the editing suggestions they made. Donna said that the writers she worked with "were willing to try and keep trying" in order to deliver the correct documentation. Brad also noted that the non-native English-speaking writers always "insist on having their work edited," and Liz said that "non-native English writers are . . . receptive to editorial input and often very motivated to improve where their English language skills may be lacking."

IMPLICATIONS FOR THE FUTURE

As noted in this chapter, new and significant dimensions have been added to the publication process due to outsourcing. Editors must rely on tools, such as style guides, much more than before to aid in unifying a document. They must also rely on technologies to help them span the distance between themselves, writers, and the client. They must negotiate the difficulties of an editor-writer relationship over these distances and try to establish, strengthen, or continue a good collaborative rapport. Adding to these difficulties are factors such as culture and language differences, which must be taken into account when collaborating with the writers or reviewing their work.

Regardless of these dimensions, however, some of the participants in the focus group believed that the basic *role* of the editor—what they actually do—changed little as a result of outsourcing. Brad stated that he did not see that his role is "any different than in previous writing or editing positions." Likewise, Liz told us that her role is "basically the same as if the whole thing was in-house." Donna, too, said that it was not her role that changed, but the "level of effort" required of an editor that had changed—in her case this level of effort had increased.

Janet, conversely, felt that "the role of the editor is more important when the writing is outsourced" because the editor "must bring the publications in line with the goals, objectives, personality, and message of the organization," and because "the editor may also need to direct the writing so that a publication written by several contract writers fits together as a unified whole." But, as Liz pointed out, this is an editor's responsibility regardless of whether they or the writers are outsourced. Nonetheless, it was John who offered a comprehensive analysis of how the editor's part in the publication process changes:

> With native speakers, or writers working in-house, the editor's job is important but probably easier since he or she works with the same people over time. With an in-house editor editing outsourced writers, the editor's job is more important to consistency in the project. With an outsourced editor editing outsourced writers, the editor's job is more difficult and even more important to the consistency in the project. When you factor in non-native English speakers, the editor's importance to the project is even greater.

The "role" then becomes that of unifier. As John notes, it is the responsibility of the editor to ensure the consistency of a project worked on by many different people who may come from many different cultures and have differing visions of what the final product should be. From these varying perspectives and writing styles, the editor creates a cohesive and usable document.

As outsourcing technical communication becomes more common, the role of the editor will grow to become the central figure that binds together the writer, the document, the reader, the subject, and the organization. Therefore, the editor can easily be seen as growing in importance to documentation projects, and as this importance grows, so too does the amount of training the editor must receive, the amount of knowledge the editor must attain, and the amount of responsibility the editor will have.

REFERENCES

Coggin, W. O., & Porter, L. R. (1993). *Editing for the technical professions.* New York: Macmillan Publishing Company.

Dayton, D. (2003). Electronic editing in technical communication: A survey of practices and attitudes. *Technical Communication, 50,* 192-206.

Dayton, D. (1998). Technical editing online: The quest for transparent technology. *Journal of Technical Writing and Communication, 28,* 3-38.

Deaton, M. (1990). Improving software documentation accuracy with writer and editor partnerships. *IPCC '90 Conference Record,* 13-15.

Duffy, T. M. (1995). Designing tools to aid technical editors: A needs analysis. *Technical Communication, 42,* 262-277.

Edmands, A. (1988). The integrated editor: Involvement of and editor in the entire information development process. *IPCC '88 Conference Record,* 119-122.

Farkas, D. K. (1987). Online editing and document review. *Technical Communication, 34,* 180-183.

Flick, U. (1998). *An introduction to qualitative research.* London, UK: Sage.

Grove, L. K. (1988). Cross-cultural editing. *IPCC '88 Conference Record,* 255-258.

Hall, E. T. (1998). The power of hidden differences. In M. J. Bennett (Ed.), *Basic concepts of intercultural communication* (pp. 53-67). Yarmouth, ME: Intercultural Press.

Hoft, N. L. (1995). *International technical communication: How to export information about high technology.* New York: John Wiley & Sons, Inc.

Hofstede, G. (2001). *Culture's consequences: Comparing values, behaviors, institutions and organizations across nations.* Thousand Oaks, CA: Sage.

Lanier, C. R. (2004). Electronic editing and the author. *Technical Communication, 51,* 526-537.

MacNealy, M. S. (1999). *Strategies for empirical research in writing.* Boston, MA: Allyn and Bacon.

Magyar, M. (1994). Do-it-yourself style guides for all occasions. *IPCC '94 Proceedings,* 85-88.

Miles, V. C., McCarthy, J. C., Dix, A. J., Harrison, M. D., & Monk A. F. (1993). Reviewing designs for a synchronous-asynchronous group editing environment. In M. Sharples (Ed.), *Computer supported collaborative writing* (pp. 137-160). London, UK: Springer-Verlag.

Pascal, C. L. (2003). Enabling chance interaction through instant messaging. *IEEE Transactions in Professional Communication, 46,* 138-141.

Perkins, J., & Maloney, C. (1998). Today's style guide: Trusted tool with added potential. *IEEE Transactions on Professional Communication, 41,* 24-32.

Ramos, A., & O'Maley, L. (2003). Offshoring of technical writing: A roundtable discussion. *The NWU BizTech offshoring project.* Retrieved February 3, 2005, from the World Wide Web: http://www.biztech-offshoring.com/roundtable.html.

Rude, C. D. (2003). *Technical editing* (3rd ed.). Boston, MA: McGraw-Hill.

Rude, C. D., & Smith, E. (1992). Use of computers in technical editing. *Technical Communication, 39,* 334-342.

Sproull, L., & Kiesler, S. (1991). *Connections: New ways of working in the networked organization.* Cambridge, MA: MIT Press.

Stocker, D. J. (1990). Technical communication: A collaborative effort between author and editor. *IPCC '90 Conference Record,* 16-18.

Thatcher, B. L. (1999). Cultural and rhetorical adaptations for South American audiences. *Technical Communication, 46,* 177-195.

Trompenaars, F., & Hampden-Turner, C. (1998). *Riding the waves of culture.* New York: McGraw-Hill.

Tse, A. C. B. (1999). Conducting electronic focus group discussions among Chinese respondents. *Journal of the Market Research Society, 41,* 407-420.

Turpin, E. R., & Bronson, J. G. (1997). Technical editing. In K. Staples & C. Ornatowski (Eds.), *Foundations for teaching technical communication: Theory, practice, and program design* (pp. 221-230), Greenwich, CT: Ablex Publishing Corporation.

PART III

Legal, Ethical, and Political Issues

CHAPTER 9

The Privacy Problems Related to International Outsourcing: A Perspective for Technical Communicators

Kirk St. Amant

International outsourcing has become one of today's most controversial topics. At the heart of this situation is a concern related to the exporting of work (and jobs) from industrialized nations to developing ones. This focus on work has caused many individuals to overlook an equally important problem: the exporting of personal medical or financial data to other nations. By sending such information abroad for processing, organizations could suddenly place personal data into a legal gray area, for data protection laws can vary greatly from nation to nation. Such variation can result in the unintended or unexpected misuse of data. Emerging business trends, moreover, indicate that organizations will increasingly use international outsourcing to process personal data.

This chapter examines how international outsourcing could lead to the abuses of personal information and explains the role technical communicators can play in addressing these problems. To achieve this end, the chapter:

- overviews the benefits/reasons that prompt organizations to use international outsourcing,
- explores international legal and market conditions that can give rise to abuses of personal data, and

- introduces strategies technical communicators can use to counter privacy threats in outsourcing.

Through understanding these ideas and implementing these strategies, technical communicators can modify professional practices to effectively address business in this new century,

AN OVERVIEW OF INTERNATIONAL OUTSOURCING

Outsourcing, in essence, is the process of transferring responsibility for completing a task from one entity to another (Bendor-Samuel, 2004). In modern business practices, the motivation for such transfers often involves cost and efficiency; that is, businesses generally outsource work to organizations that can perform it more cheaply and efficiently than the company itself can. This drive to reduce cost and improve efficiency has prompted many companies to look beyond their nation's borders when outsourcing activities.

Such international outsourcing, or offshoring, is by no means new. Rather, many companies have a long-standing practice of "exporting" a variety of skilled and unskilled manufacturing work to developing nations. Recently, however, the kind of work being sent overseas has expanded to include a variety of knowledge-based tasks including computer programming, accounting, and medical transcription work. This practice, known as business process outsourcing (BPO), often involves organizations in the industrialized nations of North America and Europe sending work to employees located in developing nations such as India, China, and the Philippines. Moreover, such international BPO has grown rapidly in recent years due to the perceived benefits many organizations think it can provide. These benefits include

- **Reduced labor costs:** Many outsourcing workers can perform skilled tasks for a fraction of what their counterparts in industrialized nations can. Gaming developers in Russia, for example, earn roughly $100 US a week (Nussbaum, 2004; Weir, 2004).
- **Enhanced management practices:** Because managers are paid less in developing nations (the average middle manager in mainland China makes $9,000 US per year), organizations can afford to increase the number of managers overseeing outsourcing activities (Hagel, 2004; Nussbaum, 2004). As a result, it is often easier for managers to identify inefficiencies and to work with employees to improve performance and avoid problems (Hagel, 2004; Lewis, 2003).
- **Decreased employee turnover:** In many developing nations, secure employment is rare, and outsourcing jobs are among the better paying ones.

Overseas outsourcing workers thus tend to stay with employers for longer periods of time (Farrell & Zainulbhai, 2004; Reuters, 2004a).

- **Shortened production time:** By distributing work to nations in other time zones, companies can keep operations going continually and complete products or processes more quickly ("America's pain," 2003; Baily & Farrell, 2004; Bierce, 1999; Friedman, 1999).

These factors have led many organizations to make international outsourcing part of their core business strategy.

THE GROWTH OF INTERNATIONAL OUTSOURCING

International outsourcing is booming. It currently accounts for some $10 billion US in worth and employs approximately 500,000 individuals in India alone (Baily & Farrell, 2004; Rosenthal, 2004b). Moreover, international outsourcing is poised to grow markedly in the future. Some observers believe it will increase by 20% a year through 2008 and account for three million business processing jobs by 2015 (Rosenthal, 2004b; Baily & Farrell, 2004). Other parties argue that at least five million jobs will be devoted to international outsourcing employees in the next 5 to 10 years (Garten, 2004).

Although much of this growth involves U.S. companies, organizations in other nations have begun including international outsourcing into their business practices. Some French companies have begun working with Senegal and Morocco on different outsourcing projects (Reuters, 2004a). German firms have started exploring outsourcing relationships with Eastern European nations, and Dutch companies now use international call centers located in South Africa (Rosenthal, 2004c). Additionally, markets in Spain, combined with the growth in the U.S. Spanish-speaking population, have led to an increase in work outsourced to Mexico and Latin America (Rosenthal, 2004a). Even India, a central outsourcing destination, is now outsourcing some work to China and to Sri Lanka (Reuters, 2004b).

As noted earlier, much of this growth encompasses knowledge-based tasks that involve the processing of personal data. Accounting practices, for example, often involve an individual's personal financial information, while medical transcription deals with a person's health records. This increased flow of information to other countries creates new and interesting situations related to the treatment of such information. To understand the significance of such transfers, one must understand the value of personal data in today's business environment.

THE VALUE OF PERSONAL INFORMATION

Marketing plays a central role in increasing corporate sales and contributing to organizational profits. Effective marketing, however, requires an understanding of consumers, for the more one knows about a prospective buyer, the easier it is to create advertising materials that will entice that person to purchase a product. Personal data is therefore an important commodity, for it can be used to create more-effective marketing materials that can increase corporate profits. This prospect of profits driven by effective marketing motivates many corporations to collect and archive as much personal data as possible, even if such data has seemingly no relation to current organizational activities. The idea is that such information might have marketing value at a later date (Davis & Meyer, 1998; Siebel & House, 1999; Whitaker, 1999).

Personal data can also help organizations conduct more-efficient research and development activities. By comparing information related to multiple individuals, companies can identify prospective consumer trends and better plan research and development to meet projected purchasing patterns. If, for example, a pharmaceutical company knows that more individuals in the United States suffer from heart disease than from pancreas disorders, they can focus their drug development efforts on medications designed to meet the needs of the larger market of individuals with heart disease.

This ability to use personal data to focus on specific consumers facilitates other business practices including the sales of goods and services to specific individuals (Teasley, 2004; "The revenge," 2003). Additionally, such data provides the organization with a database of valuable information that others might be willing to purchase. As a result, the value of personal information has skyrocketed, and so has the business imperative to collect as much of this information as possible (Davis & Meyer, 1998; Siebel & House, 1999; Whitaker, 1999).

THREATS AND RESPONSES

These trends in data collection have also given rise to consumer concerns related to privacy. For example, the data a pharmaceutical company uses to target a blood-pressure drug to a prospective consumer could be used by insurance agencies to deny coverage to the same individual. As a result of these privacy concerns, many governments have enacted laws that protect consumer information. In the United States, for example, the Fair Credit Reporting Act and the Credit Reporting Reform Act restrict how an individual's financial data may be collected (Cate, 1997). In the European Union, concerns related to the use of personal data prompted the adoption of the Data Protection Directive that strictly regulates when and how personal information can be used (Swire & Litan, 1998). Thus, while there is a market for personal data, organizations in many industrialized nations are restricted in their ability to compile or use such information.

International outsourcing, however, creates an entirely new legal situation related to data collection and distribution. By involving more than one nation in a data processing activity, offshoring also involves more than one legal system in the regulatory process. Such a situation brings with it problems of jurisdiction and enforcement.

JURISDICTION, PROTECTION, AND INTERNATIONAL OUTSOURCING

The legal concept of jurisdiction governs when a particular law can and cannot be enforced. According to this idea, the laws of one nation are often enforceable only within the borders of that nation. That is, officials in one nation cannot claim jurisdiction—or the ability to enforce the laws of their country—within another nation. As a result, once individuals or materials move beyond those borders, they are generally beyond the legal protection of that nation.

International outsourcing creates an interesting legal situation regarding jurisdiction and protection. If work is performed in another nation, then employees might be operating under a different set of laws from the company that sent them the work. Therefore, a process that might be illegal in the nation of the outsourcing client ("black market" activity) might be legally permissible in the nation of the outsourcing employees ("white market" activity). In terms of personal information and data protection, the various national laws dealing with such topics can range from the very strict (e.g., European Union's Data Protection Directive) to almost nonexistent (e.g., the People's Republic of China) (Swire & Litan, 1998). The result is a sort of gray area in international law: which laws should apply where and how (Rosenthal, 2005)? Within this gray area exists the potential for various kinds of data abuses through a process I call *gray-market informatics*.

GRAY-MARKET INFORMATICS

The conditions that allow international outsourcing workers to engage in gray-market informatics are manyfold. First, the collection and sale of certain personal data might be completely legal in the nation where the outsourcing worker is located; thus there is no legal reason (or dissuasion) for why such activities should *not* be performed. Second, such information has a relatively high market value if sold to the right individual or organization. Thus, there is incentive to misuse personal data for profit. Third, as such sales might occur overseas, the organizations or individuals who supplied such data might never realize that abuses are taking place. Such a condition mitigates the threat (and thus the deterrence) that a client might sever business ties if certain data processing conditions are not followed. Fourth, outsourcing providers often use external subcontractors—a practice that further complicates one's ability to trace how data is being "misused" and thus take action against the "violator."

In this situation, the benefits of gray-market informatics (increased earnings) are high while the risks (lost clients) remain low. Such a paradox creates an interesting temptation for international outsourcing employees making a fraction of what counterparts in industrialized nations do. Moreover, factors of physical distance and the use of subcontractors mean that such practices could go on for long periods of time before they are noticed—if they are noticed at all. In fact, it is only through a combination of intention and mistake that such practices have begun to come to light.

As of this writing, only two cases of true gray-market informatics have gained any sort of focused public attention. Both of these cases involve *data hijacking*—a type of extortion in which international outsourcing workers hold information hostage. In such situations, the outsourcing employee contacts the original supplier of the data and demands the supplier pay a certain amount of money to have that data returned. To provide incentive for such payment, the outsourcing worker also threatens that, if the requisite payment is not made, he or she will sell that data to another agency and make the news of such sale public; or post that data to an open forum, such as a Web site, and then inform others that such information is free for them to use.

In such cases, the fear of a prospective backlash related to the public disclosure of such data provides companies with the incentive to meet the extortionist's demands.

The first and more famous case involved the exploits of Lubna Baloch, a Pakistan-based outsourcing employee who worked in medical transcription. Ms. Baloch believed her client, a subcontractor working for the University of California San Francisco (UCSF) Medical Center, still owed her $500 US for the transcription services she had performed. In an attempt to recover the money she was owed, Ms. Baloch sent the UCSF Medical Center a brief but powerful e-mail:

> Your patient records are out in the open to be exposed, so you better track that person [who owes me money] and make him pay my dues otherwise I will expose all the voice files and patient records of UCSF Parnassus and Mt. Zion campuses on the Internet (Lazarus, 2004a, paragraph 4).

The message sent a shock wave through the UCSF community, and in relatively short order, arrangements were made for Ms. Baloch to received the $500 she was owed. She also vowed to honor her original promise of not releasing the related medical data: "I verify that I do not have any intent to distribute/release any patient health information out and I have destroyed the said information" (Lazarus, 2004a, paragraph 45). Thus, while the threat was seemingly averted, Ms. Baloch remains free, for such a threatened action is not against the law in Pakistan. Moreover, the UCSF Medical Center has no real proof that she indeed destroyed this information—versus having copied and sold it to other parties.

In a second case, a group of disgruntled outsourcing employees in Bangalore, India, threatened to release certain patient information to the public if the provider of that data, Heartland Information Services, failed to pay an unspecified sum of money (Lazarus, 2004b). Through a series of technical maneuvers, Heartland Information Services was able to trace the source of the threat—an e-mail message—to a particular cyber café in India. They then used records to determine which outsourcing employees with access to such data lived nearby, and through a process of luck, were able to identify the offenders, who are currently awaiting trial. (What they will be tried for and what the related sentences might be remains unclear.) Further research, moreover, revealed that the threat had been a hoax, and none of the disgruntled employees was in possession of actual medical data (Lazarus, 2004b).

In both instances, the only reason the client company (and perhaps affected individuals) became aware of this potential abuse of information was because outsourcing employees wanted the situation to become a matter of public knowledge. Although the situation in India proved to be a hoax, the one in Pakistan proves particularly problematic, for if the outsourcing employee had not sought such attention, she could have sold this medical data to a third party (e.g., a pharmaceutical company) and no one would have been the wiser. Both of these situations therefore illustrate the ease with which personal information can be abused, and the difficulties related to realizing such abuses are taking place.

THE GROWING POTENTIAL FOR ABUSE

Whereas instances of gray-market informatics have remained seemingly limited to date, certain business trends could greatly increase the prospects for future abuses of personal data. The first problematic trend is the kind of international outsourcing activities that seem poised for the greatest growth. Many managers and bankers see international outsourcing as an effective way to address different accounting practices. As a result, more personal financial data could begin moving overseas for processing, and the prospects for abuse increase.

Further contributing to this situation is Section 404 of the Sarbanes-Oxley Act of 2002. This statute requires chief executive officers and chief financial officers of U.S. public companies to review their internal controls over financial transactions ("404 tonnes," 2004). The result is that many companies must now sift through mountains of financial paperwork at a relatively high cost in terms of time and money. General Electric, for example, spent $30 million in extra payments to auditors to review such documents, while J. P. Morgan Chase has 130 full-time employees working on this project ("404 tonnes," 2004). Even in light of such expenses, some experts predict that 10%–20% of companies will fail to have such processes completed by the required legal deadline of 75 days from the end of a company's fiscal year ("404 tonnes," 2004). Such standards have also increased the time required to perform audits by 40%–60% at a time when there do not seem to be enough U.S. auditors available to meet marketplace demands (Byrnes, 2005).

Given the costs related to such activities and the fact that more complex accounting practices are being outsourced, it seems reasonable to expect that some Statute 404 activities would be prime candidates for international out sourcing. It would also seem sensible to predict that some auditing functions would be key targets for international outsourcing, especially as demand has driven up pay for U.S. auditors by 10%–20% (Byrnes, 2005). Such outsourcing would involve sending yet more kinds of sensitive financial data overseas. If, however, the current market demand for trained auditors is not met and met soon, international outsourcing might remain the only viable option in this and many other situations involving personal financial data. Financial data, moreover, is not the only kind of personal information poised for increased overseas distribution. New U.S. health-care legislation could also increase the international outsourcing of personal medical data.

The driving force behind this trends is actually a statute designed to protect patient privacy: the Health Insurance Portability and Accountability Act of 1996 (HIPAA). While HIPAA provides a mechanism for protecting patient privacy, it also requires that all of an individual's medical information be placed in electronic format so it can be easily shared (Goolsby, 2001b, 2001d). The problem is that all print medical records must now be processed into a digital format—a task that is time—consuming, costly, and monotonous (Goolsby, 2001a, 2001d). And the processing of such information from one format to another takes time, and delays can affect the quality of patient health care and patient satisfaction. These factors make HIPAA-related tasks, such as medical transcription and IT development, ideal candidates for international outsourcing (Goolsby, 2001a; Salkever, 2004; "Sink or Schwinn," 2004). These situations, however, bring the problem of abuses related to personal data. Such concerns are perhaps particularly well founded in relation to health-care data, for two of the most prominent cases of gray-market informatics involve abuses of medical data by transcritptionists in India and Pakistan (Salkever, 2004).

THE INCREASE IN INTERNATIONAL
OUTSOURCING PROVIDERS

Further complicating this situation are international trends related to economic development. In India, international outsourcing has contributed to the $420 billion US of disposable income that workers in that country have amassed in recent years (Malik, 2004). This financial growth has prompted a variety of developing nations to become more involved in international outsourcing practices. The government of China, for example, has adopted a series of government and private-sector programs that would increase online access in the country and make it a key target for the outsourcing of knowledge work ("Wired China,"

2000). Additionally, Malaysia is trying to present itself as an outsourcing alternative to India, and the Philippines has increasingly become a hub for English-language customer-service calls and IT work (Gaudin, 2003; Rosenthal, 2004c; Reuters, 2004b). In Eastern Europe, Russia and the Ukraine have developed a reputation for excellence in computer programming and have made inroads into computer-based outsourcing activities (Goolsby, 2001c; Weir, 2004).

As more nations become involved in outsourcing, the complexities related to gray-market informatics increase. Each new country brings with it a different set of laws and customs that will affect the treatment of personal data. Each nation also becomes a prospective subcontractor or "middle person" through which data can be passed. The tracking of international data flows and the isolating of where abuses take place therefore become even more complex. Such complexity might actually act as a deterrent to enforcement, for the more time and money it takes to track data flows, the less likely organizations might be to pursue violators.

The convergence of these factors means now is the time for organizations to develop methods for ensuring the safe treatment of personal data in international outsourcing situations. The fact that many financial-services providers and many health-care providers are just beginning to examine such processes means there is still time to implement data-protection systems that allow for effective international outsourcing. Moreover, the fact that many developing nations are only beginning their expansion into international outsourcing means there is still time to devise protective practices that can be adopted by these nations instead of trying to impose such practices after the fact. Finally, the current political and business climate is right for such protective measures to be developed in an atmosphere of support and interest.

GOVERNANCE AND THE ROLE OF THE TECHNICAL COMMUNICATOR

The U.S. presidential race of 2004 brought outsourcing to the forefront of public discussion by making it a central topic of each candidate's economic platform. This increased scrutiny prompted many companies to review their outsourcing practices in order to quell public concerns. Out of this review process came two key findings. First, companies needed to take a more active role in the governance, or management, of international outsourcing activities (Atwood, 2004; Bendor-Samuel, 2004; Eisner, 2002). Second, consumer privacy and IT security emerged as prospective problem areas that needed to be addressed more actively and more directly (Rosenthal, 2005; Top ten, 2005).

In response to these findings, many outsourcing researchers suggested that companies form internal governing boards that would oversee outsourcing practices (Atwood, 2004; Eisner, 2002; Goolsby, 2003). The idea would be that such governing boards would act as policymakers and distributors. To achieve these ends, such boards would need to focus on a series of core communication activities.

This focus on communication creates an important opportunity for technical communicators, for such proposed governance activities involve tasks that many practitioners and scholars consider central to technical communication practices. These governance initiatives include the following activities:

- Communicating complex ideas regularly to different audiences and across different kinds of media (e.g., newsletters, intranet sites, etc.)—something at which technical communicators are highly skilled (Atwood, 2004; Eisner, 2002; Goolsby, 2003). The idea is that the more informed employees are of critical situations, the more likely they are to address those situations effectively.
- Sharing information across different departments within an organization and across cultural barriers related to outsourcing interactions (Atwood, 2004; Goolsby, 2003). Technical communicators are trained in the significance of audience and how it affects communication, and they regularly interact with persons from other divisions as a daily matter of their jobs (e.g., working with engineering, legal, and marketing to develop product documentation). As a result, they might have the best understanding of how to work effectively across departments and to share information with audiences in different divisions.
- Addressing cultural communication factors in order to share information effectively with overseas outsourcing providers. As technical communicators are often entrusted with the tasks of working with translators and localizers—some of whom are located overseas—they often have expertise in understanding and working with cultural communication issues and working with audiences from other cultures (Flint et al., 1999; Walmer, 1999).

For these reasons, technical communicators are ideal candidates for outsourcing governance boards. Participation in such organizations would also place technical communicators in the public management roles that some individuals see as necessary to revitalizing the profession (Giammona, 2004). The question then becomes, what are some of the specific activities technical communicators can perform in relation to such governance? The answer lies with creating effective intra-organizational and external communication systems that allow information to flow efficiently and that allow organizations to track the movement of data effectively.

GOVERNANCE STRATEGIES FOR ADDRESSING OFFSHORING'S PRIVACY PROBLEMS

Although addressing such complex communication situations can be a daunting task, technical communicators can begin by focusing on a few foundational strategies that provide the groundwork essential to efficient communication and effective oversight in outsourcing situations.

Strategy 1. Develop a sensitive data classification system and share this system with employees. The key to avoiding data abuses is to determine which information is particularly sensitive and should therefore remain within a company for protection. Nonsensitive data could then be sent abroad without worry, and the processing of sensitive data would be done in house, where both organizations and national laws could oversee its uses and protect it from abuses.

As technical communicators regularly develop classification systems and definitions as part of their jobs, they are well positioned to create sensitive-data classifications. Moreover, as the in-house processing of sensitive data will likely become the task of technical communicators—who generally work with such data (e.g., results of clinical trials), it makes sense that technical communicators would be the individuals best suited to develop such a classification system; that is, they would already be familiar with what kinds of personal information that merit special treatment.

Finally, technical communicators are trained to work with different subject-matter experts (SMEs) to mediate ideas when developing materials. As a result, they would be well suited for working with an organization's legal, marketing, and other divisions to develop a definition of sensitive information that would work across an organization. The convergence of these factors provides technical communicators with the skills and knowledge needed to develop effective data categories, which is the first and most important step in creating a workable data-protection process.

Should technical communicators wish to look for models when defining sensitive data, an effective one would be the definition of "personal data" given in Chapter I of the European Union's Data Protection Directive (Directive 95/46/EC). This statute defines what personal data needs to be treated with extreme care, and it has become a foundational definition for the concept of sensitive data in other nations, including the United States (Eisner, 2002; Swire & Litan, 1998).

Strategy 2. Develop a communication plan for letting in-house employees know the importance of data security related to international outsourcing. If employees are made aware of what data is considered sensitive and how that data can be abused, they are more likely to take steps to treat the processing and the distribution of such data with care (Goolsby, 2003; Peterson, 2002). Informed employees are therefore more effective employees. The key to this situation is to remind employees regularly of such situations as well as inform them of new developments that could affect the processing or the abuses of sensitive data. Such information dissemination could be done via an organizational intranet site that is readily available. To further assist employees, such a site could have "FAQ" (Frequently Asked Questions) or "self test" modules that can answer employee questions or allow employees to test their knowledge of international outsourcing, privacy concerns, and data-processing/data-sharing policies.

Strategy 3. Work with outsourcing employees to develop data-flow charts that catalog where information goes once it is given to outsource workers. Such a chart should include the names and contact information for individual employees involved in such processes. From a data-security perspective, the single greatest problem is tracking where data goes once it is sent overseas. An organizational chart that indicates how such data moves once abroad could greatly help organizations locate where data abuses or data leaks might be taking place. This knowledge could be used to address problems or devise alternative solutions (require the outsourcer to move or treat data in different ways) that would help avoid abuses (Atwood, 2004).

For such documentation to be effective, it also needs to provide the names and the contact information of persons involved in each step of the data-transfer process. Such information creates a system of accountability that might dissuade overseas individuals from abusing data; that is, as outsourcing jobs are often the best form of employment in many areas, and the prospect of being dismissed for committing a data abuse decreases the chances of misuse in a way that an unmonitored system could not (Baily & Farrell, 2004). As a result, this documentation addresses the "accountability gap" that is a central part of gray-market informatics (Atwood, 2004; Reuters, 2004a).

Strategy 4. Develop a risk-communication plan for addressing instances when outsourced data *is* abused. Just because a system of accountability is developed does not mean that data abuses will not occur. Rather, companies should assume that such abuses will occur at some point in time. Such abuse is, after all, a continual possibility in the most secure of systems (Atis, 2003). A preformulated risk-communication plan that addresses such abuses quickly and effectively can calm consumer fears and avoid prospective backlashes from individuals or government agencies. The key, however, is to have a well formulated and well articulated plan that is accessible to all audiences. Ideally, such a communication plan would include an overview of what steps and what media the organization will use to avoid such abuses and how the organization will keep consumers apprised of other developments related to this situation. Again, the purpose of such a plan is to restore consumer confidence via a well-formed preemptive approach rather than an after-the-fact reactive one.

Strategy 5. Identify treaties and laws related to data protection in the outsourcer's own nation. The more a company knows about the legal environment in which outsourcers operate, the more effectively it can address or avoid questionable legal situations (Bierce, 1999; Eisner, 2002). By knowing the laws that govern the treatment of personal data (or lack thereof), companies can best decide what kinds of work to outsource to which nations (Doyle, 2004; Rosenthal, 2005). Also, knowing the legal enforcement mechanisms one can use to address grievances in a particular nation can help companies pressure outsourcing providers to adequately address data-processing concerns or face legal consequences.

Within this context, the role of the technical communicator would be to research such legal developments in order to provide managers and other company employees with a synopsis of what such legal agreements mean for how the company engages in outsourcing. In essence, the technical communicator would be repackaging technical materials for a variety of audiences within a company. In generating these synopses, the technical communicator could create specialized versions, each of which is geared toward the job tasks and the background of a particular company audience involved in outsourcing practices. Technical communicators could also play an active role in developing the systems for sharing such information with different company audiences (e.g., via an intranet, in a written report, etc.). They could also play an active role in making employees aware of such documentation and related legal updates on a regular basis (see Strategy 2).

Additionally, as many of these statutes will be written in other languages, they will require translation. Because technical communicators are individuals who often work with translators, they would be well positioned to pursue such processes from start (generating original translations) to finish (creating different synopses for different audiences).

Strategy 6. Create an intranet site that instructs employees (and managers) in how to recognize and address different data abuses they might encounter when working in outsourcing relationships. To help with this process, technical communicators might wish to include descriptions of how to spot certain kinds of data abuses and include a list of who to contact in which corporate office or government agency with concerns about a particular kind of violation (Peterson, 2002). By increasing the number of individuals monitoring international outsourcing activities, one decreases the chances that violations will go unnoticed. Also, by helping employees feel like they are a part of such processes, one increases the chances that they will play a more active role in these activities (Goolsby, 2003; Peterson, 2002). Such a site should also be designed to provide outsourcing-related news on a daily basis (encourages daily use of the site) and include "self test" scenarios so employees can evaluate if they are working correctly with outsourcers. Technical communicators should also make sure that outsourcing agencies are aware that the company has adopted such measures in order to provide incentive to avoid data abuses (see Strategy 3).

Strategy 7. Work with clients and suppliers to draft job tasks related to outsourcing (don't leave activities ambiguous). In the past, organizations have paid relatively little attention to how outsourcers perform tasks (Atwood, 2004; Goolsby & Whitlow, 2003). As a result, outsourcing organizations might either be lacking the direction needed to treat personal data effectively (especially if their own nation does not call for any special treatment of such data), or they might engage in standard processes that actually create the potential for data abuse (Bhagowati, 2004; Goolsby & Whitlow, 2003). By developing descriptions of how to perform specific job tasks, companies can reduce the risks that the standard processes performed in other countries might be creating privacy problems (Peterson, 2002). Included in such descriptions would be a discussion on what sensitive data is, how it should be treated, how to identify prospective abuses of that data, and what steps to take to report such abuses to both the client and to legal officials in that nation (Doyle, 2004; Peterson, 2002).

As such an approach involves the writing of instructions (i.e., how to perform certain tasks), technical communicators would be well suited to perform such tasks because these activities are at the heart of what they do on the job. Additionally, as some of the employees working for such companies might speak a language other than that of the outsourcing client, translation will become an important component of this process. Again, because technical communicators often work with translators, they are well suited to both create such job-task descriptions and have them translated for outsourcing suppliers.

Strategy 8. Create an access policy that encourages customers to regularly review their data for accuracy or abuse. Curiously, surveys indicate that most consumers believe government agencies are better equipped to maintain the security of personal data than are private companies (Goolsby, 2000). Such attitudes persist even though research indicates that privacy violations take place on a much greater scale when government agencies are in charge of processing data (Goolsby, 2000). To reduce customer concern (and the prospects for a backlash should something go wrong), companies need to take steps to make customers feel comfortable with how their personal data is treated (Goolsby & Whitlow, 2003). One way to do this is to increase transparency and help consumers feel like they can take an active role in determining how companies treat their personal information. By creating policies that encourage customers to review such data, companies can reduce customer suspicion and increase consumer confidence in the related organization.

Included in such access policies should be instructions for how to petition the company with complaints or concerns as well as provide a list of FAQs to familiarize customers with the steps a company will take to address privacy factors (Goolsby, 2003; Rosenthal, 2005). An additional measure some organizations may wish to take is to encourage customers to provide signed disclosure statements (either in writing or via digital signature) to indicate whether that individual agrees to allow his or her data to be processed by an outsourcing agent. Organizations might also wish to develop newsletters or e-mail updates on outsourcing activities and encourage customers to subscribe to such materials.

For all of these options to work effectively, technical information about a company's practices must be placed in a format that a range of customers can understand. Additionally, for customers to participate actively in such access and review processes, they need to have effective instructions on how to perform such procedures. Because technical communicators perform such tasks as a core function of their work, they would be the individuals best suited to spearhead such activities.

Strategy 9. Raise management's awareness of outsourcers using subcontractors and develop policies for when subcontractors can be used (with what activities or with what data). Include steps for registering subcontractors with the client/buyer so the buyer can track the flow of work/data to these subcontractors (Peterson, 2002). As mentioned earlier, one of the major problems with tracking privacy violations is the way in which subcontractors can complicate dataflow situations. This problem is particularly important as many outsourcing providers use such subcontractors but generally do not make the client aware of such use until something goes wrong.

This use of subcontractors can also allow outsourcing providers to circumvent legal or contractual restrictions by claiming that they were not the individuals who in fact violated privacy requirements. Additionally, the use of subcontractors can allow outsourcers to counteract the benefits of using data-communication plans to trace workflow once data is given to an outsourcing provider (see Strategy 2). Because it is imperative that both the outsourcing provider and the subcontractor understand such requirements, they might need to be translated into other languages. Again, this focus on the creation of instructional materials that require translation makes this task ideally suited for technical communicators.

Strategy 10. Work with other companies to develop a network for sharing information on international outsourcing both within specific industries and across different industries. The idea would be to create some form of easy-access registry (e.g., a Web site) in which companies could enter the names of the outsourcing providers with which they worked. Such a site would also allow users to provide a synopsis of the effectiveness with which they felt an outsourcing provider performed work. The idea would be to create a registry system, similar to the U.S. Better Business Bureau, that would record if and how certain outsourcing providers engaged in privacy (or other) violations when working with a particular company. Included in such a registry would be a listing of the violator, the nature of the violation, the client response to the violation, and the results from the action. Such a registry could help companies avoid working with "disreputable" outsourcing providers as well as offer effective strategies for addressing violations that occur in outsourcing relationships.

In this situation the prospect of lost business would again prompt outsourcing providers to avoid abuses related to personal data (Atwood, 2004). In some situations international outsourcing providers might be tempted to cross one or maybe two clients without fear of effective reprisals. The idea is that there are so many prospective clients that the loss of one or two is negligible, especially if the data provided by such clients can be used to generate greater profits than those resulting from working for those clients. Industrywide registries, however, mean that a large number of companies might now avoid suspect outsourcing providers and greatly affect their profits by creating a boycott situation. Fear of a boycott could be a powerful incentive for outsourcing providers to abide by data-processing practices required by client organizations (Atwood, 2004).

Such a registry should be online and allow users to perform internal searches for different outsourcing providers in order for it to be effective and open to the widest range of users. It should also be updated regularly. Perhaps the best organization to oversee such a registry would be industry oversight bodies or the Chamber of Commerce or the Better Business Bureau in states where a large number of companies engage in international outsourcing.

For such registries to be successful, they would need to provide users with effective instructions on how to register concerns and locate data on outsourcing providers. They would also need to provide different kinds of information to different companies depending on the size of the company (small business or multinational conglomerate) and the related industry. Such registries could also be made effective by having FAQ sheets or online help functions that facilitate use and provide information on how to address problems related to international outsourcing. Again, all of this instructional and informative work—as well as planning the design of such sites—is well suited for technical communicators who already perform such tasks.

Each of the aforementioned strategies is crucial to maintaining data security and addressing privacy concerns in outsourcing situations. Each strategy also conforms to the governance models proposed by outsourcing researchers. As a result, the individuals who spearhead such activities would be providing a valued service to their related company. Moreover, the emphasis that organizations are now placing on the oversight of international outsourcing means that these services are likely to be recognized in very public ways.

The focus such activities places on communication, instruction, translation, and addressing multiple audiences means technical communicators are ideally suited to lead such activities. In so doing, they can increase their visibility, their contributions to the management of an organization, and the value individuals within a company assign to technical communication activities. In pursuing such activities, technical communicators can establish a foundation of inherent value that would allow them to advance within an organization and would protect them from the international outsourcing trends currently affecting so many other knowledge-based professions.

The window for seizing such opportunities, however, is small. For this reason, technical communicators need to pursue such activities now, before another division or profession does. While the strategies presented in this chapter can provide technical communicators with the means for realizing such opportunities, these steps are by no means definitive. Rather, these strategies are simply models or foundations for the kinds of undertakings technical communicators can pursue to reveal their value and their role as managers within international outsourcing situations. For this reason, readers should feel free to modify the strategies presented here or to adopt new approaches to address these issues.

CONCLUSION

International outsourcing is radically affecting current perceptions of production and the workplace. Although international outsourcing offers a range of benefits, it also creates certain problem areas, especially related to the abuses of personal data. Fortunately, these problems can be addressed through governance processes that focus on effective communication. As a result, technical communicators are well positioned to use outsourcing-related concerns to reveal how the skills they possess can add value to companies. By using the strategies presented in this chapter, or by developing similar communication-based activities, technical communicators can transform the profession into a field well suited for the business demands of the new century. The time for taking advantage of this situation, however, is limited. Technical communicators must therefore act quickly in order to address this business need before another field does.

REFERENCES

404 tonnes. (2004, December 16). *The Economist*. Retrieved December 27, 2004, from http://www.economist.com/displaystory.cfm?story_id=3503931.

America's pain, India's gain. (2003, January 9). *The Economist*. Retrieved December, 27, 2004, from http://www.economist.com/displaystory.cfm?story_id=1527320.

Atis, G. (2003). Doing cross-border outsourcing deals: A quick and dirty checklist. *Outsourcing Center*. Retrieved December 27, 2004, from http://www.outsourcing-requests.com/center/jsp/requests/print/story.jsp?id=3755.

Atwood, M. (2004). The art of governance. *Outsourcing Center*. Retrieved December 27, 2004, from http://www.outsourcing-requests.com/center/jsp/requests/print/story.jsp?id=4616.

Baily, M. N., & Farrell, D. (2004, July). Exploding the myths of offshoring. *The McKinsey Quarterly*. Retrieved November 11, 2004, from http://www.mckinseyquarterly.com/article_print.aspx?L2=7&L3=10&ar=1453.

Bendor-Samuel, P. (2004). Lou Dobbs: Here's why you're wrong! *Outsourcing Center*. Retrieved December 20, 2004, from http://www.outsourcing-requests.com/center/jsp/requests/print/story.jsp?id=4565.

Bierce, B. (1999). International outsourcing: The legal view of what's different. *Outsourcing Center*. Retrieved December 12, 2004, from http://www.outsourcing-requests.com/center/jsp/requests/print/story.jsp?id=1216.

Bhagowati, B. (2004). India responds to growing concerns over data security. *Outsourcing Center*. Retrieved December 27, 2004, from http://www.outsourcing-requests.com/center/jsp/requests/print/story.jsp?id=4720.

Byrnes, N. (2005, January 1). Green eyeshades never looked so sexy. *BusinessWeek Online*. Retrieved January 5, 2005, from http://www.businessweek.com/@@na*EhYQQxu80VAkA/magazine/content/05_02/b3915041_mz011.htm.

Cate, F. H. (1997). *Privacy in the information age*. Washington, DC: Brookings Institution Press.

Davis, S., & Meyer, C. (1998). *Blur: The speed of change in the connected economy.* Reading, MA: Addison-Wesley.

Doyle, J. F. (2004). Avoiding outsourcing pitfalls. *Outsourcing Center.* Retrieved December 12, 2004, from http://www.outsourcing-requests.com/center/jsp/requests/print/story.jsp?id=4626.

Eisner, R. S. (2002). Smoothing over the privacy potholes in BPO outsourcing. *Outsourcing Center.* Retrieved December 12, 2004, from http://www.outsourcing-requests.com/center/jsp/requests/print/story.jsp?id=2451.

Farrell, D., & Zainulbhai, A. S. (2004). A richer future for India. *The McKinsey Quarterly.* Retrieved August 16, 2004, from http://www.mckinseyquarterly.com/article_page.aspx?ar=1440&L2+7&L3=10&srid=6&g.

Flint, P. et al. (1999). Going online: Helping technical communicators help translators. *Technical Communication, 46,* 238-248.

Friedman, T. L. (1999). *The Lexus and the olive tree.* New York: Farrar, Strass and Giroux.

Garten, J. E. (2004, June 21). Offshoring: You ain't seen nothin' yet. *BusinessWeek Online.* Retrieved December 30, 2004, from http://businessweek.com/print/magazine/content/04_25/b3888024_mz007.htm.

Gaudin, S. (2003, November 19). Offshoring IT jobs expected to accelerate. *ClickZ.* Retrieved November 30, 2004, from http://www.clickz.com/stats/sectors/b2b/print.php/3111321.

Giammona, B. (2004). The future of technical communication: How innovation, technology, information management, and other forces are shaping the future of the profession. *Technical Communication, 51,* 349-366.

Goolsby, K. (2000). Invasion of privacy. *Outsourcing Center.* Retrieved December 12, 2004, from http://www.outsourcing-requests.com/center/jsp/requests/print/story.jsp?id=1581.

Goolsby, K. (2001a). Healthcare's biggest challenge. *Outsourcing Center.* Retrieved December 12, 2004, from http://www.outsourcing-requests.com/center/jsp/requests/print/story.jsp?id=1660.

Goolsby, K. (2001b). How to get ready for HIPAA. *Outsourcing Center.* Retrieved December 12, 2004, from http://www.outsourcing-requests.com/center/jsp/requests/print/story.jsp?id=1686.

Goolsby, K. (2001c). Nobody does it better. *Outsourcing Center.* Retrieved December 12, 2004, from http://www.outsourcing-requests.com/center/jsp/requests/print/story.jsp?id=1816.

Goolsby, K. (2001d). *Perspectives on HIPAA.* Dallas, TX: Outsourcing Center.

Goolsby, K. (2003). *Governing attitudes: 12 best practices in managing outsourcing relationships.* Dallas, TX: Outsourcing Center.

Goolsby, K., & Whitlow, F. K. (2003). *Haste makes waste: How to avoid outsourcing problems.* Dallas, TX: Everest Group.

Hagel, J. III. (2004). Offshoring goes on the offensive. *The McKinsey Quarterly.* Retrieved November 1, 2004, from http://www.mckinseyquarterly.com/article_page.aspx?ar=1406&L2=1&L3=106&srid=11.

Lazarus, D. (2004a, March 28). Looking offshore: Outsourced UCSF notes highlight privacy risk. *San Francisco Chronicle.* Retrieved March 1, 2005, from http://www.sfgate.com/cgi-bin/article.cgi?file=/chronicle/archive/2004/03/28/MNGF S3080R264.DTL.

Lazarus, D. (2004b, April 2). Extortion threat to patients' records: Clients not informed of India staff's breach. *San Francisco Chronicle.* Retrieved March 1, 2005, from http://sfgate.com/cgi-bin/article.cgi?file=/c/a/2004/04/02/MNGI75VIEB1.DTL.

Lewis, W. W. (2003). Educating global workers. *The McKinsey Quarterly.* Retrieved November 10, 2004, from http://www.mckenseyquarterly.com/article_page.aspx?ar=1357&L2=7&L3=10.

Malik, R. (2004, July). The new land of opportunity. *Business 2.0, 5,* 72-79.

Nussbaum, B. (2004, September 20). Is outsourcing becoming outmoded? *BusinessWeek Online.* Retrieved October 11, 2004, from http://www.businessweek.com/print/bwdaaily/dnflash/sep2004/nf20040920_0654.ht m?cha.

Peterson, B. L. (2002). Information security in outsourcing agreements. *Outsourcing Center.* Retrieved December 27, 2004, from http://www.outsourcing-requests.com/center/jsp/requests/print/story.jsp?id=2355.

Reuters. (2004, July 18). France outsources, Senegal calls. *Wired.* Retrieved September 20, 2004, from http://www.wired.com/news/print/0,1294,64262,00.html.

Reuters. (2004, September 2). Outsourcing's next big thing—Malaysia? *News.Com.* Retrieved September 7, 2004, from http://news.com.com/2100-1011-5344618.html.

Rosenthal, B. E. (2004a). How real estate choices affect offshoring decisions. *Outsourcing Center.* Retrieved December 12, 2004, from http://www.outsourcing-requests.com/center/jsp/requests/print/story.jsp?id=4718.

Rosenthal, B. E. (2004b). META predicts offshoring will continue to grow at 20 percent clips through 2008. *Outsourcing Center.* Retrieved December 27, 2004, from http://www.outsourcing-requests.com/center/jsp/requests/print/story.jsp?id=4714.

Rosenthal, B. E. (2004c). Why the US and UK are calling South African call centers. *Outsourcing Center.* Retrieved December 12, 2004, from http://www.outsourcing-requests.com/center/jsp/requests/print/story.jsp?id=4717.

Rosenthal, B. E. (2005). New outsourcing risks in 2005 and how to mitigate them. *Outsourcing Center.* Retrieved January 2, 2005, from http://www.outsourcing-requests.com/center/jsp/requests/print/story.jsp?id=4721.

Salkever, A. (2004, July 7). Racing to cure sickly medical security. *BusinessWeek Online.* Retrieved December 30, 2004, from http://www.businessweek.com/print/technology/content/jul2004/tc2004077_9847_tc _171.

Siebel, T. M., & House, P. (1999). *Cyber rules: Strategies for excelling at e-business.* New York: Doubleday Press.

Sink or Schwinn. (2004, November 11). *The Economist.* Retrieved December 6, 2004, from http://www.economist.com/printedition/PrinterFriendly.cfm?Story_ID=3351542.

Swire, P. P., & Litan, R. E. (1998). *None of your business: World data flows, electronic commerce, and the European privacy directive.* Washington, DC: Brookings Institution Press.

Teasley, B. (2004, December 28). Involvement data. *ClickZ.* Retrieved December 30, 2004, from http://www.clickz.com/experts/cm/analyze_data/print.php/3450561.

The revenge of geography. (2003, March 15). *The Economist Technology Quarterly*, pp. 19-22.

Top ten e-business trends for 2005. *eMarketer*. Retrieved January 2, 2005, from http://www.emarketer.com/Article.aspx?1003202&printerFriendly=yes.

Weir, L. (2004, August 24). Boring game? Outsource it. *Wired*. Retrieved September 20, 2004, from http://www.wired.com/news/print/0,1294,64638,00.html.

Walmer, D. (1999). One company's efforts to improve translation and localization. *Technical Communication, 46*, 230-237.

Whitaker, R. (1999). *The end of privacy: How total surveillance is becoming reality.* New York: New Press.

"Wired China." (2000, July 22). *The Economist*, pp. 24-28.

CHAPTER 10

Outsourcing Technical Communication: The Policy Behind the Practice

Keith Gibson

For as long as most of us can remember, the global economy has been a reality, as products from one country are easily shipped and sold to another. There are some obvious benefits to this situation, not the least of which are Swiss chocolate in the gas station on the corner and Asian silk in the fabric store in the mall. But if products can easily flow between borders, so, in many cases, can jobs. The "giant sucking sound" of U.S. jobs heading for foreign shores has been underway for quite some time, but only in the past ten years or so has outsourcing[1] had a significant effect on white-collar professions. This has led many to rethink their position on the phenomenon, as it may no longer be a limited result of a transitioning American economy. It has also grabbed the attention of middle-class America—and when the fat part of the bell curve speaks, politicians listen. Outsourcing played a significant role in the 2004 presidential campaign, as both George W. Bush and John Kerry addressed the concerns of those Americans who are now competing for jobs with trained, capable workers able to live on a fraction of their salary. This group of Americans increasingly includes technical writers.

---

[1] There is no clear consensus on what this phenomenon should be called, nor even if it is a single phenomenon. Some prefer "offshoring" to emphasize the foreign nature of the work. Others distinguish between offshoring and outsourcing, the former designating government activity, the latter private business. The most common term to cover all aspects is "outsourcing"; to avoid confusion, I will use it throughout.

These concerns are becoming more prevalent among American technical communicators for at least two reasons. First, we are concerned about the stability of our jobs. Many positions related to information technology have made their way overseas in recent years, and Rahel Bailie (2004) indicates that "companies are increasingly comfortable outsourcing [technical writing] tasks" (para. 4). Second, we are concerned about the quality of the field. Technical writers are still in the process of defining the field—as recently as 2002, the Association of Teachers of Technical Writing (ATTW) conference featured a panel titled "Constructing Our Identity"—and the practice of American companies farming out technical writing tasks to the lowest bidder is a legitimate concern, especially when these new writers live in places that make it difficult for organizations like ATTW and the Society for Technical Communication (STC) to monitor the quality of the work.

Because of this twofold interest in outsourcing, technical writers are now becoming more interested in current public policy toward outsourcing, as well as the positions of public officials who will shape this policy for years to come. This interest, however, has not been met with particularly user-friendly examinations of the subject. Most analyses of outsourcing center around the macroeconomic effects it will have on the United States and global economies (see for instance Baily & Farrell, 2004; Drezner, 2004b; Jones, 2004; Mattoo & Wunsch, 2004); the variables are complex enough that there is more than enough disagreement on these points. Rather than add my voice to those that have explored these large-scale effects of outsourcing, I will focus on what we, as technical communicators, can or should do in response to this changing environment. To that end, this chapter contains three sections: first, I describe current U.S. laws and policies on outsourcing, specifically the free-trade agreements negotiated over the past 75 years, and portions of the U.S. tax code allowing international companies to defer paying taxes on foreign-earned income; second, I deal with the future of U.S. outsourcing policy, as indicated by American politicians' public statements; third, I connect the likely future of outsourcing policy to technical communicators, offering suggestions for us as individuals and as a community.

EXISTING OUTSOURCING POLICY

Outsourcing is an issue of fairly recent importance; as such, though many states are pursuing legislation limiting the types and numbers of jobs American companies move overseas, there are currently no laws that specifically reference the issue.[2] There are two policies that, depending on one's point of view, seem to either encourage or allow outsourcing: current (and future) free-trade agreements

---

[2] The first federal law on outsourcing, one that banned high-tech portions of government contracts from going overseas, was signed in February 2004. It was written with an expiration date of September 30, 2004, however, and, as of this writing, it has not been replaced or renewed.

and an old line in the U.S. tax code about deferring taxes on foreign-made income. Any discussion of outsourcing policy has got to begin with where we are now; the following sections will provide background needed for the later examination of where this policy is going.

Free Trade From Hawley-Smoot to the WTO

The peak of U.S. protectionism came on June 17, 1930 when President Hoover signed the Hawley-Smoot Tariff, raising duties on imported goods to the highest peacetime level in American history. The foreign retaliation (25 nations passed laws restricting the sale of U.S. goods the following year) and the role the act played in worsening the Great Depression set the U.S. on a course of tariff reduction from which we have rarely wavered in the three-quarters of a century since (Bragdon, McCutchen, & Ritchie, 1994, pp. 797-799). This trend has nearly reached its logical conclusion in the past fifteen years with a series of international agreements. The first, in 1989, established tariff-free trade between the United States and Canada. Next, President Bush reached the same deal with Mexico just before he left office in 1992. Finally, the North American Free Trade Agreement (NAFTA) was authorized by the House, ratified by the Senate, and signed by President Clinton in 1993. Protests came quickly, largely from environmental organizations and labor unions as they voiced their concerns over environmental abuses and job loss. The export of jobs gained more traction with the American public, and slogans like "Fair Trade, Not Free Trade" became rallying cries for the opposition. But with the support of U.S. Presidents from each political party, the treaty has held firm with very little opposition in the halls of Congress.

The three-country NAFTA, though, was but a drop in the free-trade bucket. April 1994, three months after NAFTA took effect, saw the signing of the General Agreement on Tariffs and Trade (GATT), a deal 46 years in the making. The original GATT involved 124 member countries, called for a 40% reduction in tariffs, and projected a $235 billion increase in worldwide income. It also established its own successor—the much-maligned World Trade Organization—to take its place on January 1, 1995. Since its inception, the WTO has expanded to 148 member nations, 32 of which are on the UN's list of 50 "least-developed" countries. The WTO establishes rules for member nations in their international dealings in goods, services, and intellectual property, but its General Agreement on Trade in Services (GATS), like U.S. law, does not specifically address outsourcing. Their guidelines state that the agreement covers "all internationally-traded services," but it categorizes these services into the following four groups:

- services supplied from one country to another (e.g., international telephone calls), officially known as "**cross-border supply**" (in WTO jargon, "mode 1")

- consumers or firms making use of a service in another country (e.g., tourism), officially **"consumption abroad"** ("mode 2")
- a foreign company setting up subsidiaries or branches to provide services in another country (e.g., foreign banks setting up operations in a country), officially **"commercial presence"** ("mode 3")
- individuals travelling [sic] from their own country to supply services in another (e.g., fashion models or consultants), officially **"presence of natural persons"** ("mode 4") (World Trade Organization, 2003, p. 36, emphasis in original)

None of these categories quite describes the phenomenon we call outsourcing, where a foreign company sets up a subsidiary to provide services in its own country. Furthermore, Mattoo and Wunsch (2004) have noted that "positive listing" in the GATS has led to further holes in the agreement: "the market access commitments of each WTO member apply only to the sectors it chooses to list. So if a service is not explicitly listed then a member remains free to restrict on trade in that service" (p. 2). Thus, not even the WTO has any explicit reference to outsourcing. The spirit of the law, however, is that there be no restriction on the exchange of services; that attitude has ruled the day to this point.

The U.S. Tax Code and Outsourcing

The second piece of public policy that is seen as having a significant effect on outsourcing is a line in the American federal tax code that allows U.S. companies with foreign subsidiaries to defer paying taxes on foreign income until that income is brought back to the United States. This foreign income is still subject to the taxes of the country in which it is earned, but U.S. tax deferment is still often significant because most countries have corporate tax rates substantially lower than America's 35%. Thus, if a company earns $100 million abroad and pays the local 20% tax rate ($20 million), it will owe another $15 million if it brings the money here.[3] This policy provides a clear incentive for the company to invest money in the foreign country rather than returning it to the United States.

Two things are worth noting. First, this loophole is not a recent addition to the tax code: the *Wall Street Journal* reports that this "active foreign income" has never been taxed at the U.S. rate since the beginning of corporate income taxes nearly 100 years ago (Liesman, 2004, para. 2). Second, America's tax code is not written in a vacuum: other countries benefit greatly from the investment of U.S. dollars encouraged by the current tax situation, and many analysts predict

---

[3] U.S. tax law credits taxes paid to another country; the 35%, then, is not on top of foreign taxes, it is the total rate paid.

retaliatory tax changes by foreign countries most affected by "active foreign income" (i.e., if we lower the corporate tax rate to 20%, Indonesia lowers theirs to 10%, maintaining the advantage of U.S. corporations investing there).

As a result, the two parts of U.S. policy that most specifically address outsourcing don't really address it at all. With all the attention outsourcing has been receiving in recent years, though, U.S. federal and state politicians are sure to act in the near future. Indeed, several state legislatures and the U.S. Congress have already drafted bills to deal with this situation. As of this writing, none have yet been successful, but since government abhors a vacuum, the U.S. stance on outsourcing is almost certain to evolve, shift, or completely change in the coming years, and concerned technical communicators would do well to pay attention to debates now taking place. With that background, I now look ahead to where outsourcing policy may be going by analyzing statements made by various politicians during and after the 2004 Presidential campaign.[4]

THE DIRECTION OF U.S. OUTSOURCING POLICY

The two major political parties in the United States spent a significant amount of television airtime talking about the causes, effects, and future of outsourcing. Their rhetoric can be analyzed in a number of ways; I will here focus on two *topoi* that consistently appeared in the discussions: patriotism and intellectualism. I will first examine the emotional appeals to patriotism and, in some cases, jingoism as the "Buy American" slogans made a brief reappearance in the national discourse. I will then describe Donald Wood's theory of anti-intellectualism and analyze how each candidate appealed to intellectual or anti-intellectual positions on outsourcing. This linguistic and rhetorical examination will uncover some of the complexities involved in the outsourcing debate, but the focus throughout will be on how this debate is and will be affecting the changing occupational landscape for technical communicators.

Made in the USA:
How Patriotism Shaped the Outsourcing Debate

The use of patriotism, even jingoism, in economic discussions gained wide attention in the 1970s when the International Ladies' Garment Workers' Union made "Look for the Union Label" a household phrase. The 1980s saw an increase in the use and violence of such campaigns, as autoworkers took sledgehammers

---

[4] John Kerry was obviously the most quoted Democrat during 2004, and most of the statements I analyze from his party come from him. It is less clear that he represents the future of the Democratic Party, even if he decides to run for President again. Thus, my analysis of his statements will be compared not only to his positions and ideas, but also to those of the party as a whole; this should give us a better picture of where the Democrats plan to go with this issue.

to foreign cars, insisting that we "Buy American." These campaigns played on the union sympathies of liberals and the feelings of American superiority of conservatives to craft a surprisingly effective argument, one that spawned bumper stickers, T-shirts, and a resurgence in American manufacturing (Frank, 1999, pp. 226-240).

The 1990s, though, saw a deterioration of the "Buy American" movement as consumers realized quality and value could be found in foreign-made products and as manufacturers gained a sense of international solidarity with workers performing similar labor in similar factories, often for the same company (Frank, 1999, pp. 244-250). This solidarity was particularly evident in the information technology (IT) sector of the global economy: qualified computer programmers, software technicians, and technical communicators were soon coming from all parts of the globe, and in the late 1990s the American IT industry was grateful for the help. The Information Technology Association of America (ITAA) (2004) reports that IT outsourcing began in earnest in 1998, but the economy was growing quickly enough to more than accommodate any U.S. worker who lost a job (p. 2). The presence of international co-workers, then, did not seem like competition so much as a growing fraternity; the STC, for instance, has seen rapid growth in the past ten years, and now boasts local chapters in 22 different countries.

This global marketplace was fine while the economy grew worldwide in the 1990s; when times get tough, however, all economics, like politics, turns out to be local. The downturn in the IT industry in 2000 did not just slow growth in the field, it forced many companies to drastically cut their expenses or go out of business completely. Many companies chose to adapt by hiring more international workers at a fraction of the cost of American employees; the ITAA (2004) estimated that from 1998 to 2003, 104,000 IT jobs were lost due to outsourcing.[5] Many other companies simply laid off employees; from 2000 to 2003, the IT industry lost 268,000 jobs for nonoutsourcing reasons, such as the end of the internet boom, the recession of 2001, and the productivity gains that accompanied technological advances (pp. 2-3). The IT job losses due to outsourcing, though significantly fewer than those lost for other reasons, were enough, especially when combined with increased media attention, to stir a minirevival of the old union rallying cries.

Many of John Kerry's 2004 speeches on outsourcing featured these "Buy American" sentiments. The most famous was his statement on February 19, just nine days after the Council of Economic Advisors report labeled outsourcing "a new way of doing international trade" (as cited in Weisman, 2004,

---

[5] According to their report, this figure includes "not only jobs that were eliminated by some U.S. companies that substituted offshore resources for domestic resources, but it also includes jobs that were never created as other U.S. companies expanded their IT activities using offshore resources without reducing their domestic resources" (ITAA, 2004, p. 2).

para. 6). As discussed below, many in Washington did not agree with this characterization—chief among them was John Kerry. He declared he would "repeal every tax break and loophole that rewards any Benedict Arnold CEO or corporation for shipping American jobs overseas" (as cited in Jones, 2004, para. 4). His campaign Web site featured the very phrase of the 1980s movements: "John Kerry believes that federal contracts where possible should be performed by American workers. John Kerry supports stronger 'Buy American' guidelines for defense and homeland security" (Kerry, 2004, para. 2). In a September 7 speech, he invoked the label that so many had worn so proudly: "My value is a good, old-fashioned four words: 'Made in the USA'" (as cited in Superville, 2004, para. 9). Ted Kennedy appealed to a similar sentiment when he called the CEA report "unpatriotic economics" (as cited in "Bush adviser backs," 2004, para. 22).

The Bush administration has played to the nationalism of the American worker as well, but in a slightly different way: insisting that Americans can successfully compete with foreign manufacturers without adding rules or tariffs. In a September 2003 interview regarding increasing outsourcing in technical fields, Chris Israel, a Commerce Department deputy assistant secretary, stated that "the answer to economic challenges is growth and innovation" (as cited in Thibodeau, 2003, para. 2). The day the CEA report was issued, White House spokeswoman Claire Buchan was asked about its implications for American workers. She responded, "The president's view is that American workers are the best workers in the world" (as cited in Weisman, 2004, para. 9). In the debates, Bush (2004, October 9) expanded on that theme, arguing that the best way to reduce the effects of outsourcing is to "make sure we've got a workforce that's productive and competitive" (as cited in *Debate transcript: October 8, 2004*). This led, in the second and third debates, to his claim that new laws are not the solution, but rather "education is how to help the person who's lost a job" (as cited in *Debate transcript: October 13, 2004*).

American patriotism is a powerful emotion, and both candidates appealed to it in their own way. John Kerry hearkened back to the "Buy American" campaigns of the 1970s and 80s, hoping to regain the solid union support for Democrats that had been slipping since NAFTA became law during the Clinton administration. George Bush likewise appealed to his base, insisting that Americans don't need extra protections; we either are or can become "the best workers in the world." These appeals to patriotism were fairly predictable, relatively safe, and probably mildly effective. However, the implied "us vs. them" mentality is simply not in line with the current nature of the global economy, especially in the IT sector. Precisely because of the current state of information technology, American workers can no longer pretend that there is such a thing as "an American job," and these emotional arguments that equate outsourcing with high treason simply distract our attention from a more calm analysis of what is indeed a difficult situation.

Postintellectualism and the Loss of Perspective

Donald Wood (1996) has studied what he describes as our descent into a postintellectual period, "a loss of open-mindedness and intellectual inquiry" that keeps us from dealing with our societal crises rationally (p. 8). One of the main features of this postintellectualism is a vocational specialization that has led to a loss of the "broad liberal arts perspective," formerly a common feature of even elementary education (Wood, 1996, p. 45). Lack of this perspective leaves most of us without "the ability to cope with the totality of our social environment, [so] we entrust the management of society to the specialists and technocrats" (Wood, 1996, p. 45).

This phenomenon is perhaps nowhere more apparent than in dealings with economic issues. Many Americans graduate from high school and college having never taken an economics course, and the level of economic illiteracy among otherwise-educated adults is, according to the President of the National Council on Economic Education, "disturbing" (Duvall, 2004, para. 2). A recent Harris poll found that two-thirds of Americans do not understand that active competition in the market place reduces prices and improves quality, and half do not know the stock market is where the public can buy and sell stocks (as cited in Duvall, 2004, paras. 11-12). This is an example of the "lack of a liberal arts perspective," of which Wood writes, and it leads to another type of lost perspective: a focus on the small picture rather than the big one. Those without a clear understanding of economic theory tend to focus on microeconomics—they make judgments about the economy based on their situation or their neighbors' or their community's. But no system with the size and complexity of the U.S. economy (much less the world economy) can be properly understood by examining but a small part—the big picture must be viewed. For instance, few would dispute that the rise of the personal computer has been a good thing for the American economy (Internet bubble notwithstanding), but the typewriter repairpersons who were driven into early retirement were probably not thrilled by it. Those with economic "perspective" see things one way; those without it see them another.

Jonathan Larson (1993) claims most economic disagreements, and free trade disputes in particular, tend to fall along these lines; specifically, he argues that "the battle lines over NAFTA are not drawn between Democrats and Republicans but between economic and academic elites and the populist revolt" (para. 5). These same battle lines have been shaping up in the fight over outsourcing as well, and they affect how both the government and technical communicators view the issue.

One of the purposes of representative government is to relieve the general public of needing to master every single policy issue the country faces; the challenge for the representatives, however, is that they must balance their under-standing (or, at least, their advisors' understanding) of the issues with the way they must address these issues to the public. This tension was perhaps never clearer than during the outsourcing kerfuffle that erupted over two very busy days in the life of President Bush's Chief Economic Advisor, Gregory Mankiw in early February 2004. On February 9, in a briefing to introduce the Council of Economic Advisor's "Economic Report of the President," he said, "I think outsourcing is a growing phenomenon, but it's something that we should realize is probably a plus for the economy in the long run" (as cited in "Bush adviser backs," 2004, para. 3). The next day he delivered "The Economic Report of the President," which expanded on the sentiment:

> New types of trade deliver new benefits to consumers and firms in open economies. Growing international demand for goods such as movies, pharmaceuticals, and recordings offers new opportunities for US exporters. A burgeoning trade in services provides an important outlet for US expertise in sectors such as banking, engineering, and higher education. The ability to buy less expensive goods and services from new producers has made household budgets go further, while the ability of firms to distribute their production around the world has cut costs and thus prices to consumers. The benefits from new forms of trade, such as in services, are no different from the benefits from traditional trade in goods. Outsourcing of professional services is a prominent example of a new type of trade. The gains from trade that take place over the internet or telephone lines are no different than the gains from trade in physical goods transported by ship or plane. When a good or service is produced at a lower cost in another country, it makes sense to import it rather than produce it domestically. This allows the United States to devote its resources to more productive purposes (U.S. Council of Economic Advisors, 2004, p. 7).

Following the presentation of the report, Mankiw continued to reporters, "Outsourcing is just a new way of doing international trade. More things are tradable than were tradable in the past and that's a good thing" (as cited in Weisman, 2004, para. 6).

According to Daniel Drezner (2004b, May/June), "No economist really disputed Mankiw's observation" (para. 2)[6]: Alan Greenspan, for instance, defended Mankiw's claims two days later ("Greenspan," 2004); *The Economist* published an editorial supporting the contention that outsourcing makes the economies on both ends stronger ("Great," 2004); and former Clinton administration economist Martin Baily made an almost identical argument five months later in *The McKinsey Quarterly* (Baily & Farrell, 2004). To those without Wood's "broad

---

[6] This is, of course, a difficult claim to prove, but both Drezner (2004a, March) and the Committee of 100 (2004) have compiled extensive bibliographies of a wide variety of economic theorists, nearly all of them arguing against the notion that outsourcing is particularly harmful. In addition, NBC financial correspondent Mike Jensen concluded a 1999 report on the WTO with the statement that "most experts say getting rid of trade barriers on both sides is a good thing for American workers and consumers" (as cited in Ackerman, 2000, para. 5).

liberal arts perspective," however, hearing outsourcing described as "a plus for the economy" or a "new benefit" simply did not make sense.

So, in a rare show of bipartisan agreement, Congressional leaders of both parties stepped forward to lead from behind, telling the American people what they wanted to hear. Republican Congressman Daniel Manzullo immediately called for Mankiw's resignation, stating, "I know the president cannot believe what this man has said. He ought to walk away, and return to his ivy-covered office at Harvard" (as cited in Weisman, 2004, para. 4). On February 11, Speaker of the House Dennis Hastert said Mankiw's "theory fails a basic test of real economics," and House Minority Leader Nancy Pelosi criticized what she called "the president's embracing of outsourcing" (as cited in "Bush econ," 2004, paras. 4, 7). The same day Senate Minority Leader Tom Daschle and Senator Ted Kennedy held a joint press conference in which Daschle called Mankiw's statements "Alice in Wonderland economics," and Kennedy said the president's economic report was "an insult to every hard-working American" (as cited in "Bush adviser backs," 2004, paras. 20, 22). Daschle further emphasized the difference between academic elitism and what he believed was common sense: "Nearly every state in the nation has lost manufacturing jobs, and, contrary to the administration's economic *theories*, there is nothing good about it" (as cited in "Bush adviser backs," 2004, para. 21, emphasis added). Even President Bush backpedaled from his adviser's comments; in a speech in Pennsylvania, he noted that "there are people looking for work because jobs have gone overseas. And we need to act in this country. We need to act to make sure there are more jobs at home and people are more likely to retain a job" (as cited in "Bush econ," 2004, para. 6). Kerry responded quickly as well, claiming Mankiw's statements were proof that Bush believed "that shipping American jobs overseas is good for America" (as cited in "Bush adviser supports," 2004, para. 11). Speaking to reporters, he even mused aloud, "What in the world are they thinking?" (as cited in Weisman, 2004, para. 2).

The ensuing tension between theorists and politicians did not go away quietly. On March 30, 2004, when Treasury Secretary John Snow was asked if he would advise U.S. companies to slow down their outsourcing, he reiterated Mankiw's general claim that outsourcing is not harmful to the economy as a whole: "I think American companies need to do what they need to do to be competitive, and as they're competitive, it's good for shareholders, it's good for their consumers, and it's good for their employees" (as cited in Treasury, 2004, para. 3). Kerry spokeswoman Stephanie Cutter quickly responded that Snow was "again emphasizing the administration's support for sending US jobs overseas, because it's 'cheaper' for the companies" (as cited in Jones, 2004, para. 7).

The noise made over outsourcing during the campaign is strong evidence indeed for Larson's claim that these kinds of arguments tend to occur between "academic and economic elites and the populist revolt." Outsourcing in IT fields has led to similar disagreements. Catherine Mann (2003), a senior fellow at the Institute for International Economics, wrote in December 2003 that the globalization of IT hardware in the 1990s was a key part of the economic boom of the period, leading to the "'trifecta' of faster income growth, lower inflation, and more employment" and that our previous experience with outsourcing hardware should serve as "a model for the global evolution of IT services and software" (p. 1). She argues that "globally integrated production of IT software and services will reduce [their] prices and . . . will promote further diffusion of IT use and transformation throughout the US economy" (Mann, 2003, p. 2). The Information Technology Association of America (ITAA) (2004) likewise forecasts an improved economy through outsourcing, noting that "while global IT software and service outsourcing displaces some IT workers, total employment in the United States increases as the benefits ripple through the economy. . . . IT outsourcing created over 90,000 net new jobs as of 2003 and is expected to create 317,000 net new jobs by 2008" (p. 1).

Norman Matloff (2004), a computer-science professor, argues that this "big picture" is only one side of the story; even if the ITAA is right about the rising number of jobs, "the vast majority of these jobs will not be of the high-level variety. . . . Thus the US would lose IT jobs requiring a more rigorous level of education in exchange for gaining jobs requiring a less-demanding education" (p. 28). Further, Matloff (2004) claims the trend of outsourcing is not likely to slow down anytime soon, meaning that even if the industry creates new types of jobs for our IT workers, "the technological ones are likely to be offshored . . . [leaving] sales and marketing jobs in the US but with R&D done offshore" (p. 28). Matloff's arguments underscore the complexities of outsourcing policy. Those who argue the microeconomic case—outsourcing is bad because I lost my job—may indeed be seeing only the small picture; but the news that the economy as a whole has more jobs will be small consolation if they are not in fields in which those individuals are trained. A technical writer in Texas who loses her job to a writer in India may not be helped no matter how many roofing jobs open up in Dallas.

These difficulties plague those politicians charged with making public policy on outsourcing. Slowing outsourcing means restricting free trade, something the United States has been hesitant to do, especially in the last couple decades. It would also mean ignoring what economists claim is the welfare of the many for the benefit of the few; this would not be unprecedented, but it is not exactly the formula for winning elections. And if the current administration is maintaining a stance on outsourcing that is not particularly popular with technical writers, it is worth noting that a Kerry administration likely would have been no different: since the election, Kerry has reportedly "backpedaled" on his outsourcing stance "after he realized it was not so harmful to the US economy" (as cited in Envoy, 2005, para. 5).

LOOKING TO THE FUTURE

The reason for this analysis was to assess the future of U.S. outsourcing policy, specifically how it will affect technical writers' two concerns: our jobs and our field. If the first concern can be addressed, if something can be done to stop technical writing jobs from crossing borders, our employment futures will seem more secure, and we will find it much easier to ensure the quality of the work our field produces. If not, we will need to be much more creative in both endeavors.

Concerning the first, the federal government has two main options if it wishes to stem the tide of jobs moving overseas: executive orders and legislation. In 2003 assistant deputy secretary Chris Israel indicated that there are several options open to a White House inclined to make outsourcing difficult: it can set requirements on government contracts, it can use national security as an excuse to discourage sending certain work overseas, or it can even restrict certain types of work visas international corporations use to develop offshore subsidiaries (as cited in Thibodeau, 2003).

As Bush's economic advisers have indicated, however, the current administration is not anxious to restrict this new part of the global economy. The U.S. ambassador to India, David Mulford, has repeatedly assured the Indian government that the Bush White House is not going to act to reduce outsourcing, largely because the current thinking is that it helps all sides: "there's a realisation [sic] now that there is an economic logic behind outsourcing. Every dollar that is going out by way of outsourcing is bringing in more than a dollar" (as cited in Envoy, 2005, para. 2).

Congress is an entirely different matter. There are several Congresspersons whose constituents are very uneasy about the continued outsourcing trend, and the coming session is likely to see continued efforts to specifically address outsourcing through legislation. Public policy being what it is, these efforts will likely affect the public sector first and the private sector, if at all, much later. A look at what may be ahead on a national level can be seen in a threesome of bills passed by the California legislature in late 2004. These bills sought to prohibit three specific activities:

- outsourcing of essential state homeland security work;
- state agencies or local government from contracting for services to be performed by workers outside the United States; and
- health-care businesses from transmitting personally identifiable information outside the United States without authorization. (Short, 2004)

Gov. Schwarzenegger vetoed all three, citing reasons similar to those found in the pro-business arguments discussed above. Short is confident that outsourcing legislation will come up again, but he argues it is likely to be similar in substance to that put forth by the California legislature, particularly as it applies only to government employees. Indeed, without some large-scale changes to current international trade agreements, there seems to be little direct action to be taken against private companies moving jobs overseas. David Mulford, in his dealings with India, has pointed out "I don't think US legislation can change the course of global business. And, I don't think private US business is willing to accept any intrusive government interference on this issue" (as cited in "US Poll," 2004, para. 8). The implications of any near-future legislation for technical writers, then, appears to be minimal. The Bureau of Labor Statistics (2004) reports that, of the approximately 50,000 technical writers in the United States, relatively few are employed in the public sector (Employment section, para. 1). The private companies that employ most technical writers are unlikely to be bound by outsourcing restrictions in the near future, even if any are signed into law.

Thus, the likelihood of executive action is small, and the future of outsourcing legislation is largely irrelevant to most IT workers; what, then, is the future for technical writers? On one hand, economists are nearly unanimous in insisting that outsourcing is not as damaging to the American economy as it seems; it may even lead to a stronger economy with more opportunity. On the other hand, a number of technical writing jobs are sure to be sent abroad, and the Bureau of Labor Statistics (2004) projection that "[d]emand for technical writers . . . is likely to increase" could turn out to be more muted than they suggest (Job Outlook section, para. 3). In this situation, technical writers, as a group, have (at least) two options. One is to do nothing collectively, encouraging members to individually prepare themselves for a job market that has been softened by outsourcing. Generally speaking, this preparation consists of making oneself valuable in a variety of ways; specifically, technical writers need to make a conscious effort to stay on top of the ever-changing technologies that dictate the modes of communication we use. We can also make ourselves valuable by becoming more versed in the subject matters on which we write—we may never actually be the engineers, but if we can communicate with them more easily in their own language, we will be more integral parts of the team. A roundtable discussion on outsourcing featuring members of the STC, the National Writer's Union, and the Bay Area Publication Managers Forum encouraged technical writers to "retrain into editors" and "look into writing white papers [and] business plans" for industries that are now becoming computerized (Ramos, 2003, Summary section, para. 2). The best-case scenario is for this extra training to be superfluous, but more skills will lead to more flexibility; in an evolving economy, flexibility is a valuable asset.

The second option is to try to influence government policy. Republicans will control the White House and be able to block attempts to override vetoes through at least 2008, and they seem very reluctant to initiate any sweeping regulations on their own. But Washington D.C. has never met a special interest group it didn't like, and the 18,000 member Society for Technical Communication is headquartered just across the Potomac in Arlington, VA. The mission of the STC is "Creating and supporting a forum for communities of practice in the profession of technical communication" (Society for Technical Communication, 2005), but, according to the "STC Strategic Plan 2002–2007," forming any kind of lobbying group is not even on the radar (Society for Technical Communication, 2002). Maurice Martin, the STC Communication Director, pointed out that STC is a 501 (c) 3 organization, which means they are allowed to lobby Congress, but, he said, the current Board of Directors has specifically passed on the idea of such action (personal communication, June 6, 2005). Organizational momentum being what it is, any movement on these issues will probably take some time, but if we want to make our voices heard, we have got to speak up.

There is a distinct possibility that outsourcing is not going to cause any major problems—our own career paths may never be threatened, and the U.S. economy may grow because of it. Even so, a growing number of foreign-based technical writers producing materials for American readers will have an impact on the nature and the reputation of our field, a reputation that is vital to our position as valued members of the workplace. One way to ensure a high quality of technical communication is an increased emphasis on international certification. The good news here is that the infrastructure for a program like this is already in place. The STC is very influential in North and South America and Asia, and they work closely with INTECOM, which has a large presence in Europe, Australia, and New Zealand. The International Organization for Standardization (ISO) (2004) has an extensive list of technical-documentation guidelines that could be readily transformed into a set of certification procedures; combined with the worldwide presence of the above organizations, companies around the world could be strongly encouraged to hire writers who meet or who produce writing that meets a set of international criteria. In terms of protecting, and even enhancing, the reputation of technical communicators across the globe, international certification may be an efficient and effective solution.

A final need, as almost every academic musing suggests, is further research. Outsourcing is a topic in which anecdotal evidence tends to carry a lot of weight, but informed decisions require data that is as specific as possible. We need numbers on the rate of job movement across borders, and we need to know the actual effect of these transfers on the American and world economies. If the STC or INTECOM are to act, we need survey information to decide what the membership wishes to do. And if we are to establish international standards for certification, we need to interview writers, users, and subject-matter experts to determine the most helpful guidelines.

Outsourcing is understandably a cause of anxiety for technical writers, but it need not be viewed as a death knell to the field in the United States. Though there may be little that can or will be done to stop companies from moving jobs overseas, American companies will continue to need technical communicators in large numbers. Indeed, if we prepare ourselves for the changing marketplace, we may become, individually and collectively, stronger and more productive members of an evolving global economy.

REFERENCES

Ackerman, S. (2000, January). *Prattle in Seattle: WTO coverage misrepresented issues, protests.* Retrieved November 10, 2004 from http://www.fair.org/extra/0001/wto-prattle.html.

America cries foul as Bush advocates outsourcing. (2004, February 15). *Sify.com.* Retrieved December 10, 2004 from http://sify.com/news/internet/fullstory.php?id=13389626.

Bailie, R. A. (2003, October). *What color is your future job: Commodity writer or strategic communicator?* Retrieved November 15, 2004 from http://www.stcnymetro.org/metro_voice/mv_102003/mv_102003.html.

Baily, M., & Farrell, D. (2004, July). Exploding the myths of offshoring. *McKinsey Quarterly.* Retrieved January 5, 2005 from http://www.mckinseyquarterly.com/.

Bragdon, H. W., McCutchen, S. P., & Ritchie, D. A. (1994). *History of a free nation.* New York: Macmillan/McGraw-Hill.

Bureau of Labor Statistics. (2004, February 27). Writers and editors. *Occupational outlook handbook 2004-05 edition.* Retrieved December 1, 2004 from http://www.bls.gov/oco/ocos089.htm.

Bush adviser backs off pro-outsourcing comment. (2004, February 12). *CNN.com.* Retrieved September 21, 2004 from http://www.cnn.com/2004/US/02/12/bush.outsourcing/.

Bush adviser supports outsourcing. (2004, February 12). *FoxNews.com.* Retrieved September 16, 2004 from http://www.foxnews.com/story/0,2933,111225,00.html.

Bush econ adviser: outsourcing ok. (2004, February 13). *CBSNews.com.* Retrieved September 15, 2004 from http://www.cbsnews.com/stories/2004/02/13/opinion/main600351.shtml.

Committee of 100. (2004, June). *Outsourcing bibliography.* Retrieved September 10, 2004 from http://www.committee100.org/About/outsourcing%20articles/outsourcing%20biblio graphy.doc.

Debate transcript: October 8, 2004. (2004, October 9). Retrieved October 10, 2004 from http://www.debates.org/pages/trans2004c.html.

Debate transcript: October 13, 2004. (2004, October 14). Retrieved October 15, 2004 from http://www.debates.org/pages/trans2004d.html.

Drezner, D. (2004a, March). *An outsourcing bibliography.* Retrieved December 1, 2004 from http://www.danieldrezner.com/archives/001155.html.

Drezner, D. (2004b, May/June). *The outsourcing bogeyman.* Retrieved September 15, 2004 from http://www.danieldrezner.com/policy/outsourcing.htm.

Duvall, R. F. (2004, March 30). *Testimony of Dr. Robert F. Duvall President and Chief Executive Officer National Council on Economic Education before the Subcommittee on Financial Management, the Budget, and International Security of the Senate Committee on Governmental Affairs.* Retrieved October 16, 2004 from http://www.ncee.net/news/story.php?story_id=51.

Economy, the: People's chief concerns. (2004, January). Retrieved September 10, 2004 from http://www.publicagenda.org/issues/pcc_detail.cfm?issue_type=economy&list=1.

Envoy sees no threat to outsourcing in India. (2005, January 28). *The Times of India.* Retrieved February 1, 2005 from http://timesofindia.indiatimes.com/.

Frank, D. (1999). *Buy American: The untold story of economic nationalism.* Boston: Beacon Press.

Great hollowing-out myth, the. (2004, February 19). *The Economist.* Retrieved September 20, 2004 from http://www.economist.com/.

Greenspan too defends outsourcing. (2004, February 21). *Rediff.com.* Retrieved September 21, 2004 from http://www.rediff.com/money/2004/feb/21bpo.htm.

Jones, S. (2004, March 31). Outsourcing sends jobs away, but others come in, supporters say. *CNSNews.com.* Retrieved September 21, 2004 from http://www.cnsnews.com/Politics/Archive/200403/POL.20040331a.html.

International Organization for Standardization. (2004). *Technical product documentation.* Retrieved April 13, 2005 from http://www.iso.org/iso/en/CatalogueListPage.CatalogueList?ICS1=1&ICS2=&ICS3=&scopelist=.

Information Technology Association of America. (2004, March). *Executive summary: The comprehensive impact of offshore IT software and services outsourcing on the US economy and the IT industry.* Retrieved June 10, 2004 from http://www.itaa.org/itserv/docs/execsumm.pdf.

Kerry, J. (2004, August 31). *Statement by John Kerry on World Trade Organization ruling on the Byrd Amendment.* Retrieved September 10, 2004 from http://www.johnkerry.com/pressroom/releases/pr_2004_0831d.html.

Larson, J. (1993). *The history of 'free trade.'* Retrieved November 15, 2004 from http://villa.lakes.com/eltechno/TVAfretr.html.

Liesman, S. (2004, March 12). US tax code provisions encourage offshore jobs. *The Wall Street Journal.* Retrieved September 25, 2004 from http://online.wsj.com.

Mann, C. L. (2003, December). Globalization of IT services and white collar jobs: The next wave of productivity growth. [Electronic version]. *International Economics Policy Briefs PB03* (11), 1-10.

Matloff, N. (2004, November). Globalization and the American IT worker [Electronic version]. *Communications of the ACM, 47*(11), 27-29.

Mattoo, A., & Wunsch, S. (2004, March). *Pre-empting protectionism in services: The WTO and outsourcing.* Retrieved October 12, 2004 from http://econ.worldbank.org/files/34010_wps3237.pdf.

Ramos, A. (2003, July). *The NWU BizTech Offshoring Project.* Retrieved June 18, 2005 from http://www.biztech-offshoring.com/roundtable.html.

Short, G. (2004). *Vetoing the legislation against outsourcing in California.* Retrieved December 10, 2004 from http://www.outsourcing-law.com/Vetoing.outsourcing.11.2004.htm.

Society for Technical Communication. (2002). *STC strategic plan 2002-2007.* Retrieved April 21, 2005 from http://www.stc.org/PDF_Files/StrategicPlan.pdf.

Society for Technical Communication. (2005). *About STC.* Retrieved April 2, 2005 from http://www.stc.org/about.asp.

Superville, D. (2004, September 7). Kerry assails deficit as Bush's fault. *Miami Herald.* Retrieved September 21, 2004 from http://www.miami.com/mld/miamiherald/.

Thibodeau, P. (2003, September 29). Bush administration won't impede offshore outsourcing. *Computer World.* Retrieved November 11, 2004 from http://www.computerworld.com/careertopics/careers/labor/story/0,10801,85468,00.html.

Treasury Secretary defends outsourcing. (2004, February 24). *MSNBC.com*. Retrieved November 1, 2004 from http://www.msnbc.msn.com/id/4365553.

U.S. Council of Economic Advisors. (2004, February 10). *The Economic Report of the President*. Retrieved September 20, 2004 from http://www.whitehouse.gov/cea/text/economic_report_20040210.html.

US poll results won't hit outsourcing: Mulford. (2004, April 30). *Rediff.com*. Retrieved January 10, 2005 from http://www.rediff.com/money/2004/apr/30bpo1.htm.

Weisman, J. (2004, February 11). Bush, adviser assailed for stance on 'offshoring' jobs. *Washington Post*. Retrieved September 16, 2004 from http://www.washingtonpost.com/.

Wood, D. (1996). *Post-intellectualism and the decline of democracy*. Westport, CT: Praeger Publishing.

World Trade Organization. (2003). *Understanding the WTO*. Geneva: WTO Publications.

CHAPTER 11

Obligations and Opportunities: Legal Issues in Offshore Outsourcing Technical Communication

Charlsye Smith Diaz

To date, only the work of the World Trade Organization and several acts such as the General Agreement on Trade in Services (GATS) and the Agreement on Trade-Related Aspects of Intellectual Property Rights (TRIPS)—provide negotiated uniform rules among member countries for offshore outsourcing. Case law, the common law of the United States that is established through judicial decision making rather than legislation, is more or less rendered useless in international or multinational enterprises; instead, these enterprises turn to what is known as "soft law"—individual agreements between corporations (Hillgenberg, 1999, p. 499). Without the benefit of legislation or the precedent established through case law, U.S. attorneys are advising their clients to proceed with caution when outsourcing work offshore.

In the bleak light that attorneys paint—and their rhetorical job is to paint things in such a light—the offshore employee becomes a potential corporate saboteur or potential spy, ready to take trade secrets, proprietary business methods, or manufacturing plans to another company. Pink (2004), an attorney, explains why intellectual property must be controlled: "The countries in which . . . outsourcing is sent usually have less developed data protection and intellectual property laws. . . . There is the risk of industrial espionage in bitterly poor nations that often do not have laws protecting foreign companies and rarely enforce whatever laws may exist" (p. 370). Being able to recognize the potential for sabotage as

203

well as other legal concerns enables technical communicators to envision changes to their job descriptions that result from sending work offshore.

Becoming a technical communicator who understands the legal concerns related to offshore outsourcing helps prepare for change in the field, a change that author and *New York Times* foreign affairs columnist Friedman (2005) describes in *The World is Flat: A Brief History of the Twenty-First Century*: "It's time to think about the obligations of off-shoring as well as the opportunities. . . . Every person, just as every corporation, must tend to his or her own economic destiny, just as our parents and grandparents in the mills, shoe shops and factories did" (p. 21). Technical communicators who take on the challenge of understanding the legal concerns of offshore outsourcing will redefine the field's obligations and opportunities while fiercely protecting the heart of their organizations—the intellectual capital.

PURPOSE AND SCOPE

Writing about the legal concerns of offshore outsourcing requires that I preface the discussion with two qualifications: Although I have logged more than a decade working on complex business litigation, I am not an attorney, and this text should not be construed as legal advice. Second, the governance in offshore outsourcing changes quickly, and technical communicators need to approach this text as follows: today, this chapter may be useful and informative, but tomorrow, this chapter may serve only as a starting point in the challenge of determining the legal concerns of taking technical communication work offshore.

To identify the legal concerns in offshore outsourcing, I reviewed print and online materials, including book-length texts, law journals, and legal news, and I interviewed two attorneys who specialize in outsourcing and technology, Marc S. Friedman and Benjamin M. Dean. Marc S. Friedman, a member of Sills Cummis Epstein & Gross P.C. in New Jersey, has written more than 150 articles and speaks extensively in the United States and abroad about computer law. In addition, he is the former president of the International Computer Law Association. Benjamin M. Dean, an attorney at Pillsbury Winthrop Shaw Pittman LLP in Washington, D.C., focuses his practice on complex technology transactions, including software licensing, software development, and outsourcing. In addition to participating in interviews, both attorneys read and commented on drafts of this text.

I excluded from this review any texts that focus on privacy issues and control of personal medical information, topics that Kirk St.Amant addresses in his chapter, "The Privacy Problems Related to International Outsourcing: A Primer for Technical Communicators." In this chapter, I focus on the legal concerns of offshore outsourcing the craft of technical communication.

Based on this research, I organized this primer into four sections: (1) an explanation of the governance of offshore outsourcing; (2) a discussion of how this governance influences decision making about the kinds of intellectual capital that need protecting; (3) an overview of the legal concerns when developing outsourcing agreements; and (4) I conclude with questions and thoughts about how a technical communicator might prepare for working for a company that is considering offshoring or that is already offshoring technical communication.

GOVERNANCE OF OFFSHORE OUTSOURCING

Governance of offshore outsourcing is handled in a combination of ways, usually guided by the negotiated rules of the World Trade Organization (WTO), negotiated contracts, and governmental control. The major legal concern that results from multiple sources of governance is that not all countries play by the negotiated rules. Because the work of technical communicators is intellectual property under copyright law, companies considering outsourcing technical communication need to understand how the enforcement of intellectual property laws occurs in the country where the work will be outsourced.

For example, the current rule of thumb, according to attorney Marc Friedman, is that companies should consider outsourcing work involving intellectual property (IP) only to countries that have good records of enforcement of intellectual property ownership (personal communication, June 10, 2005). When considering whether to outsource work that yields material that can be protected under copyright law, Friedman advises that "unless a corporation is prepared to roll up its sleeves to assess the risks and take on those activities that control the risks, it ought not go outside the United States." To do this, he advises that "If you are going to outsource technical communication, you would want to outsource to a company in a jurisdiction where IP laws are respected and enforced." A good assessment for determining where to outsource technical communication would be looking first to see whether a country is a member of the WTO and then examining the country's record for enforcing intellectual property.

Two member countries, India and China, have very different track records. India, for example, is working to improve its enforcement of intellectual property as both a requirement of being a member of the WTO and in order to encourage companies in other countries to consider doing business there (Dean, personal communication, June 8 and 10, 2005). According to Fitzgerald (2003), India "actually has a much *better* cultural and legal climate for IP protection than many other nations offering offshore coding. Observers say India has a culture that generally seems to respect intellectual property. . . ." China, on the other hand, joined the WTO in 2001, but remained lax in its protection and enforcement of intellectual property laws. In 2002, for example, software copyright violations occurring in China "cost U.S. businesses $1.85 billion" according to some estimates (Josephberg, Pollack, Victoriano, Gitig, van Ness, Wagner, & Eremitaggio,

2003, p. 22). Lately, however, China has ramped up enforcement of intellectual property rights so much that the world is taking notice. Friedman (2005) suggests that China's "real long-term strategy is to outrace America and the E.U. countries to the top . . ." (p. 118). Still, Friedman cautions that offshore outsourcing and the protection of intellectual property need to be considered together:

> "Who owns what" is sure to emerge as one of the most contentious political and geopolitical questions in a flat world—especially if more and more American companies start feeling ripped off by more and more Chinese companies. If you are in the business of selling words, music, pharmaceuticals and you are not worried about protecting your intellectual property, you are not paying attention (2005, p. 218).

By the time this text hits the market, China's intent may be clearer. The advice of counsel is to wait and see but also to prepare by writing contracts that delineate ownership of intellectual property very carefully.

In anticipation of some of the problems attorney Marc Friedman describes, the WTO was established January 1, 1995 with the purpose of managing "the rules of trade between nations at a global or near-global level" (World Trade Organization (WTO), 2003, p. 9). The WTO grew out of an agreement established in 1948, called the General Agreement on Tariffs and Trade (GATT). The WTO serves as a sort of clearinghouse for trade between nations—a forum for negotiating trade agreements and a place to settle trade disputes. Member nations—150 nations are participating as of January 11, 2007—participate by agreeing to follow the negotiated rules. Two agreements are of particular interest to technical communicators: GATS and TRIPS.

GATS focuses on trade in services. According to the WTO (2003), GATS "is the first and only set of multilateral rules governing international trade in services," and "was developed in response to the huge growth of the service economy" (p. 33). The principles of GATS can be somewhat delineated as follows, although the agreement itself identifies countries' specific agreements in relation to trade (p. 33):

- GATS covers all services, but because not all services are equal, air travel, for example has specific needs that are not governed by GATS.
- All services must receive the "most-favoured nation" (MFN) treatment. MFN is a nondiscriminatory concept that demands that countries not discriminate among trading partners or give particular "foreign products, services, or nationals" better treatment. The idea is to bring equality among trading partners.
- Once a foreign entity enters the market, it must receive the same national treatment as local entities receive.

- The regulations and oversight must be objective, reasonable, and transparent; the rules need to be published and bureaucracies must have points of contact established and their contact information available.

In addition to setting trade standards, one of GATS's goals is to further negotiate the liberalization of cross-border trading ("progressive liberalization" of trade).

The negotiations that yielded GATS, for instance, occurred during a seven-year negotiation called the "Uruguay Round." The next round of negotiations began in 2000 and is known as the Doha Development Agenda (WTO, 2003, p. 36). The Doha Development Agenda continues to focus on trade in services among nation members. Another important result of the Uruguay Round is the Agreement on TRIPS.

According to WTO (2003), the TRIPS agreement is "an attempt to narrow the gaps in the way that these rights are protected around the world, and to bring them under common international rules" (p. 39). The WTO explains the agreement as follows:

The agreement focuses on five basic issues (p. 39):

- how basic **principles** of the trading system and other international intellectual property agreements should be applied
- how to give adequate **protection** to intellectual property rights
- how countries should **enforce** those rights adequately in their own territories
- how to **settle disputes** on intellectual property between members of the WTO
- **special transitional agreements** during the period when the new system is being introduced

With TRIPS, countries know what the expectations are when working with each other to buy and sell goods and services. TRIPS requires that member countries have and enforce specific intellectual property protection laws in their countries. Essentially, GATS and TRIPS begin to define boundaries for working with other nations and to further the goals of the WTO to open borders for globalization of trade in goods, services, and intellectual property.

Within these boundaries, attorney Marc Friedman recommends taking a multifaceted approach to outsourcing: "If I were outsourcing technical writing, I would enter into an outsourcing agreement. We would build into that agreement as many intellectual property protections as we could. Also, I would do some fundamental research on copyright law. I would also want to speak to a lawyer in the jurisdiction where the outsourcing would occur" (personal communication June 10, 2005). Ensuring that proprietary work product and protected intellectual property are secure is important in planning an offshore venture.

MAKING DECISIONS ABOUT OUTSOURCING

Attorney Marc Friedman recommends a multifront approach to outsourcing technical communication because outsourcing requires attention to many areas. Friedman advises that offshore outsourcing is "risky," and companies should proceed "with a plan to minimize those risks" (personal communication, June 10, 2005). Writing an offshore outsourcing agreement requires thinking about bad things you never want to happen; a good outsourcing agreement helps. Contracts govern most outsourcing agreements to make clear the realities of working from and within multiple legal systems. Contracts also enable companies to do things differently from methods set forth by the WTO. Contracts, therefore, serve as a method for minimizing risk and serve to define the relationships of parties.

Contract agreements can be as general or as specific as the negotiating parties want. Attorneys Dean and Friedman recommend writing very specific contracts that address the needs that are unique to an organization. Dean describes the job of an attorney working out the complex agreements that outsourcing requires as working "in the weeds," or in the specific details that must be addressed. Attorneys Friedman and Dean identify the following five issues as important for working through offshore agreements for technical communication: conducting due diligence, preparing for knowledge transfer and training, considering business continuity, preparing a disaster plan, and considering other issues (Dean, personal communication, June 8 and 10, 2005; Friedman, personal communication, June 10, 2005).

Many of these issues are defined in a preliminary step called "due diligence" that occurs (or should occur) at the beginning of seeking an offshore vendor. By understanding the larger concerns and cautions, technical communicators may be better able to make recommendations, identify potential problems, and make good arguments about how to proceed with offshoring technical communication work.

Due Diligence

Due diligence is the legal term for getting to know a company, its financial standing, its agreements, its employees and their abilities, and its stability. In addition to a general understanding of the company, due diligence in offshore outsourcing also requires examining the host country to determine whether its legal system is effective in protecting and enforcing intellectual and industrial property. Due diligence requires assessing the needs of a particular kind of outsourcing, such as technical communication. When outsourcing technical communication, for example, the problem of copyright law is one of the immediate concerns because most written products are covered by the copyright laws where the work is produced, according to attorneys Friedman and Dean (Dean, personal communication, June 10, 2005; Friedman, personal communication, June 8 and 10, 2005).

One of the primary concerns during due diligence is a country's treatment of intellectual property. According to Raysman and Brown (2003), attorneys writing for the *New York Law Journal*, "Intellectual property laws and enforcement vary considerably around the world, and one of the primary concerns for customers entering into technology-related outsourcing agreements is that they retain ownership of their existing intellectual property and gain appropriate ownership of materials generated in the outsourcing relationship." To gain ownership of copyright-protected work, according to Marc Friedman, outsourcing agreements need to be written so that the copyright ownership falls within the control of U.S. laws. Contracts can be written so that they specifically are governed by U.S. laws, rather than the law of the country where the work is created (which local country's law would govern copyright-protected material, absent contractual provisions stating otherwise). According to Friedman, to understand how intellectual property, and specifically copyright-protected material, is handled within a specific country, due diligence should include an initial investigation of the potential country's legal system (Friedman, personal communication, June 10, 2005).

One of the first considerations a company must undertake when exploring offshore outsourcing is the enforcement of the laws of the country where outsourcing might occur. Working with a known local attorney who can be candid about the foreign legal system is vital, Marc Friedman explains (personal communication, June 10, 2005). Asking whether the country is a member of the WTO is a good start, according to Friedman. U.S. attorneys see membership in the WTO as a starting point: Are the laws aligned? Does the country have a good reputation for enforcing intellectual property? These questions must be asked before access to intellectual property and access to proprietary structures and business methods can be released to the offshore entity.

Due diligence provides an overview for the issues that will be important in contract negotiation and in decision making about what kinds of work are appropriate to outsource. Raysman and Brown (2003) explain:

> . . . a customer may consider dealing only with vendors that have a United States presence, only outsourcing projects that do not involve sensitive property, maintaining computer code in the United States and limiting the vendor's ability to make local copies. . . .

Attorneys Friedman and Dean agree. Friedman concurs that "what I've gleaned from attending to many, many clients is that as a matter of politics and culture, many countries are not effectively enforcing their intellectual property laws." Dean explains further that some U.S. companies "really aggressively prosecute all over the world" in order to protect their intellectual property. He states that "There's a lot of fear to outsource to countries where there is widespread infringement" (personal communication, June 8 and 10, 2005). Both Friedman and Dean urge clients to undertake a careful due diligence examination of potential companies and their countries.

In addition to examining the issue of intellectual property protection, other major issues include determining how knowledge will be transferred and how employees will be trained; writing a business-continuity plan; preparing for disaster; and other considerations unique to a specific field.

Knowledge Transfer/Training

A vital consideration during due diligence is to determine how the transfer of knowledge and training of employees at the offshore entity will occur. When companies enter into outsourcing agreements, information needs to be transferred expediently from the U.S.-based bricks-and-mortar building to the offshore counterpart or vendor. This data transfer includes information sent over networks and human-to-human transfer via training of new employees. To transfer information, equipment must be secured that enables the transfer, and employees must be hired, or the vendor's employees must be trained. Three concerns include the time and costs involved; the vendors' abilities to scale—reduce or add—employees as necessary; and the way that turnover will be handled. Dean cautions that each of these items must be considered carefully (personal communication, June 8 and 10, 2005).

The cost of transition and time involved may be surprising, according to Overby (2003), writing for *CIO Magazine*. Overby holds that this transitional period is "one of the most expensive stages of an offshore endeavor." She estimates that it takes "three months to a full year to completely hand operations to an offshore partner. If company executives aren't aware that there will be no savings—but rather significant expenses—during this period, they are in for a nasty surprise." Transitions of people and information often require having employees work in both America and offshore. In addition, work in the offshore counterpart needs to be mentored closely at first. Equipment delays and failure to take time to build relationships often cause project delays and other expensive outcomes, according to Overby.

In addition to the initial training and transfer of information, Dean recommends that a company needs to make sure the offshore entity has the ability to "scale" its personnel when needed, or to increase its employee base if new demands for service or products need to be met. If, for example, a call center located in India serves an insurance company that gets a new corporate client with 50,000 employees, the call center in India needs to be able to increase its staff to handle the increase in call center volume. Of course, Dean explains, the ramp up would not usually have to occur overnight, because most companies have advance notice of a start date for handling a new client's business (Dean, personal communication, June 8 and 10, 2005).

Finally, in addition to the ability to scale, turnover can be a concern in some countries (Dean, personal communication, June 8 and 10, 2005). This problem was illustrated at the National Writers Union (NWU, 2003) roundtable discussion about offshore outsourcing of technical writing in Silicon Valley, where one company reported that in India "the top performers get experience, quit and went to other companies for higher pay" (NWU). Dean seconds this assessment. He estimates that in the software-development market in India, key personnel recently have had turnover rates of 40% to 50% each year. The problem of turnover requires that companies think about how information will be transferred initially and then subsequently, as turnover occurs. For example, the American company might pay for initial training of offshore personnel, but subsequent employee training might be the responsibility of the offshore entity (Dean, personal communication, June 8 and 10, 2005).

The transfer of information and training of offshore employees are vital considerations when developing outsourcing agreements. The relationships built during training and transition may provide the basis for building and maintaining efficient and effective offshore relationships. Knowing how information will be transferred originally and then how the transfer will continue when new offshore employees come on board prepares a company for maintaining business operations.

Business Continuity

Business continuity—or maintaining day-to-day operations—focuses on "the normal steps [taken] every day to make sure all is okay," Dean explains (personal communication, June 8 and 10, 2005). For technical writers, business continuity has two components: the larger picture of maintaining business operations—ensuring that work product is stored and transferred appropriately; and also ensuring that the writing is clear, ethical, and meets legal standards. Business continuity, then, requires maintaining control over data systems as well as ensuring the quality of the technical communication produced offshore.

When maintaining control over work product, the idea is to create a method for understanding the work and the progress of the work being completed in the offshore entity on a day-to-day basis. For example, some companies require backups of work product each day, require that hard copies of information be shipped to the United States, and require certain reporting functions daily or regularly (Dean, personal communication, June 8 and 10, 2005). Some entities maintain a business-continuity center in the same offshore country but located away from the primary work facility, so that a back-up location is available should something happen to the main facility or its employees, according to Dean.

The ultimate purpose of a business-continuity plan is to enable work to continue if something goes wrong. What if the collaboration does not work? Having plans in place can preserve business relationships with current customers. Guyer (2004), writing for *Network World Fusion*, provides an example:

Everdream, an IT services provider in Fremont, California, shifted some of its work to Costa Rica, expecting to reduce its call center expenses by 25%. Instead, problems that should have taken 5 minutes to solve were taking an hour. . . . Today, Everdream has phased out its Costa Rica operation and reopened its U.S. centers.

Having a plan in place that ensures a smooth transition back to the United States in the event of a failed working relationship is important in working through negotiations with potential outsourcing vendors.

Disaster Recovery

Related to, but separate from, business continuity is the problem of disaster recovery. Whereas business continuity focuses on the day-to-day understanding of the work that occurs in the offshore entity, disaster recovery is a planned method for continuing to do business should a disaster occur—either naturally or by act of war or terrorism. The difference in the two terms involves *when* each occurs. Schwartz (2005), writing for *Managing Offshore*, describes it this way: "Simply put, a [business continuity plan] is an action plan that lays out processes and procedures to ensure that critical business functions will continue with minimal disruption should a disaster occur." Although both are planned, the business-continuity plan is carried out on a daily or regular basis, while the disaster-recovery plan becomes operational only after disaster strikes.

A disaster could be anything beyond the reasonable control of a party: a natural disaster such as the tsunami of December 2004, an act of war, or if the offshore country is no longer viable as a place to do business (due to political realities or otherwise) (Dean, personal communication June 8 and 10, 2005). If a disaster strikes, the company needs to be able to respond quickly. The company's business-continuity center might provide assistance when the disaster-recovery plan goes into action by maintaining an office where key personnel can go to access information and perform job duties.

Dean recommends that companies address disaster recovery when writing contracts by determining what should happen if a facility is destroyed or staff members are unable to perform job functions. Who will take control of operations and how quickly will the change occur? If the host country is no longer a viable location for operations, what will happen to force recovery? The political realities of doing business overseas must be addressed at the beginning, according to Dean, because the cost of recovering from disaster must be considered.

TREADING CAREFULLY:
HOW TECHNICAL COMMUNICATORS CAN PREPARE

To meet the obligations and challenges of a changing work environment, technical communicators can ask and assess how their duties may shift in relation to the process of offshore outsourcing. Notes from the National Writers Union roundtable on outsourcing, for example, suggest that outsourcing decisions about technical communication are made at the CEO level, a practice that may be problematic, given how specific the contract negotiations need to be to protect the work product and to ensure its quality.

As the field of technical communication convenes offshore agreements for knowledge work, other issues may arise. These issues may come from technical communicators who know the field better than their company's management who focuses on macro-issues and better than their company's counsel who may not know the concerns specific to the field of technical communication. Technical communicators who understand the questions that legal counsel needs to ask will be integral to the challenges and changes ahead.

In addition, although offshore outsourcing has been occurring for a long time, some intellectual questions remain. For example, Dean explains that in the United States and overseas some technology services are taxed in different ways (personal communication, June 8 and 10, 2005). One question that must be asked is whether—and when—technical communication can be considered a "technology service." (Writing instructions for operating a lawn mower may not be considered "technology service," but writing instructions for software may be.) Another question concerns watching to see how the world takes on business-methods patents, something the WTO has not yet addressed. How will these patents hold up in the worldwide market?

Related to this, technical communicators can work as facilitators who convene offshore outsourcing relationships; as developers and overseers of business-continuity and disaster-recovery plans; as monitors and administrators who measure the success of the relationship; or as scouts and technical writers who pursue securing nontraditional patents for business methods and industrial property that may not fit into traditional patenting categories. A panel at the Philadelphia Metro Chapter of the Society for Technical Communication also suggested that technical communicators recognize changes, as reported by Rosenberg (2004) in *Intercom*:

> The documents we work on change constantly, and so, it seems, does the technology we use and the business culture in which we work. The global economy presents us with challenges that are essentially not very different from those we've conquered in the past. So, as always, it's up to us to enhance our skills, sharpen our business instincts, and expand our flexibility to succeed in this ever-changing world (p. 23).

Right now, many areas are open for technical communicators to take an entrepreneurial approach to meeting the "obligations and opportunities" created by offshore outsourcing.

REFERENCES

Fitzgerald, M. (2003, November 15). At risk offshore. *CIO Magazine*. Retrieved June 2005, from http://www.cio.com.

Friedman, T. L. (2005). *The world is flat: A brief history of the twenty-first century*. New York: Farrar, Straus and Giroux.

Guyer, L. (2004, July 6). Cracks are appearing in offshoring plans. *Network world fusion*. Retrieved March 2, 2005, from http://www.nwfusion.com.

Hillgenberg, H. (1999). A fresh look at soft law. *European Journal of International Law, 10*, 499-515.

Josephberg, K., Pollack, J., Victoriano, J., Gitig, O., van Ness, A., Wagner, S., & Eremitaggio, P. (2005, May.) Software piracy carries heavy cost for US. *Intellectual Property & Technology Law Journal, 15*(5), 22-23. Retrieved February 17, 2005, from ABI/INFORM Global.

National Writers Union (NWU). (2003, July 24). Offshoring of technical writing: A roundtable discussion. Retrieved May 1, 2005, from http://www.biztech-offshoring.com/roundtable.html.

Overby, S. (2003, September 1). The hidden costs of offshoring. *CIO Magazine*. Retrieved July 11, 2005, from http://www.cio.com.

Pink, S. W. (2004, March). Recent trends in outsourcing: Understanding and managing the legal issues and risk. *Patents, Copyrights, Trademarks, and Literary Property Course Handbook Series*. 24th Annual Institute on Computer Law, 365-387.

Raysman, R., & Brown, P. (2003, March 27). Offshore outsourcing means careful legal planning. *Law.com*. Retrieved February 17, 2005, from http://www.law.com.

Rosenberg, N. (2004, July/August). What does it mean for us?" *Intercom*, 23.

Schwartz, K. D. (2005, March). Preparing for the worst. *Managing offshore*. Retrieved June 2005 from http://www.managingoffshore.com.

World Trade Organization (WTO). (2003, September). The World Trade Organization. Retrieved January 2005, from http://www.wto.org.

Conclusion:
Personal Reflection
on Developing a Viable Trajectory
for Outsourcing Technical
Communications

Barry Thatcher

As many chapters of this collection have documented, technical communications that were once developed in the United States or Western Europe are now being developed in Asia, Africa, Latin America, and other parts of the world. Thus, technical communication is following other fields such as information technologies, electronics manufacturing, and even textiles; consequently, the outsourcing of technical communication products and jobs will continue to influence our profession. Among many things, perhaps the greatest change is the profile of technical communicator's job in the United States. This profile is dramatically and permanently changing in light of the world economy and rapidly developing communications technologies. As explored in this collection, this new profile includes more emphasis of value added and disruptive practices (Hackos & Hackos), managing international editing (Lanier), collaboration (Melton), and understanding international education in technical communications (Evia). Furthermore, this collection highlights new knowledge that technical communicators will need to have in the global context, such as privacy (St. Amant), legal (Diaz) and political (Gibson). Finally, this edited collection examines how technical communications is being practiced in various outsourcing contexts including India (Natarajan & Pandit), Africa (Bokor), Germany (Kaempf & Drewer), and Mexico (Thatcher & Garza-Almanza). Understanding these different rhetorical traditions is critical for effectively managing global communication processes and products.

Collectively, this edition lays out the larger picture of outsourcing and technical communications, but specifically, it perhaps has not answered adequately these questions: What kinds of jobs will remain in the United States? Which jobs are more efficiently handled outside the United States? How can U.S. technical communicators develop a "comparative advantage" in the global economy? As a summary to the issues developed in this collection, the following three sections project a trajectory of the technical communication profession in the United States and worldwide.

Interdependence and Specialization

As most research has documented, the outsourcing context is making the world much more interdependent *and* specialized, a contradictory variable that has important ramifications for technical communication. For example, one of the outsourcing factories that I studied produces all of the cruise controls for a global automobile manufacturer, so automobile assembly plants all over the world have to rely on and communicate regularly with this small plant in Chihuahua, Mexico. Not surprisingly, effective technical communications is critical for this outsourcing endeavor, but as explored in this collection, this new kind of technical communication is essentially *intercultural* and *international*; and thus, it needs to be sensitive to critical differences in culture, law, politics, and technologies.

How U.S. technical communication researchers and practitioners react to the essentially intercultural element of outsourcing communications is the key issue, one that could either move us forward with strength or downsize us dramatically. If we can develop theory, research, and practice that addresses intercultural technical communication and see its potential strength in the outsourcing context, we have a bright future. However, as one who regularly researches, teaches, and practices intercultural technical communication, I feel we have a long way to go and are most likely behind much of the world for a number of reasons. First, predominant cultural values in the United States (see Stewart & Bennett, 1991, on U.S. ethnocentrism) and within the U.S. technical communication industry and academia work against intercultural approaches to technical communications. These problematic values include a strong sense of individualism, self-reliance, and universalism (Stewart & Bennett, 1991; Trompenaars & Hampden-Turner, 2000). These problematic variables create a disposition to believe that one's communication patterns are the norm that others should follow. In other words, the direct, reader-friendly, deductive, low-context, and analytical approach to technical communication has been naturalized among most U.S. technical communication theory, research, and practice for so long that many U.S. technical communicators cannot think otherwise (see Thatcher, 1999, 2000). This ethnocentrism works against adjusting communication styles for international or non-U.S. audiences.

This sense of ethnocentrism is also greatly compounded by predominant views in U.S. academia that foster "the local approach" (Thatcher, 2005) to cultural relations rather than developing viable intercultural and international frameworks for research, theory, and practice. This local approach strongly encourages what I call *naïve individualism*, the belief that all humans are different and all cultures are too complicated to compare; thus incommensurability of cultures and humans should prevail rather than reasoned, evidence-based comparisons of how cultural and rhetorical traditions encourage distinct communication patterns. This localized approach is often supplemented by corresponding ideological critiques of intercultural relations, which have importance in certain contexts, but in many intercultural contexts, they provide "little light and much heat" (Bennett, 1998, p. 11). As documented extensively elsewhere, this difference-based, local approach does not permit the kind of cross-cultural theorizing and research methods necessary to understand the relations of technical communication at truly a global level (see Bhawuk & Triandis 1996; Lucy, 1996; Thatcher 2005).

In conclusion, in order for U.S. technical communication practice, theory, and research to contribute to outsourcing technical communications in the global context, we must break out of our ethnocentric beliefs about what good technical communications are, we must move beyond the localized approaches to cultural theory, and we must develop viable, ethical, and effective (culturally adapted) communications for the interdependence and specialization of the outsourcing context.

English as Tyrannosaurus Rex

I have copied the title of one of my favorite articles (Swales, 1997) about the international influence of English to explore some possible ramifications for outsourced technical communications. Put simply, English has become the dominant language of science, business, academia, and information technologies. From Swales' analogy (1997), it is the T-rex of all languages. In the light of contrastive rhetoric (Kaplan, 2001) and second-language studies (Pennycook, 1995), the cultural and rhetorical implications of this dominant language is very significant. Pennycook (1995) argues that English is significantly influencing world cultural patterns; and Kaplan (2001) documents the difficulty of ESL writers adapting to U.S. rhetorical traditions. U.S. technical communication theory, research, and practice are in a unique position regarding the influence of English. The advantage is that almost all U.S. technical communication theory and practice is based on English as the default language; thus, the huge learning curve of mastering English is mostly nonexistent. The disadvantage of English being the default language is that U.S. technical communicators can easily ignore other rhetorical patterns based on different language and cultural traditions.

U.S. researchers and practitioners must acknowledge this worldwide influence of English when developing technical communication for outsourced markets. However, this acknowledgement must not be of the ethnocentric type; that is, because English is the dominant language, then the rest of the world must simply adapt to it and its corresponding rhetorical and cultural patterns. In a real way, English gives U.S. technical communication theory, practice, and research a comparative advantage if it does not fall into ethnocentrism, but rather, uses it to develop ethical and effective means of mediating the interdependence and specialization brought about by the outsourcing context. How that can be done is explored in the next section.

Predominant U.S. Cultural Values as Virtues Rather Than Vices

As Hampden-Turner (2000) argue, cultural values produce both virtues and vices; thus, effective intercultural research and practice should marshal the virtues of many cultural traditions (Stewart & Bennett, 1991, pp. 149-176) to create synergy in a specific global context. In other words, intercultural researchers should draw on the strengths of a specific set of cultural and rhetorical values given a specific situation. Accordingly, U.S. technical communication researchers and practitioners can develop a comparative advantage in the outsourced context if they draw on the virtues of some of their rhetorical and cultural traditions. The first value to be addressed is individualism, a value of extraordinary importance to the United States (Hampden-Turner & Trompenaars, 2000; Stewart & Bennett, 1991). The vice side of individualism has already been addressed, in terms of ethnocentrism and singular world views. However, the virtue of individualism is innovation and development (Hampden-Turner & Trompenaars, 2000), especially in technology, industry, and business. Theoretically, individualism provides the freedom to experiment and develop concepts and products without the constraints of community influence. Communitarian cultures, as argued by Hampden-Turner and Trompenaars (2000), have a smaller propensity for innovation but a much larger capacity to fine tune already-developed products into more marketable dimensions.

The U.S. innovative tradition should be an important value for U.S. technical communicators, perhaps following Hacko's concept of disruption. From my perspective as an intercultural researcher and technical communicator, useful technical communication innovators would draw on the multimedia capacity of communications technologies to develop formats, genres, and forms of instruction that are more easily localized into non-U.S. rhetorical traditions. This is precisely my challenge when working with environmental and health literacy along the U.S.-Mexico border. It is important to remember, however, that this virtue of individualism must be checked continually with the virtue of communitarianism—of making sure of the fit to a target context.

The last value that could give a comparative advantage to the United States (and other Western countries) is the concept of universalism (Hampden-Turner & Trompenaars, 2000; Hofstede, 1997). Universalism means creating a level playing field so that people are judged not on their relationships but on predetermined rules; in essence, rule of law, rather than rule of will or relationship. This value is reflected in the strong push for antidiscrimination laws in the United States and other universalist countries. It is also reflected in the various international standards such as ISO. Particularism is the counter to universalism, and it encourages context and relationship-based rules and exceptional thinking. The vice of universalism is using the level playing field as a hypocritical and discriminatory excuse when exceptions to the rules are justified but not allowed. The vice of particularism is simply corruption—using a relationship to gain advantage. Relatively speaking, the United States has a strong ideal of universalism, perhaps because it is almost entirely an immigrant nation (although in practice, it falls very short). Since outsourcing is encouraging specialization and interdependence among various rhetorical and cultural traditions, the universalist impulse is critical for mediating these complex relationships. U.S. technical communicators can draw from this tradition and help develop international and intercultural standards for technical communication products. However, as with all cultural values, U.S. technical communicators must temper this universalist value with a strong sense of particularism, of how relationships and rules are related, especially because of the predominant influence of English and U.S. expertise in technology development.

My proposal for U.S. technical communicators is to draw on our strengths in English, innovation, and universalism in ethically and culturally sensitive ways. That's the trajectory and challenge: Outsourcing is moving U.S. technical communication theory and practice to an intercultural or international realm. U.S. technical communication theory and practice can embrace this change and make the necessary adjustments for it, or it can continue in the status quo and watch as more jobs move to other countries. If we move forward strategically and ethically, we can develop innovative and ethical approaches to this interdependent and specialized global context.

REFERENCES

Bhawuk, D. P., & Triandis, H. C. (1996). The role of culture theory in the study of culture and intercultural training. In H. C. Landis & Rabi S. Bhagat (Eds.), *Handbook of intercultural training* (2nd ed., pp. 17-34). Thousand Oaks, CA: Sage Publications.

Bennett, M. J. (1998). Intercultural communication: A current perspective. In M. Bennett (Ed.), *Basic concepts of intercultural communication* (pp. 1-34). Yarmouth, ME: Intercultural Press.

Hampden-Turner, C., & Trompenaars, F. (2000). *Building cross-cultural competence: How to create wealth from conflicting values.* New Haven, CT: Yale University Press.

Hofstede, G. (1997). *Cultures and organizations: Software of the mind.* New York: McGraw-Hill.

Kaplan, R. (2001). *Contrastive rhetoric revisited and redefined.* Mahwah, NJ: Lawrence Erlbaum Associates.

Lucy, J. (1996). The scope of linguistic relativity. In J. J. Gumperez & _. Levinson (Eds.), *Rethinking linguistic relativity* (pp. 37-69). Cambridge: Cambridge University Press.

Pennycook, A. (1995). *The cultural politics of English as an international language.* London: Addison Wesley Publishing Company.

Stewart, E., & Bennett, M. (1991). *American cultural patterns: A cross-cultural perspective* (Rev. ed.). Yarmouth, ME: Intercultural Press, Inc.

Swales, J. (1997). English as Tyrannosaurus Rex. *World Englishes, 16*, 373-382.

Thatcher, B. L. (2005). Situating L2 writing in global communication technologies. *Computers and Composition, 22*, 279-295.

Thatcher, B. L. (2000). L2 professional writing in a U.S. and South American context. *Journal of Second Language Writing, 9*(1), 41-69.

Thatcher, B. L. (1999). Cultural and rhetorical adaptations for South American audiences. *Technical Communication, 46*(2), 177-195.

Trompenaars, F., & Hampden-Turner, C. (1998). *Riding the waves of culture: Understanding diversity in global business* (2nd ed.). New York: McGraw-Hill.

Contributors

MICHAEL JARVIS KWADZO BOKOR is a PhD candidate in the English Studies program (technical communication specialization, focusing on cross-cultural dimensions of international technical communication) at Illinois State University. He holds a Diploma in Journalism and Public Relations (June 1984) and practiced journalism in Ghana, West Africa, before enrolling at Illinois State in the fall of 2001. He has been subeditor of the Association of Teachers of Technical Writing (ATTW) Bibliography. His research interests include post-colonial studies, cultural literacy, cross-cultural communication, World Englishes, and language attitudes of native English speakers.

CHARLSYE SMITH DIAZ received an MA in Professional Writing (University of Massachusetts Dartmouth, 1997) and a PhD in Technical Communication and Rhetoric (Texas Tech University, 2004). She is an assistant professor at and director of the Professional and Technical Writing Program at the University of Hartford. Her research focuses on U.S. and international legal issues related to the informal and formal writing of engineers and scientists, including documentation—especially intellectual property—that results from research and development.

PETRA DREWER received an MA in Technical Translation (Hildesheim, 1996), and a PhD in Cognitive Linguistics (Hildesheim, 2003). Her main focus of research is on the influence of metaphorical thinking on cognition, but she is also interested in technical language and terminology, with close links to computer-aided and machine translation. She teaches language and text design in the degree program Technical Communication (University of Applied Sciences, Karlsruhe).

CARLOS EVIA is an Assistant Professor of Professional Writing at Virginia Tech. He received his PhD in Technical Communication and Rhetoric from Texas Tech University, and his Master's in Computer Systems from Universidad LaSalle in Mexico City. Carlos has workplace and academic experience in technical writing and international localization of technological products. His research interests are located in the intersection of information technology, technical communication, and multiculturalism. He can be contacted at carlos.evia@vt.edu.

VICTORIANO GARZA-ALMANZA received his PhD at La Universidad Autónoma de Nuevo León in Mexico. He is a full-time professor at la Universidad Autónoma de Ciudad Juárez. He is also a founding member of El Colegio de Chihuahua and director of its Observatorio Ambiental. He is a former environmental health consultant of the Pan American Health Organization/World Health Organization on the U.S.-Mexico border and South America. He is also a member of El Sistema Nacional de Investigadores del CONACYT de México.

KEITH GIBSON earned his PhD from Penn State University in 2003 and joined the Auburn faculty as an Assistant Professor the same year. His research focuses on the intersections of rhetorical theories and scientific discourse; he is particularly interested in how rhetorical pursuits shape scientific knowledge. Keith has focused much of his work on research surrounding artificial intelligence in the last 50 years; he is currently working on a book project that analyzes the various rhetorical strategies being employed in efforts to pass the Turing Test, and he has an article critiquing the digital computer as a metaphor for mind. Keith also investigates the way science influences public policy; in addition to this chapter on outsourcing, he has published an article on the rhetoric of the anti-nuclear-power movement.

JOANN T. HACKOS is president of Comtech Services, Inc. and executive director of the Center for Information-Development Management. She has published four books with John Wiley & Sons, including *Managing your Documentation Projects* (1994), *Standards for Online Communication* (1996), *User and Task Analysis for Interface Design* with Janice Redish (1997), and *Content Management for Dynamic Web Delivery* (2002). She expects to publish a new management book for information development in late 2006. Her team recently released *Introduction to the Darwin Information Typing Architecture* (2006). Dr. Hackos speaks frequently to organizations worldwide on trends in information development, structured authoring, minimalism, content management strategies, and offshore outsourcing. She consults with information managers on the process maturity of their organizations and their implementation of content management. She is a fellow and past president of the Society for Technical Communication.

WILLIAM HACKOS, JR. is Vice President of Comtech Services, Inc., an information management and design firm located in Denver, Colorado. Dr. Hackos consults with corporations worldwide to develop strategies for information management and information design, organizational management, user and task analysis, information architecture, and tools and technology selection. Dr. Hackos also leads frequent workshops related to information management and design throughout the United States.

CHARLOTTE KAEMPF received an MSc in Biology (Goettingen, 1978), a PhD in Microbiology (Konstanz, 1984), and an MA in Technical Communication (Texas Tech University, 2004; online). She is a student in the Technical Communication and Rhetoric PhD program at Texas Tech University (online). Her research interest shifted from bacterial photosynthesis and chemotaxis to environmental sciences and risk communication. She teaches ecology and environmental management to civil engineering majors (Universität Karlsruhe (TH), Germany).

CLINTON R. LANIER is an Assistant Professor of Professional Writing at the University of Memphis. He has previously been employed as an information developer for IBM and most recently as a technical editor for the United States Army. He is an active consultant to professional organizations for a number of topics concerning professional communications. His research interests include technical editing, international professional communication, and computer program documentation.

JAMES MELTON is an Assistant Professor of Business Communication at Central Michigan University. In addition to writing about professional communication competencies necessary in offshore outsourcing, he has also written articles about language use in globally networked learning environments and teaching international professional communication. He is interested in pursuing research in these areas, as well as examining the influence of business information systems on global communication.

PRASHANT NATARAJAN is a business consultant whose areas of expertise include software project management, usability, information architecture, and international technical communication. Prashant's articles on global project management, usability, and international technical communication have been published in both nonscholarly and scholarly publications. He has also presented well-received papers on these topics at several international conferences. Prashant is a regional representative of the IEEE Professional Communication Society (USA). He is also a peer reviewer for the society's journal, Transactions on Professional Communication. In the past he has also served as membership manager and nominating committee manager for the Society for Technical Communication (India chapter). You can contact him at prashant.natarajan@gmail.com.

MAKARAND (MAK) PANDIT is the CEO of Technowrites Pvt. Ltd., a Technical Writing Service Provider company in India. He has worked on the projects of several Fortune 500 companies and India's top IT companies. He is a bachelor in Electronics Engineering and a postgraduate in Marketing Management and has published several articles related to freelancing and estimation in Indus (newsletter of STC India Chapter) and Intercom (Newsletter of STC). Mak has served the STC India Chapter in various volunteer positions, including President in 2005. He is also a visiting lecturer at the University of Pune and an award-winning speaker. He can be reached at mp@vsnl.com.

KIRK ST. AMANT is an Assistant Professor in the Department of English at Texas Tech University. He has a background in anthropology, international government, and technical communication, and his research interests include intercultural exchanges via online media and international outsourcing. He has taught online and conventional courses in technical and professional communication and in intercultural communication for Texas Tech University, Mercer University, and James Madison University. He has also taught courses in e-commerce, distance education, and business communication in Ukraine as a part of the USAID-sponsored Consortium for the Enhancement of Ukrainian Management Education (CEUME). He can be contacted at kirk.st-amant@ttu.edu.

BARRY THATCHER is an Associate Professor of Rhetoric and Professional Communication at New Mexico State University. He has worked in international technical communication for more than 12 years. He has taught technical communications in South America for four years, and currently he is researching and teaching cross-cultural technical communication along the U.S.-Mexico border. His work in Mexico focuses on the issues of technical communications needed for outsourcing new technologies to *maquilas* (U.S.-owned manufacturing plants in Mexican border cities). Thatcher has published numerous articles on cross-cultural issues in technical and professional communication.

Index

["Privacy Problems Related to
    International Outsourcing . . ."
    (St. Amant)]
  Health Insurance Portability and
    Accountability Act of 1996, 172
  increase in international outsourcing
    providers, 172-173
  jurisdiction and protection, 169
  overview, 165-167
  personal information, value of, 168
  Sarbanes-Oxley Act of 2002, 171-172
  summary/conclusions, 181
  threats and responses, 168-169
Production time, shortened, 167
Programa Nacional Fronterizo
    (PRONAF), 93-94
Protectionism, U.S., 187

Quality concerns, 32, 42-43, 60, 78, 186

Raynor, Michael E., 109
Registry for entering names of the
    outsourcing providers, 179-180
Research and development (R&D), 71-72,
    75, 111
Responding to cheap labor from foreign
    workers. See "Information
    Developer's Dilemma, The";
    "Language, Culture, and
    Collaboration in Offshore
    Outsourcing"; "Personal
    Reflection on Developing a Viable
    Trajectory for Outsourcing
    Technical Communications"
Rhetorical traditions. See "Approaching
    Outsourcing in Rhetoric and
    Professional Communication . . ."
Rig Veda, 11, 12
Rising Data, 57-58
Risk-communication plans and governing
    boards overseeing outsourcing
    practices, 176
Roosevelt, Franklin D., 93
Russia, 173

S.A. International Limited, 40
Sanskrit, 13, 14
Savings, demonstrating cost, 127-129
Scale, ability to, 210
Schwarzenegger, Arnold, 196
Scientific tradition in India, 11-12
"Second Circle" (Kachru), 15
Senegal, 49
Shulba Sutras, 13
Simon Fraser University, 40
Simplified Technical English, 79
Single sourcing content, 117
Small markets and disruptive innovation,
    111
Snow, John, 194
Social-epistemic theory of rhetoric, 133
Society for Technical Communication
    (STC)
  editing, technical, 149
  Germany, 70, 72
  government policy, influencing,
    197-198
  India, 12, 28
  lexicology and outsourcing from
    German-speaking contexts, 70
  quality concerns, 186
  See also "Defining Technical
    Communication in the United
    States and India . . ."
Soft, 54
Software Futures, 53
Software services and India, 11, 15, 40
South Africa, 51-54, 60-61
South African Broadcasting Corporation,
    53
Southern African Development and
    Coordinating Council (SADCC),
    53
Spain, 88, 90
Specialization and interdependence,
    216-217
St. Amant, Kirk, 6
Standard American English (SAE), 12,
    22-23, 25
"Standard Englishes and World
    Englishes . . ." (Gilsdorf), 14-15

SELECTED TITLES FROM

Baywood's Technical Communications Serie

Series Editor, *Charles H. Sides*

ASSESSMENT IN TECHNICAL AND PROFESSIONAL COMUNICATION
Edited by *Margaret Hundleby and Jo Allen*
— WINNER OF THE CPTSC AWARD FOR EXCELLENCE —
IN PROGRAM ASSESSMENT

CONTENT MANAGEMENT
Bridging the Gap Between Theory and Practice
Edited by *George Pullman and Baotong Gu*

CONNECTING PEOPLE WITH TECHNOLOGY
Issues in Professional Communication
Edited by *George F. Hayhoe and Helen M. Grady*

OUTSOURCING TECHNICAL COMMUNICATION
Issues, Policies and Practices
Edited by *Barry L. Thatcher and Carlos Evia*

**MOTIVES FOR METAPHOR IN SCIENTIFIC
AND TECHNICAL COMMUNICATION**
Timothy D. Giles

TOGETHER WITH TECHNOLOGY
Writing Review, Enculturation and Technological Mediation
Jason Swarts
— WINNER OF THE 2009 NCTE AWARD FOR BEST BOOK —
IN TECHNICAL OR SCIENTIFIC COMMUNICATION

RESOURCES IN TECHNICAL COMMUNICATION
Outcomes and Approaches
Edited by *Cynthia L. Selfe*
— WINNER OF THE 2007 STC AWARD OF EXCELLENCE —
NY METRO CHAPTER

COMMUNICATIVE PRACTICES IN WORKPLACES AND THE PROFESSIONS
Cultural Perspectives on the Regulation of Discourse and Organizations
Edited by *Mark Zachry and Charlotte Thralls*
— WINNER OF THE 2008 NCTE AWARD FOR BEST COLLECTION OF ESSAYS —
IN TECHNICAL OR SCIENTIFIC COMMUNICATION

ONLINE EDUCATION
Global Questions, Local Answers
Edited by *Kelli Cargile Cook and Keith Grant-Davie*
— WINNER OF THE 2006 NCTE AWARD FOR BEST COLLECTION OF ESSAYS —
IN TECHNICAL OR SCIENTIFIC COMMUNICATION